GOVERNING THE LONDON REGION

A publication of the
Franklin K. Lane Memorial Fund,
Institute of Governmental Studies,
University of California, Berkeley

The Franklin K. Lane Memorial Fund takes its name from Franklin Knight Lane (1864–1921), a distinguished Californian who was successively New York correspondent for the San Francisco *Chronicle*, City and County Attorney of San Francisco, member and later chairman of the United States Interstate Commerce Commission, and Secretary of the Interior in the cabinet of President Woodrow Wilson.

The general purposes of the endowment are to promote "better understanding of the nature and working of the American system of democratic government, particularly in its political, economic and social aspects," and the "study and development of the most suitable methods for its improvement in the light of experience."

GOVERNING THE LONDON REGION: REORGANIZATION AND PLANNING IN THE 1960's

By DONALD L. FOLEY

Published for the

INSTITUTE OF GOVERNMENTAL STUDIES

UNIVERSITY OF CALIFORNIA PRESS

Berkeley, Los Angeles, London

University of California Press
Berkeley and Los Angeles, California

University of California Press, Ltd.
London, England

First Printing, 1972

First Paperback Edition, 1972

ISBN: 0-520-02248-3 (paper)
        0-520-0240-5 (cloth)

Library of Congress Catalog Card Number: 76-157822

Printed in the United States of America

FOREWORD

T HE UNITED STATES became a metropolitan nation before fully realizing that it was even urban. This "new" condition has been extensively described, analyzed, praised, and deplored. Moreover, metropolitanization has met with a variety of responses. Some people have virtually ignored it. Some have stoically or willingly accepted it. Others have prescribed extensive treatments for its real and alleged ills.

Although institutional change is typically slow—in the United States and elsewhere—the governance of metropolitan areas is responding to growth pressures and to increasing awareness of urban community interdependence. All levels of government now openly participate in the governance of metropolitan areas. People and organizations habitually turn from one level to another, and back again, to get desired results or to forestall unwanted developments. Nowhere, however, does the organizational machinery seem to be functioning well.

Charles E. Merriam's telling comment is perhaps even more pertinent today than when first written in 1942: "The adequate organization of modern metropolitan areas is one of the great unsolved problems of modern politics. This is true of all large urban aggregations of population in all countries, especially all growing cities." [1]

Everywhere metropolitan agglomerations are burgeoning. For at least a century, rapid growth has characterized urban populations throughout the world. Although these high rates of increase may decline before we enter the twenty-first century, urban growth will probably continue. Much of the increase will take place in and around large cities. Man's foreseeable future is metropolitan.

One hundred years ago the world had only seven metropolitan areas with a million or more inhabitants each. Their combined population was only 13 million, less than today's total for either the Tokyo-Yokohama or New York regions. By 1951, 90 of the world's metropolitan areas had more than one million inhabitants each. Since then the further increase has been phenomenal. Thus by 1968 the number of areas with one million or more inhabitants had jumped to 150, a rise of 70 per cent in only 17 years. The recency, rapidity, and magnitude of these developments all help account for the intense attention that urban governmental institutions have been receiving in many countries, and especially in the past few years.

It is appropriate that we begin this study of metropolitan governance by exploring how the urban offspring of an old imperial city—whose very name rolls like thunder on the Thames—reorganized itself for the closing third of the twentieth century. London's long collective memory recalls marching Roman legionnaires, intertribal wars of Celt and Anglo-Saxon, the Norman Conquest of 1066, the dawning promise of Chaucer's England and the heady ferment of Shakespeare's, the civic admiration of a dyspeptic Dr. Johnson, the pomp and circumstance of Victoria's capital, the stubborn courage of the Battle of Britain, the hopeful genesis of the Greenbelt, the agonizing struggle with postwar urbanization, and, finally, the emergence of a new, swinging London, blossoming with mod styles, permissive ways, and miniskirted ladies.

London's metropolis is rich in color and fascination, legend and accomplishment, fact and folklore, as well as human values. Drawing on its wealth of experience, London should have much to tell us by the way it approaches the seemingly intractable problems of urban government. Even if the organizational results are neither wholly successful nor fully satisfactory, the political struggle and intellectual effort can help illuminate some murky problems of governing urban man in democratic societies.

Despite the differences between Britain and the United States, there are important similarities in the organizational dilemmas, and in the basic relationships among actors and institutions. Even more important is the restatement of the classical theory of local government in a democratic nation, as well as the appropriate revision of governmental theory to account for changes in the goals, values, and problems that form part of our changing Western heritage. The governance of metropolitan areas is part of the larger problems of economic, social, and political organization of a nation. The theoretical and pragmatic contributions of the British experience will help us guide our own local government through its revolutionary transformation, so that, as Charles Merriam has said, "local values will appear in a new light, in a new and finer setting than before."

The United States census of 1970 showed that 55 of the nation's 243 metropolitan areas had reached populations of more than 500,-000. More than half of the 55 exceed one million. Obviously, many of America's metropolitan communities are large and intricately diversified. These big and complicated agglomerations are more likely to find relevant clues to satisfactory relationships among their parts from the experiences of large and complex urban communities in other areas of the world—Britain and elsewhere—than in America's smaller, simpler, single-county metropolitan areas.

London's experiment is best viewed as part of a larger picture. The studies that led to London's reorganization were the first in what has now become a comprehensive series of investigations of urban governance covering all of Great Britain. These new non-London efforts are also analyzed clearly and succinctly in Donald L. Foley's book. The comparisons and contrasts help greatly to elucidate the significance of London's experiment, and to show how it fits in the larger scene.

Governmental complexities in London and Britain's other metropolitan areas emphasize what we already knew, or should have known. That is, the answer to metropolitan problems is not a simplistic consolidation of many "fractionated" local authorities into a single regional entity. This simple model cannot accommodate the extreme complexities of large urban communities. Instead, urban government is part of a *national system,* and all levels participate in a variety of roles that depend on the nation's mix of institutions, traditions, history, and other relevant factors. One of the substantial strengths of Foley's study lies in its perspectives on Britain's national system of urban governance, as embodied in the new London.

But there is a larger picture, still. Efforts at improving governmental ability to deal with metropolitan regions are becoming worldwide. In Canada, Scandinavia, western Europe, Latin America, and other areas, responsible people are worrying about how their governments are organized to serve large urban communities—and many are doing something about it.

Although in some respects the United States is different, it is by no means exempt from these influences. As one of the editors commented previously:

A pluralistic system like America's militates against comprehensive, long-range planning and governmental change. *Laissez-faire* policies and solicitude for "private enterprise" reinforce these restraining influences. So do theories of local home rule and institutionalized veto mechanisms. The United States *is* different, but it is showing signs of change. Also, the United States is using universal methods to try to achieve some of the same urban goals of the other societies. . . .

All the world is an organizational laboratory. And all the urban regions are intricate complexes of governmental experimentation. Each one of them is worthy of study, and each has some relevance for the others, despite geographic distance, environmental difference, or institutional disparity.

The Berkeley physicist who is unaware of relevant work in the laboratories of Chicago, London, or Tokyo, is severely handicapped. Perhaps the student of urban government suffers from an analogous handicap if he has no access to the results of the "real-life" experiments going on in Minneapolis, Toronto, London, Paris, Stockholm, Zagreb, Warsaw, Sydney. . . .[2]

With sophistication and insight, students of metropolitan government can help us understand the full meaning and larger significance of these varied efforts to deal with urbanization and the problems of growth. Such clues are needed because—short of war-and-peace, life-and-death issues—the world's parlous urban condition accounts for some of the most difficult social and environmental problems that confront all mankind. These problems desperately demand solution if future life styles in the cities of this planet are to offer a modicum of human dignity and humane quality. Achieving workable systems of government could be a crucial step, helping to determine what happens to the future of urban communities.

Foley's book is the first of a projected series on many metropolitan regions of the world, in the United States and elsewhere. Albert Rose has virtually completed the second contribution, a volume on Toronto, whose governmental system was recently reorganized for the second time in less than 20 years. Similar efforts have been commissioned for some 20 other major metropolitan regions. With luck, and hard work, several of these will come to fruition in 1972 and 1973.

STANLEY SCOTT   VICTOR JONES
Editor, Lane Fund   *Coeditor, Lane Studies in*
Publications   *Regional Government*

CONTENTS

Chapter VIII

IMPLICATIONS: WHAT DOES IT ALL MEAN?

PREFACE

G<small>REATER LONDON</small> is a distinctive and exciting metropolis. It has great historic depth, as was amply demonstrated by the magnificent special exhibition, "Growth of London, A.D. 43–1964," for which the Victoria and Albert Museum assembled exceptional items from the City's capacious storehouse. Any outside observer is hard pressed to comprehend and do justice to the richness of London's past, or the subtlety with which earlier development patterns have influenced subsequent stages of growth.

In an altogether remarkable fashion, during the past decade this great metropolitan area has received a thoroughgoing reform of its local government. Thus we have been witnessing the superimposition of a major rational modernization effort applied to a tradition-laden structure. The many complexities make it a formidable assignment to prepare a compact account that can also successfully focus on significant recent developments and satisfactorily master the intricate relations among London, the larger realms of the surrounding South East England region, and the omnipresent British central government.

Moreover it has been exceedingly difficult to draft a final text in a situation that has proved so fluid during these lively recent years. A veritable succession of major studies affecting London deserves to be taken into account, and at any point in the writing, the procession is still moving past. We have opted to deal primarily with these main topics: the governmental reorganization of Greater London; main problems confronting London, with emphasis on planning; regional planning for South East England; and proposals for governmental reorganization in other parts of Great Britain.

Our indebtedness extends to many. Included are officials serving with the Greater London Council, selected London boroughs, and the Ministry of Housing and Local Government; the Ditchley Foundation seminar on metropolitan planning, July 1964; the University of Toronto seminar on metropolitan reorganization, October 1965; the American Philosophical Society for a grant and the Committee on Research at the Berkeley campus for funds helping to finance research in London, spring and summer 1968; typing services from the Department of City and Regional Planning, and the Center for Planning and Development Research; editorial assistance by Mrs. Judith Riggs; continued encouragement and support from the Institute of Governmental Studies, especially Mr. Stanley Scott for reviewing the manuscript and steering it through revisions, and Mrs. Harriet Nathan, for editorial care; finally, Mr. Max Knight and others at the University of California Press for their help. We specifically acknowledge the assistance of the Ministry of Housing and Local Government in making available maps that have been used or adapted—for Maps 2, 3, 6, and 7. Mrs. Adrienne Morgan prepared most of the maps for publication.

As an adviser on this Institute of Governmental Studies series, Professor Victor Jones provided detailed, searching criticism. Comments on a shorter first draft were provided by Mr. Geoffrey Chipperfield, Ministry of Housing and Local Government, and Professor Daniel Mandelker, Washington University. For extremely helpful critical reviews of the manuscript during autumn 1970, we are also particularly grateful to Professor David Donnison, Director, Center for Environmental Studies, London; Professor C. D. Foster, London School of Economics and Political Science; Mr. Brandon Howell, Technical Secretary, Standing Conference on London and South East England; Professor Emeritus W. A. Robson, London School of Economics and Political Science; and Visiting Professor L. J. Sharpe, Queen's University, Kingston, Ontario. We have footnoted their specific contributions only where their written comments were literally quoted, and where they materially changed the points made in earlier drafts.

Berkeley, California
February, 1971

D. L. F.

CHAPTER I

MANY LONDONS: THE DIMENSIONS OF A WORLD METROPOLIS

LONDON IS a city rich in tradition. The geographical form of what might loosely be called Metropolitan London can be seen most clearly in terms of historical growth. Like an archaeologist, one discovers successive layers, beginning with the ancient City and continuing outward to the most recent suburban development. Each layer has added new buildings, new ways of handling problems, and new units of government. In ordinary conversation, people simply refer to "London," but any description of the form and government of London runs the risk of semantic confusion, for there are many Londons.

SEVEN CONCENTRIC AREAS

This section discusses the seven concentric areas or rings in London's orbit, and the accompanying geographical labels that are used for statistical and planning purposes for the areas. Map 1 gives a visual picture of the entire area discussed. Table 1 provides a convenient summary. The terms used are also explained in the Glossary, pp. 190–196.

1. The smallest area is the central one-square-mile City of London. It is a geographical and governmental unit, but more than that it is a unique area, a financial and commercial hub with its own traditions and characteristics.

2. The Central Area, lying roughly within the ring of main railway stations, contains such specialized precincts as the West End and

1

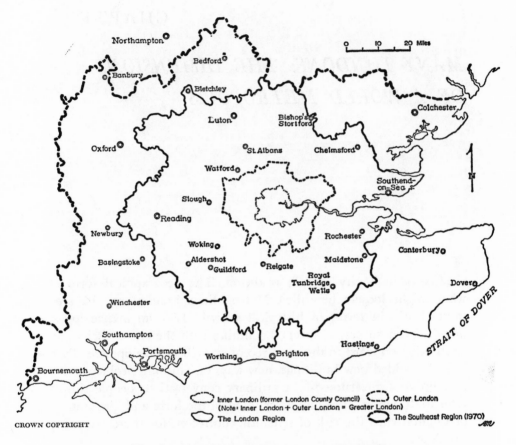

MAP 1—COMPONENT AREAS OF THE LONDON REGION

Bloomsbury, in addition to the City of London. Comprising 8.5 square miles, it corresponds to the central business district in an American city, but it is neither a governmental nor a formal statistical unit.*

3. Inner London is a designation, new since 1965, for the area previously known as the Administrative County of London for three-quarters of a century. More precisely, before 1965 this area consisted of the County of London, governed by the London County Council (the LCC), and the City of London, the square-mile governmental island within the LCC, governed by its own common

---

* Central London has also been given other definitions. See "Central Area" in the Glossary.

Council. Like most American central cities, Inner London has been losing population steadily. In 1901 its population was 4.5 million; in 1970 it was down to 3 million people. Its present governmental character will be described in Chapter Two.

As it has grown, London has spread outward from the center. By the mid-1960's it had filled in an area roughly elliptical in shape, with an east-west diameter of about 30 miles and a north-south diameter of about 25 miles. This solidly developed area has, in turn, been surrounded since the late 1940's by a great Metropolitan Greenbelt, roughly six to ten miles in width (see Map 2). This circular Greenbelt is unique among the major metropolitan areas of the world. By the early 1960's the area within the Greenbelt contained approximately 8 million residents.

4. It was logical that the Registrar General, responsible for the

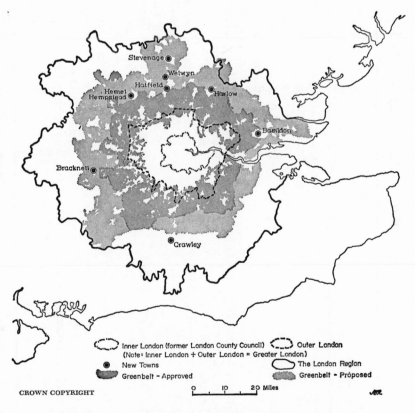

Inner London (former London County Council) Outer London
(Note: Inner London + Outer London = Greater London)
New Towns   The London Region
Greenbelt – Approved   Greenbelt – Proposed

CROWN COPYRIGHT   0   10   20 Miles

MAP 2—LONDON METROPOLITAN GREENBELT AND NEW TOWNS

3

Table 1

Area Units Descriptive of London

Area Designation	Population (millions)	Area (square miles)	Current Governmental Jurisdiction or Usage	Usage Before Formation of Greater London Council, 1965
1. City of London	0.004	1	Governed by its own Common Council	Same as current usage
2. Central Area	0.2	8.5	Statistical area, within the ring of major railroad stations	Same as current usage
3. Inner London	3.1	118	Inner London Education Authority controls education within this area	Formerly the Administrative County of London (London County Council and City of London)
4. Greater London (also Greater London Conurbation)	7.8	616	Area governed by Greater London Council (and census statistical area adjusted to match)	Greater London Conurbation previously had an area of 722 square miles
5. London Metropolitan Region	13.0	4,412	Statistical area designated by Ministry of Housing and Local Government to identify commuting area	Same as current usage
6. South East Region	17.0	10,558	Area of the South East Economic Planning Council (advisory to the central government); also used by the Standing Conference on London and South East Regional Planning, an association of local governments.	Area covered by the Standing Conference was once smaller, but was expanded in 1966 to match that used by Economic Planning Council
7. "South East Study" Region	18.5	16,000	Not currently used	Statistical area used by Ministry of Housing and Local Government for its 1964 report

SOURCES: Various standard publications by the Greater London Council and the British Government.

British census, should identify essentially this same area, 722 square miles in extent, as the Greater London Conurbation. The "conurbation" concept used roughly parallels the "urbanized area" concept used by the U.S. Bureau of the Census. Until 1965, this statistical Greater London Conurbation encompassed more than 100 local governments, ranging in importance from districts and parishes to boroughs and counties.

With the reorganization of London government in 1965 (to which much of this volume will be devoted), most of the area within the Greater London Conurbation became the responsibility of a new metropolitan government, the Greater London Council (GLC), and virtually all of the existing local governments were dissolved. This new geographical area that the GLC came to govern may be designated Greater London. For a brief period after 1965, Greater London, with its 616 square miles, remained distinct from and a little smaller than the Greater London Conurbation. Subsequently the Greater London Conurbation was redefined and reduced in area to coincide exactly with Greater London. (This deliberate merging has proved convenient for most purposes. It does mean, however, that the conurbation area, as a census concept, may no longer be expanded periodically in area to match outward growth of population. However, the existence of an encircling Metropolitan Greenbelt constrains such expansion and provides an unusually fixed outer boundary for Greater London.)

In recent years, Greater London's overall population has been declining. Growth has shifted outward beyond the contiguously developed conurbation proper into sections of the Metropolitan Greenbelt and has jumped beyond to areas entirely outside the Greenbelt. By the late 1950's, the Ministry of Housing and Local Government (MHLG) had identified a new and larger area for statistical purposes.

5. Thus the London Metropolitan Region was designated, with a diameter ranging from 80 to 100 miles. This region includes Greater London and the Outer Metropolitan Area beyond the Metropolitan Greenbelt. All told, the Metropolitan Region includes some 4,400 square miles and a population of 13 million. (It is labeled as "The London Region" in Maps 1 and 2.)

6. A still larger region identified for statistical and planning purposes is the South East Region. This is based on an expanded definition of London's hinterland. It covers more than 10,000 square miles

5

in a huge ring which encircles and incorporates the conurbation, and contains 17 million residents.* This region is the official domain of the South East Economic Planning Council, established in 1965, and is also the area served by the Standing Conference on London and South East Regional Planning. (The Planning Council and the Standing Conference are discussed in detail in Chapter Four.)

7. For working purposes in its investigations, which culminated in *The South East Study*,[1] the MHLG elected to employ an even larger special region with 18 million residents, nearly two-fifths of the entire population of England and Wales. This region, which we designate the "South East Study" Region, adds East Anglia (the traditional name for the region to the northeast) and Dorset (a small county to the southwest) to the South East Region, and lies roughly southeast of a line from the Wash to Dorset. (This study by the MHLG is discussed in Chapter Four.)

The preceding outline of geographical and governmental terms used in this study illustrates clearly the spread of Metropolitan London into South East England. The motor age has freed both individuals and industries from the necessity of remaining near established rail and transit lines. Their use of this freedom to choose other criteria of location has resulted in a far-ranging expansion into the countryside around London, and has naturally brought vast changes to the character and spatial structure of London. This raises the stubborn question of how far the Metropolitan Region extends. It is easy to draw arbitrary boundary lines on a map and indicate governmental and census districts, but for purposes of realistic analysis it is difficult to find a clear line separating Metropolitan London from South East England.

We recognize similar difficulties and developments in the United States. Hundreds of regional councils have been coming into existence, some of the largest of which blur the lines between metropolitan and broader regional definitions. Symbolically, their very names indicate the degree to which some of these entities, having one or more metropolitan cores, are very large in geographic coverage: the Northeastern Illinois Planning Commission, the Delaware

---

* For descriptions of two slightly different versions of the South East Region, see "South East Region" in Glossary.

Valley Regional Planning Commission, and the Southern California Association of Governments are examples.

"THE CENTER OF THINGS"

London is so clearly at the center of things in Britain that its dominance is simply taken for granted. It houses royalty, Parliament, and the central government. It serves the Commonwealth as well as the United Kingdom. It contains a financial nucleus of international importance, and a continuously growing headquarters-office complex. Cultural, professional, and educational specialties and headquarters are concentrated in London. In addition, while old and established businesses have continued to prosper, London has also attracted a larger proportion of new "growth" industries than has the rest of Britain.

London's importance is supported by several contemporary developments. Governmental and corporate reorganization in recent years has encouraged greater administrative centralization, and London has provided an attractive locale for both giant nationalized industries and large private companies. The emergence of a revitalized Europe, including the potential pull of the Common Market, has increased reliance on London, with its favorable location in South East England and its outstanding airport and seaport facilities. Construction of a tunnel under the English Channel (which now seems likely), and other improvements in transportation across the Channel, would further enhance London's position as a gateway metropolis.[2]

A subsequent section discusses the serious problems raised by the relentless growth of Metropolitan London as they relate to physical planning and governmental organization. From a national perspective, the probability of growth keeps alive the worries of the Barlow Commission, which concluded in the late 1930's that London's vitality and growth were being bought at the expense of the economic and social health of other less favored parts of Britain.[3] The issue is persistent and perplexing. The view that the provinces deserve economic bolstering comes into conflict with an alternate view that the fostering of London's development may be a direct way of ensuring essential national economic growth.

In addition, since London as a complex, functioning whole in-

7

creasingly merges into an organizational pattern embracing much of South East England, the problem becomes the relative prosperity and growth of the entire South East. Gradually Britain has become divided into (1) a rich "nation" centered on London, embracing the South East, and extending into the Midlands, and (2) a poor "nation," geographically more distant from London, and including the depressed industrial centers of South Wales, Merseyside, the North East, Scotland, and Northern Ireland.[4]

In sum, it is hardly surprising that the London Region continues to grow, since it provides such a favorable locale for the people and activities that are responsible for a vigorous British political economy. London offers access to a set of functional centers, possesses a great variety of the specialized services that help incubate developing industries, and is thought to provide cultural and other amenities lacking in the provinces.

GROWTH OF EMPLOYMENT

The dimensions of London's growth can perhaps best be conveyed by reviewing what has been happening to employment, and by examining demographic trends. A synopsis of employment trends serves two purposes. First, it indicates changes in the location of job opportunities, and helps to explain changes in the distribution of population, since job seekers move toward job opportunities. Second, it supplies indicators of the economic growth in one area vis-à-vis the nation.* This is important where, as in the case of Metropolitan London, there is no adequate reporting of the relationship between the economy of the metropolitan area and the economy of the nation (such as was reported for the New York Metropolitan Region in 1959–1960).

During the 1920's and 1930's London and the Home Counties accounted for about half of the employment increases for all of Great Britain, although they contain only a quarter of Britain's total employment. It was concern about this situation that led to the forma-

---

* Appropriate income measures would be useful, if they were available. Because of rising productivity per worker, gross national product has been rising at about 2.5 per cent to 3.0 per cent annually, while employment has increased at only an average of some 0.6 per cent per year. Thus it is obvious that employment increases are by no means directly proportional to other measures of economic activity.

8

tion of the Barlow Commission and the publication of its warnings. To head off further concentration, in 1945 the central government began regulating the growth of manufacturing establishments in Metropolitan London; the Board of Trade has administered the controls. But until recently, nonmanufacturing employment was not regulated, and office activity thrived in London.[5]

It is now clear that the disproportionately large employment growth in Metropolitan London during the 1950's had tapered off by the 1960's. Thus from 1951 to 1961, the London Metropolitan Region accounted for 51 per cent of the employment increase in England and Wales. On the other hand, for the period 1961 to 1966 (date of the latest available figures), this same region accounted for only 26 per cent of the national employment increase. But the Outer South East increased its proportion of the national employment increase from 11 per cent for 1951–1961 to 15 per cent for 1961–1966.* Viewing this phenomenon in a slightly different way, recent average annual percentage increases in employment for Greater London are seen to have remained low, while the rates for the Outer Metropolitan Area† and for the rest of England and Wales increased noticeably, as the following figures show (for greater detail, see the Appendix, Table I).

	Average Annual Percentage Increase in Employment	
	1951–1961	*1961–1966*
Greater London	0.4	0.2
Outer Metropolitan Area	2.4	3.7
London Metropolitan Region	0.9	1.2
Outer South East	0.7	2.8
South East Region	0.8	1.5
Remainder of England and Wales	0.3	1.2
England and Wales	0.5	1.4

These figures make it clear that Greater London's growth has slowed down, and also that employment in the Outer Metropolitan Area and in the larger South East Region has been growing far more

* "Outer South East" is that part of the South East Region outside of the London Metropolitan Region.

† "Outer Metropolitan Area" is that part of the London Metropolitan Area outside of Greater London.

vigorously than in the rest of England and in Wales. Thus it is only Greater London's remarkably low growth rate that holds down the overall figures for the entire Metropolitan Region.

But the full dynamics of shifts in employment only emerge when one also examines data broken down by type of industry. For the period 1961–1966, a pronounced dispersal of manufacturing employment occurred, with Greater London losing (1.7 per cent annually) and the Outer South East showing strong gains (3.0 per cent annually); in contrast, the rest of England and Wales was gaining moderately in manufacturing employment (0.7 per cent annually). Gains in the services and construction sectors within Greater London were less than those for England and Wales outside of the South East Region, but the rate of increase in service employment in the Outer South East was nearly double that for England and Wales (see the Appendix, Table II). As would be expected, the South East Region continues to receive more than its share of employment increases from those main industrial sectors exhibiting vigorous growth, and less than its share from those industrial sectors showing lower rates of growth or actual declines:[6]

Overall Change in Employment in England and Wales
1961–1966

Industrial Sector	In Thousands	In Per Cent	Per Cent of National Change Accounted for by the South East Region
Services	1,074	10.3	44.4
Construction	291	20.5	32.3
Manufacturing	216	2.8	12.0
Primary	−169	−12.6	8.9

Thus, during the 1961–1966 period the South East Region, which was responsible for 36.5 per cent of national employment in 1961, accounted for 44 per cent and 32 per cent respectively of the national increases for the two industrial sectors that were growing fastest, but received only 12 per cent of the national increase in manufacturing. Other analyses have also revealed differentials among manufacturing groups, and have shown that the South East Region gained employment in growth groups such as radio and electronics, motor vehicles, scientific and optical instruments, printing and publishing, and selected metal and machinery industries.[7]

During the past three or four years Great Britain has been facing a labor shortage, reflecting very slow growth in the working-age population, compared with the growth of the total population. Because London's total population is dropping, this has been and will probably continue to be a more acute problem for Greater London than for other parts of Britain.[8] These trends may produce an altered equilibrium between Greater London and other parts of Britain.

GROWTH AND REDISTRIBUTION OF POPULATION

Employment shifts have direct counterparts in demographic trends. Until about 1961 the London Metropolitan Region had been growing in both absolute and relative terms. Thus by 1961 this region, with 12.5 million residents, accounted for more than 27 per cent of the population of England and Wales. More recent figures suggest, however, that growth is slowing and that the region's share of the national population may be expected to decrease.

A summary of trends from 1931 to 1968, with estimates for 1981 (see the Appendix, Table III) shows the characteristic growth pattern of large and mature metropolitan areas: Inner London has steadily lost population for several decades; the remainder of Greater London has lost population since 1951; and active growth areas have spread outward, first to the Outer Metropolitan Area and, more recently, to the Outer South East. This outward spread of growth is summarized below:

	Average Annual Percentage Increase in Population	
	1951–1961	*1961–1966*
Inner London	−0.5	−0.7
Rest of Greater London	−0.1	−0.2
Greater London	−0.3	−0.4
Outer Metropolitan Area	+2.9	+2.1
London Metropolitan Region	+0.7	+0.5
Outer South East	+1.0	+1.6
South East Region	+0.7	+0.8
Remainder of England and Wales	+0.4	+0.7
England and Wales	+0.5	+0.7

These aggregate population figures, like the aggregate employment figures reported above, disguise extremely dynamic developments in the restructuring of Metropolitan London. Further changes in the

11

intra-metropolitan distribution of employment and population may be highly significant. Despite the heavy concentration of office-type employment in central portions of Inner London, an increasing amount of office employment is now spreading to other parts of the Metropolitan Region. Manufacturing employment has been actively dispersed. While inward commuting to the center retains its prime importance, other trip patterns to scattered employment destinations are increasing. Land use and transportation implications are further discussed below.

Population growth in Outer London not only responds to a combination of emerging employment opportunities and suburban-linked amenities, but in turn triggers increased service employment with the growth of outer shopping centers, schools, governmental offices, and related activities. Though distributed in relatively low densities, this outer growth has had a remarkable cumulative effect in redressing the balance between the old London and the new. This is illustrated by these population shifts within the South East Region, including prospective changes estimated for 1981:

| | Percentage Distribution of Population | | | |
	1951	1961	1968	Est. 1981
Inner London	22.0	19.4	17.5	13.9
Remainder of Greater London	32.0	29.4	27.5	25.1
Outer Metropolitan Area	23.0	27.6	30.0	32.8
Outer South East	23.0	23.5	24.9	28.2
SOUTH EAST REGION	100.0	100.0	100.0	100.0
Population (in millions)	15.2	16.4	17.2	18.5

Note: Percentages may not add to 100.0 due to rounding.

Within this thirty-year period that part of the South East outside of Greater London is expected to rise from 46 per cent to 61 per cent of the total for the South East Region. This clear evidence of outward redistribution, however, is by no means as dramatic as that which may be expected during a comparable period in most large, rapidly growing American metropolitan areas. It is possible, too, that increased automobile use and a preference for single-family dwellings may promote future development at lower densities, which would disperse the population even more than the official projections suggest.

Natural increase, despite some vicissitudes in birthrate, remains a major component of population change. Births rose from about 1955 to 1964, but since then have dropped perceptibly. In addition, the migrations in and out of Greater London, and in and out of the Outer Metropolitan Area, remain exceedingly complex and are subject to major swings depending upon employment opportunities. Components of net migration for two recent years are summarized here; negative figures mean net outflow from Greater London and positive figures mean net inflow to Greater London:[9]

Migration between Greater London and:	Net Population Flow	
	1960–1961	1965–1966
Outer South East	−100,000	−93,000
Rest of England and Wales	−1,000	−21,000
Rest of Great Britain and Overseas	+61,000	+27,000
TOTALS	−40,000	−87,000

These data show that there has characteristically been a substantial net in-migration from other parts of Britain and from overseas, a modest out-migration to England and Wales (other than the South East Region), and a marked out-migration to the Outer South East. These combine into a total net out-migration outnumbering natural increase (births minus deaths) by about 3 to 2. Here are average annual figures for Greater London:[10]

	Population Changes, Greater London		
	1951–1961	1961–1966	1966–1968
Natural Increase	+33,600	+52,600	+46,300
Net Migration	−54,000	−79,600	−82,400
NET CHANGES	−20,400	−27,000	−36,200

Note: Figures may not add to totals due to rounding.

The rise in net out-migration is thus seen to be a major contributing factor in Greater London's declining population.

In contrast, strong net in-migration reinforces relatively high rates of natural increase and pushes up population growth in both the Outer Metropolitan Area and the Outer South East. For example, here are the average annual figures for the Outer Metropolitan Area:[11]

13

	Population Changes, Outer Metropoliton Area		
	1951–1961	*1961–1966*	*1966–1968*
Natural Increase	+24,200	+43,400	+42,300
Net Migration	+77,000	+54,900	+42,500
NET CHANGES	+101,200	+98,300	+84,800

To grasp the full impact of population trends, it is also essential to consider how these are translated into changes in numbers and types of households. During recent years, owing to a perceptible drop in the average size of households, the number of households has tended to increase more rapidly than the total count of population might suggest (or, atlernatively, not to decrease in proportion to population losses). Average household size for Greater London has dropped from 3.02 persons per household in 1951 to 2.85 in 1961 and to 2.67 in 1966. The number of households in the South East Region increased by 13 per cent, while population increased by only 7 per cent during the 1951–1961 period. Within Greater London, for that same ten-year period, population registered a 2 per cent loss, but the number of households rose about 2 per cent. The change in the distribution of households by size in Greater London is shown by this summary tabulation:[12]

	All Households		*1–2 Person Households (per cent)*	*3–5 Person Households (per cent)*	*6 Persons and Over (per cent)*
	Number	*Per Cent*			
1951	2,619,000	100.0	42.0	51.9	6.1
1966	2,690,000	100.0	49.9	44.6	5.5

There have also been significant changes in the social characteristics of Greater London's households. As middle-class families move out beyond the boundaries of Greater London, there is an ever-growing tendency toward polarization between the rich and the poor, although undoubtedly this is less pronounced than in metropolitan areas in the United States.

The implications of these shifts in the character of households, and the housing problems to which these trends have contributed, are treated in Chapter Six.

THE CHANGING PHYSICAL PATTERN

The London Metropolitan Region has been growing at rates that look modest when compared with the increases in most large metropolitan areas in the United States. But the region's growth is vigorous by British standards. In absolute terms, the increase during recent years has amounted to an annual average of about 65,000 residents and about 50,000 employed persons. As we have indicated, the resident population has undergone a marked dispersal, while employment, despite its considerable growth in outer sections of the Metropolitan Region, continues to be far more centrally located. In central London alone, the construction of new office space has been particularly impressive, increasing from 153 million square feet in 1957 to 175 million in 1962, but with growth slowing so that there were only 179 million square feet of space by 1967. The 1967 figure represented 60 per cent of the total office space in all of Greater London.[13]

Nevertheless, an increasing amount of the newest office construction has been occurring in parts of Inner London other than the central area. The rapid buildup of Croydon, 12 miles south of the heart of London, provides a notable example. While it still has not been dispersed as much as new manufacturing facilities, office construction in outer areas is also increasing. Here are the net increases in office and industrial floor space from 1964 to 1967:[14]

	Increases in Office Space Millions of sq. ft.	Per Cent of Increase in South East Region	Increases in Industrial Space Millions of sq. ft.	Per Cent of Increase in South East Region
Greater London	12.9	67	2.9	10
Outer Metropolitan Area	4.4	22	14.2	49
Outer South East	2.1	11	11.7	41
South East Region	19.4	100	28.7	100

Note: Figures may not add to totals because of rounding.

It follows that vast changes have been underway in land use and, more important, in the fundamental relationships between place of residence and place of work.

The volume of longer-distance commuting has increased, and trips from the outer suburbs are common. This has taxed the main radial underground and railroad lines. The remarkable upsurge in automobile ownership and use for commuting has seriously congested roads running into central London. The number of persons entering central London by rail increased 20 per cent during the ten-year period to 1962, and those entering by private car 109 per cent, while

15

the number using busses dropped 25 per cent. The overall number of persons entering rose 12 per cent, bringing the total to 1,238,000 entrants for the peak period, 7 to 10 o'clock in the morning.[15] Despite the tremendous increase in the use of the automobile (and in contrast to American cities), nine out of every ten persons still reach the center by public transport: about two-fifths come by rail, two-fifths by the underground (subway), and a steadily diminishing one-fifth by bus.

For the most part, London avoids New York's very high residential densities. Flats characteristically do not exceed three or four stories, and much of London still has the tree-lined streets more characteristic of smaller cities. As of the late 1950's, the average residential density for Inner London was 85 persons per net acre; the density north of the river was 115, and that south of the river 67.[16] Because of extensive war damage, large sections of London, such as the areas in the East End north of the older docks, formerly characterized by high residential densities, were rebuilt at moderate densities. In Stepney, for example, the number of persons per net acre fell from 184 to a new standard of 136; the planned reduction in residents was from 200,000 to 94,000; and the actual area in residential use in the main development area was increased from 424 to 461 net acres.

One can view the density pattern of the Greater London Conurbation as resembling the cross-section of a low-rise volcanic cone. There is an inner area of reduced gross residential densities in the office-commercial center. Next there is a close-in encircling high ridge with densities of up to about 50 persons per gross acre (for example, in Holborn and Stepney). Finally, one observes a gradual downslope beyond, dropping to less than 40 per gross acre, then generally dropping to about 18 to 20 per gross acre toward the outskirts of Inner London and to less than 10 per gross acre near the edge of the built-up conurbation.*

Perhaps the most unusual features of London's contemporary physical pattern—excluding the dominant historical physiography of

---

* "Gross density" is defined as persons per "gross acre," meaning that all land is included, nonresidential as well as residential. "Net density" restricts the land to direct residential usage. See Coppock's initial article in J. T. Coppock and Hugh C. Prince, eds., *Greater London* (London: Faber and Faber, 1964), pp. 36–37.

the central area and the absorbed villages—are the Metropolitan Greenbelt and the set of publicly developed outer new towns. These represent major impacts of the *Greater London Plan of 1944,* as implemented in the postwar years.* The main rather solidly built-up portion of Greater London, containing something less than 600 square miles—the average radius from the center being about 14 miles—has been encircled by a green girdle 6 to 10 miles wide and covering 840 square miles.

The Greenbelt is used mainly for agriculture, along with the other uses that existed before the Greenbelt policy was established in the late 1940's. Some residential communities or smaller clusters are to be found within the Greenbelt and, under special circumstances, permission is granted for further building inside these established settlements. The land remains largely in private ownership, but use is painstakingly controlled by planning authorities under central government policy. Under the monumental Town and Country Planning Act of 1947, compensation was provided where planning permission for other uses was refused, but that arrangement was subsequently scrapped. Present land use controls in the Metropolitan Greenbelt and elsewhere now operate primarily without compensation to the landowners. Once the Greenbelt area is defined by the various development plans, permission to develop can be refused under planning powers, without compensation.

In the outer parts of the Metropolitan Greenbelt, or just beyond it, eight new towns have been built with average planned capacities of about 65,000 residents each, although not all are completed. These new towns are planned to accommodate gross densities of about 12 to 15 persons per acre. Net residential densities are typically in the 40 to 65 range, with an average of about 15 dwelling units per net acre. The new town corporations, which are special public organizations created by the central government, have sought to create full

---

* Patrick Abercrombie, *Greater London Plan, 1944* (London: HMSO, 1945). The plan is known both as the Greater London Plan and as the Abercrombie Plan. Supplemented by various affirmations of policy by the central government, this plan became the bulwark of broad development policy for Greater London for the next 20 years. Sir Patrick Abercrombie was also leader of the planning team that prepared an earlier companion plan for the County of London: J. H. Forshaw and Patrick Abercrombie, *County of London Plan* (Prepared for the LCC; London: Macmillan, 1943).

and varied employment opportunities; they have generally been successful in attracting industry and offices, as well as retail stores and the usual services.[17]

All told, these new towns and other planned public efforts to build new communities or to expand existing ones outside of Greater London have accommodated an estimated 600,000 residents since World War II.[18] The scale and boldness of this public initiative have had no direct parallel in the United States. Moreover, the plan has attracted worldwide attention as a positive way of relieving overcrowding in the central city, and of controlling the physical pattern of urban growth. British political leaders are convinced that the resulting growth pattern is more desirable than the suburban development typical of the United States.

CHAPTER II

THE GREATER LONDON
REORGANIZATION OF 1965

THIS CHAPTER concentrates on the new London metropolitan government that went into effect on April 1, 1965. The characteristics of this two-tiered governmental structure warrant detailed examination, because the new system of local government is widely hailed as a model for analogous governmental reform elsewhere.

Before reporting the process that produced the new government, or describing its principal features, it is appropriate to review the general characteristics of British government, and to offer a brief history of London's evolving governmental structure. The chief purpose is to identify some of the historical and cultural differences between Britain and the United States that bear on government in large metropolitan areas. This will help the American reader grapple with the question: how relevant to metropolitan problems in the United States, and how adaptable to the American cultural-institutional context, are the lessons from London that this book attempts to elucidate?

THE BRITISH GOVERNMENTAL SYSTEM

With its long history of evolution through incremental refinements, British government is unquestionably complex and tradition-laden, especially in its detailed working. To an American, it may become almost unfathomable or take on a certain mystical quality. Yet the essential structure is simpler than government in the United States. A look at the British system will help the non-British reader understand this discussion of the government of Greater London, and its reform.

First of all, central government in Britain is very strong, so strong that it is generally referred to as "the Government." There are no intervening states or provinces, so that central government deals directly with local government. There are far fewer checks and balances between executive and legislative branches; in the British cabinet system those holding key executive posts are members of Parliament, and are usually tied together by a party-related and cabinet-centered mechanism of cooperation and discipline. Sharing in the administration, although taking their political and policy clues from the ministers, is a cadre of elite administrative officers—the higher civil servants with "Rolls Royce minds." *

Great Britain contrasts sharply with the United States, because British central government leaders in office *are empowered and entrusted to govern.* Certain rules of the game seek to preserve fair play and to provide ample opportunity for critical review, but there is nothing comparable to the checks and power limitations that characterize government in the United States. The British system rests on an elitist tradition of responsible leadership. It presumes that a pragmatic consensus can be achieved. While in power, party leaders forming the government are given great leeway, although the representatives of the opposing parties are expected to question and criticize. But until the leaders in power are forced out by loss of an election, their government is given great scope for decision and action.

To a remarkable degree the system functions on the basis of acceptance of *authority.* The elite conceives of government service as a readily assumed responsibility. In contrast, the general citizenry appears to be very tolerant of government and its leaders. This shared expectancy that it is natural to be led provides the consensual support sustaining the system.

Local government in Britain, for all its trappings of democracy and autonomy, can usefully be viewed as a decentralized administrative mechanism for carrying out the bidding of central government. This

* " 'They have very silky minds,' R. A. Butler said to me, about higher civil servants: 'they've Rolls Royce minds. In fact, the civil service is a bit like a Rolls Royce—you know it's the best machine in the world, but you're not quite sure what to do with it. I think it's a bit too smooth: it needs *rubbing up* a bit.' " Anthony Sampson, *The Anatomy of Britain Today* (New York: Harper Colophon, 1966), pp. 262–263.

20

does not mean that specific local governments may not also undertake responsibilities on their own initiative. But as compared with the situation in the United States, British local government is unquestionably far more constrained by central government checks, and is much more dependent upon specific authority delegated by central government. At first the visiting American observer may not sense how different the central-local relationship is from that in the United States. The controls and the power of central government are smoothly and unobtrusively exercised—this is a special forte of the higher civil service. Indeed, the preponderant acceptance of the system even by local government leaders provides further evidence of the pervasiveness with which the authority of central government is both expected and respected. This stands in great contrast to the ideological bases of grass-roots government and of federalism, which lead to such basic and bitter cleavages between distinct governmental levels in the United States.

The British central government, usually acting through its various ministries and departments, maintains firm control of virtually every functional sphere. Whether the question relates to education, housing, transport, or economic development, an appropriate ministry is ready with its policy group, inspectors, and other officials hovering over and guiding the activities of local governmental officers and staff. Local governmental representatives exercise considerable initiative, but always with the realization that central governmental agencies hold veto power. A veto may be cloaked in persuasion when the central government wishes to avoid openly flouting local opinion. But it is still a veto.

Thus the central government maintains direct responsibility for such explorations of possible governmental reform as may, however irregularly, from time to time be judged important. The history of the last hundred years or so shows few major and effective overall reviews of London government. But the review in the late 1950's and the subsequent steps to translate its major recommendations into effective action were taken by the central government. One key to such a process of institutionalized change is the device of the commission of inquiry, the most important being a royal commission. In Britain a carefully selected royal commission representing a spread of viewpoints and interests and carrying great prestige can search out possible major alternative approaches to a given problem and can produce an ordered set of recommendations providing a base for legislative action. The royal commission mechanism works in Britain because it coincides with expectations that the government in power will initiate needed reforms. Moreover, the commissions are able to reach a consensus that provides a practicable basis for doing a necessary job. Thus it is expected that a royal commission will present a completed and packaged proposal that is feasible—political, financial and other considerations having already been taken into account. This contrasts with the greater proclivity of American review commissions for making a large number of proposals, often seemingly quite separate from any serious expectation that the entire package might be a practical basis for legislation.

Three major points relating to government in Britain have thus been introduced that bear on the subsequent discussion. First, central and local government are intricately related in a national system. Second, local government is a device for administrative decentralization within this system. Third, structural reforms within this system are responsibilities of the central government. Thus the reform of local government for Greater London is but one sector of a much broader commitment to local governmental reform throughout Brittain. Consequently Chapter Seven asks whether the main ideas carried through in the creation of the Greater London Council, and in the reorganization of the entire London government, have been judged sufficiently valid and practicable to serve as models for metropolitan reform proposals in other parts of Britain. Chapter Eight also suggests that the appropriate American counterpart of British central government's responsibility for local governmental reform is strong initiative—plus firm and continuing programmatic action—by our national and state governments in recognizing the essential wholeness of the United States governmental system. In sum, we seem to have a good deal to learn from Britain although it may be quite unrealistic to assume that particular features of British local governmental reorganization will be acceptable in the United States at the level of local referenda. The full discussion of these points is reserved for Chapter Eight.

THE STRUCTURE OF LOCAL GOVERNMENT

In Britain, local governments are known generically as "local authorities." As in the United States, several varieties are found—

counties, county boroughs (independent of and parallel to counties), and other less important lower-tier authorities over which counties serve as upper-tier umbrellas. All local authorities are governed by elected councils. These councils are notable for their size, which on the average is considerably larger than comparable governing councils in the United States and in other leading European countries. The largest authorities are counties and county boroughs with more than 600,000 population; they have councils ranging from 85 to 166 members. Authorities in the 200,000 to 600,000 population class have council memberships ranging from 64 to 121. Those in the 100,000 to 200,000 class have council memberships ranging from 57 to 93. Local authorities with populations between 30,000 and 100,000 have from 18 to 70 council members. Finally, those with populations between 10,000 and 30,000 have from 8 to 60 council members.[1]

There appears to be a double or triple rationale for these very large local authority councils. It can be argued that they are more representative and include a greater variety of membership than is the case with small councils. It is also clear that they encourage heavy reliance by each local authority on a large number of council working committees that assume responsibility for specific functional spheres. The large council follows something of the pattern of Parliament, and it is also consistent with a political-party approach to council organization, where one of the parties is recognized as in power, and the other major party (as well as splinter minority parties) accepts the role of opposition. A recent investigation of local organization sponsored by the central government—the Maud Committee (on the management of local government)—concluded that excessively large councils should be avoided, and recommended a maximum of 75 council members. But the concept of councils that are much larger than most in America seems firmly accepted.

Characteristically, the county councils meet only once every three months, and the other local authority councils meet monthly. The principal work, as we have noted, is carried on by council committees. Whereas the largest councils may have as many as 35 committees, the smaller ones tend to have far fewer, sometimes as few as only three or four committees. Counties and county boroughs usually have about 20 committees each. On the average, county council committees meet five times per year, but the council committees of other local authorities tend to meet once a month.

In the larger councils, each member serves on an average of from six to ten committees or subcommittees. Council members in county boroughs, for example, spend more than 75 hours per month on council business. Slightly under 20 hours of this is taken up by council and committee attendance. Traditionally, so-called co-opted members (persons who are not council members) are also added to some committees, particularly in the field of education.

The committee system has both merits and defects. Within the British context it permits a local authority council to delegate to committees most of the detailed administrative-executive concern for the management of specific functions. This enables the councils to reserve responsibility for overseeing committee work, and for discussing broader and sometimes multi-functional issues. It also permits council members to have their fingers on a fair amount of detail, which seems to be what the British have interpreted as appropriate for local democratic government. Despite extensive delegation, the British system makes each of the committees finally responsible to the council, in marked contrast to the American tendency to delegate functions—education in particular, but also city planning, housing, and others—to separate and autonomous boards or commissions.

The searching Maud Committee report also identified basic difficulties in the committee system, and in the existing local governmental structure. Thus, the Maud Committee concluded that the various council committees are often far too independent of the council, and are not properly part of any concerted effort to coordinate diverse committee operations. The Maud Committee also argued for mechanisms deliberately created to ensure direction and coordination. Each local authority has a clerk to the council, and he serves as something of a coordinator or administrator. But clerks are peers of the department heads, rather than being administratively over them. Consequently the clerks' coordinative leadership is more a matter of personal influence than of hierarchical position. Local authorities lack executives or administrators approximating the roles of American mayors or city managers. The Maud Committee suggested, among other things, a stronger role for the clerk, a management board made up of five or six council members, more central information, and the deliberate delegation of more administrative power to professional department heads and to staff, with the council and council committees concentrating on policy matters.

As already noted, local authorities are subject to detailed guidance by the central government. They cannot expand their functional responsibilities without specific central government sanction. They are subject to ministerial regulations at every turn. Moreover, particularly in fiscal matters, the local authorities depend very heavily upon the central government, both for funds and for clearance on the manner of expenditure. This, too, is under review, for it is recognized that a restructured local government should also be strengthened and given correspondingly greater leeway for action.

The evidence points to no great enthusiasm by citizens for becoming directly involved in British local government. Voting tends to be fairly light: only about 40 per cent of voters turn out for local elections. Further, a substantial number of council seats are uncontested. The British system, by its very emphasis on central government, appears to foster far greater interest in national elections than in local. It also seems to stress the political importance of delivering votes in order to influence the outcome of national elections, rather than contributing to the winning of local elections. Thus, paradoxically, the citizens and voters, whom British local authorities are supposed to serve, are actually rather detached from them.

One final characteristic of local authority councils is worth noting: the indirect election by the elected councillors of a further group of aldermen who in turn come to serve as additional council members. At present, aldermen may number up to one-sixth of the elected councillors. Aldermen are often persons with experience as council members, who have failed to achieve reelection, or older or retired persons with ample time for such work. They bring a continuity of experience, but they also dilute the concept of direct democratic election by the citizenry. The aldermanic system has come under heavy criticism, especially by the Maud Committee. It is possible that aldermen will be excluded from local authority councils in the future, further reducing council size and strengthening representation by direct election.

LONDON'S GOVERNMENT: A BRIEF HISTORY [2]

London's long and complex evolution can be summarized by pointing to three especially significant acts of Parliament passed in 1855, 1888, and 1899. The Metropolitan Management Act of 1855 created a relatively weak Metropolitan Board of Works, which was given direct responsibilities mainly for sewage and drainage. Most municipal functions remained with a welter of 99 untouched parishes. The new, indirectly elected, limited-purpose governmental unit encompassed 2.8 million residents and included the 116 square mile area that was subsequently to become the County of London. During the next 20 years, the board's functions were gradually extended or amplified. Significantly, however, no powers in the health and welfare spheres were given to the board. Some functions became separate: the Metropolitan Police had been removed from local control in the 1830's, and a separate London School Board was created in 1870.

By the mid-1880's, local governmental reform was receiving national attention, and serious scandals attributed to a corrupt Metropolitan Board of Works insured the inclusion of London in this broader consideration. Thus, as a counterpart to legislation establishing elected councils in counties throughout England, the Local Government Act of 1888 also created a new Administrative County of London, carved from neighboring counties to take in the geographic area previously under the jurisdiction of the Metropolitan Board of Works. This Administrative County consisted primarily of a new London County Council (LCC). It included, for some administrative purposes, the City of London, which was relatively untouched by the reforms. While the local governmental units remained much as they had existed under the previous board, William A. Robson, an authority on London government, stresses that the new LCC brought a complete change of atmosphere. Very able councillors were attracted, and open debates characterized its operations.

Eleven years passed before order was brought to the disarray of subsidiary local governments that had persisted. The London Government Act of 1899 established 28 metropolitan boroughs and abolished the previous local units, although respecting the continued separate existence of the City of London. These metropolitan boroughs were, however, granted so much authority that they rivaled the LCC. Thus, the boroughs took on a broad range of functions, such as public health, welfare, street maintenance, and inspections of many sorts. Only gradually were the powers of the LCC expanded, for example, by taking over from the London School Board in 1904 the responsibilities for education, and later assuming responsibilities for public assistance, town planning, and, concurrently with the metropolitan boroughs, housing.

No major reorganization was accomplished during the 61 years from 1899 until the Herbert Commission presented its report. The primary effort was that of the Royal Commission on London Government (the Ullswater Commission), in session from 1921 to 1923. It resulted in no direct effective reform action. During this period, the number of separate specialized authorities completely outside of the LCC's jurisdiction, if anything, increased.[3] These included: the Metropolitan Water Board (1902); the Port of London Authority (1908); the London and Home Counties Traffic Advisory Committee (1924); the Metropolitan Area Licensing Authority (1930), controlling the licensing of public service vehicles and goods vehicles; the London Passenger Transport Board (1933), becoming the London Transport Executive (1947); nationalized regional gas and electricity boards cutting across Greater London (1948); and a nationalized hospital service with boards also cutting across Greater London (1948).

For the dozen years from 1945 until 1957, limited efforts were made to review and to patch up local government. In desultory fashion these were reported out, but they carried admonitions not to meddle with the LCC and not to consider major reorganization within Middlesex County, an almost solidly urbanized set of suburbs located north of the LCC. While the Labor Party was in power (1945–1951), its leaders were most concerned with major nationalization efforts, and were in any event not disposed to direct critical inquiry at the LCC, which had traditionally been dominated by Labor. But as the Conservatives came into power in 1951, significant local governmental review efforts were undertaken. Three white papers were issued by the central government in 1956 and 1957. They proposed local government commissions for England and Wales to review the situation further. It appeared, however, that such inquiries would be of restricted scope and that no reform moves would be undertaken unless concurred in by a majority of the local governments affected. This was largely the course of events over the next several years, so far as the rest of England and Wales was concerned. The Local Government Act of 1958 authorized the Local Government Commission of England to review, under some-

27

what limited powers, the organization of local government outside the London Area.

It came as something of a surprise, then, that Henry Brooke, appointed Minister of Housing and Local Government in January 1957, moved ahead vigorously during the summer and fall of that year to gain the authorization for, and to see that members were appointed to, a new Royal Commission on Local Government in Greater London. This commission of inquiry had none of the limitations placed upon the Local Government Commission of England. The chairman, Sir Edwin Herbert, and six other members were to prove remarkably independent of ties to local governmental consensus.* Thus was established—in the best spirit of British central governmental responsibility—a royal commission that was to prove thoroughly resourceful in analyzing problems, identifying the most promising alternatives, and designing a completely new governmental system.[4]

THE HERBERT COMMISSION

The Herbert Commission was directed "To examine the present system and working of local government in the Greater London area; to recommend whether any, and if so what, changes in the local government structure and the distribution of local authority functions in the area, or in any part of it, would better secure effective and convenient local government. . . ." Excluded from the commission's consideration were police (a central government function, in the case of London), water (under the Metropolitan Water Board), and, tacitly at least, public transport (a responsibility of the London Transport Executive, a public corporation under central government supervision).

The Herbert Commission invited evidence from more than 200 authorities or organizations. There were 117 local governmental units within the commission's review area of 840 square miles. (See Map 3.) In addition to reading the large volumes of written evidence, and an additional 174 communications from the public at large, the commission held 70 sessions to take oral evidence, spent 88 days visiting local authorities in the review area, and held 44 other meetings. Major central government departments submitted

---

* Sir Edwin Herbert subsequently became Lord Tangley.

BOUNDARIES
- - - - - Greater London
———— County
————— Local government

CROWN COPYRIGHT

0 | | | | | 5 Miles

City of London   [1]
County boroughs
  West Ham   [2]
  East Ham   [3]
  Croyden   [4]

MAP 3—FORMER LOCAL GOVERNMENTS WITHIN THE AREA TO
BECOME GREATER LONDON

recommendations, as did the political parties, many professional organizations, associations of local authorities, and individual local authorities within the review area. As might be expected, most of this evidence was restricted to mundane matters. Much of it was defensive of the status quo. In contrast, however, some reports, including those by some academic groups, sought to identify major theoretical alternatives. For example, an influential document was submitted by a working group at the London School of Economics, under Professor William A. Robson's chairmanship. This report urged radical reorganization into two levels of government, with functions separated into those that could be handled locally and those that were metropolitan in scope.

29

Perhaps as much as any other bit of evidence, this report pointed in the direction that the commission followed: proposing two levels and examining the balance of functions between them. The commission evolved two main criteria for judging reorganization proposals: first, that administrative efficiency be sought (suggesting local units large enough to attract competent officials and to cause a minimum of duplication of effort); and second, that the authorities remain responsive to the people in the best democratic traditions of local self-government (suggesting that functional responsibilities be assigned to local units of the smallest feasible size). The rationale for a two-tiered structure was imbedded in the idea that each specific governmental function should be analyzed and allocated accordingly. It would be assigned to a metropolitan-wide upper tier, if the preferred emphasis were to be on overall coordination, or on a single metropolitan service system. It would go to a more localized lower tier, if the emphasis were to be on distinctly local responsiveness, with a greater degree of local self-determination. The meticulous examination of functions as a basis for optimal allocation became a major undertaking and a distinctive contribution of the Herbert Commission.

Persuasive evidence, including that given by the Center for Urban Studies at the University of London, argued that rather than relying on direct reorganization of local government, it would be better to leave local government essentially alone and to rely on the strong coordinating powers of the central government to achieve metropolitan and regional unity of policy and action. Complementary arguments favoring joint consultation among the local units also supported the argument that local governmental structure might best be left in its current form. It was argued, too, that the proposal for a Greater London government was unduly restricted to the built-up area within the Greenbelt and that this would hamper the strengthening of broader regional government.

In the millions of words of evidence presented to the commission, one set of oral exchanges between Dame Evelyn Sharp, Permanent Secretary, Ministry of Housing and Local Government, and the members of the commission (on January 12, 1960) effectively summarizes the alternatives. As the Permanent Secretary was queried about possible arrangements for Greater London, she spoke of the great temptation to assume that planning doctrine—she particularly referred to the still revered Abercrombie Plan—best comes from the central government, and that local governments can then expect to comply with the policies laid down from above. She argued that this was a dangerous notion. Here is a portion of her extended remarks:

No Ministry sitting in Whitehall can ever be as successful negotiating the planning for a whole region as the authority for that region. Its angle is a different one—we are looking from the top down, not from the bottom up, and I think it makes a great deal of difference to the sort of plan that will result. . . . [In] the planning world there is an obvious case, a strong case, for having *an* authority—and I am not saying what kind of an authority at this stage—which is thinking of the planning of Greater London. . . .

[If] a local authority is not to have a major say on how its land should be used and developed and what should be done with it, I think local government would be fatally impoverished. . . .

You can of course in a country like the United Kingdom argue yourself into thinking that local government is not a good idea at all; every part is so caught up with every other part, the problems are so much common problems. You can, I think, make a very good case for something like a perfect system if you do not in fact believe, as I believe, that local government is an absolutely essential part of our system of government and that whatever price you have to pay for it you must pay.[5]

It follows that since an expanded local government designed to serve a metropolis offsets central government authority, it might be preferable to a strengthened central government as a means of solving metropolitan problems.

The commission came to agree that a reformed and expanded two-tier metropolitan government was preferable to reliance on the central government as metropolitan coordinator. In its final report, after reviewing the main alternatives, the Herbert Commission said:

We conclude, therefore, that the solution lies not in a surrender of vital local government functions to central government but in the reorganization of local government institutions within the Review Area so as to enable those functions to be performed by and through the machinery of local government. Such a surrender is not necessary and is undesirable for a number of specific reasons.[6]

Accordingly, in its report of October 1960, the commission recommended that a two-tier governmental structure be created. This was to include 52 new Greater London boroughs, each with a population of 100,000 to 250,000, to which as many functions as possible would be given. A Greater London Council (GLC), would also be created, encompassing an area with about 8 million residents. The GLC would assume responsibilities for such functions as might be dealt with over the whole area. All previous multi-function local governments would be superseded, except for the City of London. The organization of the metropolitan police, already under the control of the Commissioners for Metropolitan Police, appointed by the central government's Home Secretary and serving an area roughly coterminous with that dealt with by the Herbert Commission, would not be affected. Nor would operations of the Metropolitan Water Board be affected.

The Herbert Commission report evoked diverse reactions and acrimonious debate.[7] It was bitterly opposed by the existing London County Council (LCC), and by the London Labor Party, as representing a Conservative move to dismember the Labor Party stronghold within the County of London. Forceful arguments were raised that it would be inadvisable to break up the excellent LCC government by distributing to the boroughs such major functions as education, health, welfare, and housing. Some outer suburban areas strongly resisted inclusion within the proposed Greater London Council. As the drafting of the London Government bill proceeded, a number of important changes were introduced, and the Herbert Commission recommendations underwent substantial changes. In the end, the voting which carried the London Government Act of 1963 through Parliament was heavily partisan, and the Labor Party opposed the legislation to the end.

THE NEW GOVERNMENTAL SYSTEM

The London Government Act excluded nine urban districts and boroughs in five outer counties from the area under the jurisdiction of the GLC. This reduced the proposed area of inclusion to 616 square miles, compared with the commission recommendation of 760 square miles, and the original commission review area of 840 square miles. The number of new London boroughs was reduced to 32 (plus the City, recognized as a special case) with populations from 146,000 to 340,000, averaging about 250,000.* Clearly, each would be sufficiently large to be a viable government.

Thus a new set of 34 governments—the GLC, 32 London boroughs, and the City—replaced the greater complexity of 92 earlier governments in the same geographic area. Two counties, London and Middlesex, were replaced completely. Parts of four other counties—Essex, Kent, Surrey, and a small segment of Hertfordshire—were separated from their home counties and incorporated into the GLC. Three county boroughs—Croydon, East Ham, and West Ham—were fully absorbed. The counties had been upper-tier governments, and the county boroughs single-tier. Lower-tier governmental units that were also absorbed included 28 metropolitan boroughs within the old LCC, and 39 municipal boroughs and 15 urban districts within the counties outside the LCC. Only the City of London managed to remain intact as a government, and only Harrow kept its geographic boundaries, while being transformed from a municipal borough into a new London borough. (Table 2 shows the former units incorporated in each London borough. See also Map 3, p. 29.)

The London Government Act also made a fundamental change in the handling of education, a most important local function. The Herbert Commission had recommended that the GLC be the education authority, but that the operation of most schools be assigned to the boroughs. "The broad division should be that the [GLC] should be responsible for the provision of a statutory standard of education throughout the area and that the boroughs should be responsible for the discharge of the executive work, subject to budgetary and other controls by the [GLC]." [8] The threat to dismantle the LCC education service, which was respected for its high standards, and to entrust the schools to boroughs, which had no experience in administering education, caused a fiery debate. Just before

---

* The City Corporation of London, governed by its Common Council, was given its charter in 1070, and has understandably been able to defy efforts to absorb it within larger local governmental units. The Herbert Commission recommended that it be permitted to continue its special status as before, but that it be allocated functional responsibilities as though it were a London borough. So it is both different from the London boroughs (and not included in the ordinary count of 32 boroughs) and a parallel lower-tier authority (so that for most purposes we may conveniently include it as a 33rd borough-level government).

Table 2

The London Boroughs and Their Former Status

London Boroughs with 1968 Populations	Former Governmental Status
Barking (169,520)	Barking MB[a] (part), Dagenham MB (part)
Barnet (316,240)	Barnet UD[a], East Barnet UD, Finchley MB, Friern Barnet UD, Hendon MB
Bexley (215,470)	Bexley MB, Chislehurst and Sidcup UD (part), Crayford UD, Erith MB
Brent (284,460)	Wembley MB, Willesden MB
Bromley (304,230)	Beckenham MB, Bromley MB, Chislehurst and Sidcup UD (part), Orpington UD, Penge UD
Camden I[a] (231,680)	Hampstead MetB[a], Holborn MetB, St. Pancras MetB
Croydon (329,210)	Couldsdon and Purley UD, Croydon CB[a]
Ealing (298,720)	Acton MB, Ealing MB, Southall MB
Enfield (267,830)	Edmonton MB, Enfield MB, Southgate MB
Greenwich I (229,700)	Greenwich MetB, Woolwich MetB (part)
Hackney I (243,180)	Hackney MetB, Shoreditch MetB, Stoke Newington MetB
Hammersmith I (197,590)	Fulham MetB, Hammersmith MetB
Haringey (245,270)	Hornsey MB, Tottenham MB, Wood Green MB
Harrow (208,220)	Harrow MB
Havering (252,290)	Hornchurch UD, Romford MB
Hillingdon (236,990)	Hayes and Harlington UD, Ruislip-Northwood UD, Uxbridge MB, Yiewsley and West Drayton UD
Hounslow (205,580)	Brentford and Chiswick MB, Feltham UD, Heston and Isleworth MB
Islington I (241,890)	Finsbury MetB, Islington MetB
Kensington and Chelsea, Royal Borough I (210,720)	Chelsea MetB, Kensington MetB
Kingston-upon-Thames, Royal Borough (144,480)	Kingston-upon-Thames MB, Malden and Coombe MB, Surbiton MB
Lambeth I (329,250)	Lambeth MetB, Wandsworth MetB (part)
Lewisham I (281,140)	Deptford MetB, Lewisham MetB
Merton (184,220)	Merton and Morden UD, Mitcham MB, Wimbledon MB
Newham (255,130)	Barking MB (part), East Ham CB, West Ham CB, Woolwich MetB (part)
Redbridge (246,090)	Chigwell UD (part), Dagenham MB (part), Ilford MB, Wanstead and Woodford MB

Table 2 (*Continued*)

London Boroughs with 1968 Populations	Former Governmental Status
Richmond-upon-Thames (177,130)	Barnes MB, Richmond MB, Twickenham MB
Southwark I (293,120)	Bermondsey MetB, Camberwell MetB, Southwark MetB
Sutton (165,430)	Beddington and Wallington MB, Carshalton UD, Sutton and Cheam MB
Tower Hamlets I (192,250)	Bethnal Green MetB, Poplar MetB, Stepney MetB
Waltham Forest (236,900)	Chingford MB, Leyton MB, Walthamstow MB
Wandsworth I (321,720)	Battersea MetB, Wandsworth MetB (part)
Westminster, City of I (243,960)	City of Westminster, Paddington MetB, St. Marylebone MetB
City of London I (4,210)	City of London

ᵃ Abbreviations: I, Inner London Borough; MetB, Metropolitan Borough; MB, Municipal Borough; CB, County Borough; UD, Urban District.

SOURCES: *1966 Annual Abstract of Greater London Statistics* (London: GLC, 1968), Table 1, p. 1; Gerald Rhodes, *The Government of London: The Struggle for Reform* (London: London School of Economics and Political Science, and Weidenfeld and Nicolson, 1970), Appendix 3, pp. 255–260.

the local elections, the London Teachers' Association took to the streets in defense of the LCC education service. The opposition also received strong behind-the-scenes support from within the Ministry of Education. In the end, the government backed down, and in subsequent statements concluded that the two-tiered approach to education would prove too cumbersome. Consequently, the act assigned education in the inner boroughs (equivalent to the former LCC area) completely to an Inner London Education Authority (ILEA) and in the outer boroughs (the remainder of Greater London) completely to the boroughs. The ILEA has 53 members, of whom 40 are the GLC councillors for the 12 Inner London boroughs and the other 13 are representatives, one from each council, of the Inner London borough councils and the common council of the City of London. This arrangement for Inner London was to be subject to review at the end of the first five years, but was made permanent by the Local Government (Termination of Reviews) Act of 1967. The outer borough councils handle their responsibilities through educa-

35

tion committees. Map 4 shows the London boroughs and their distribution between Inner and Outer London.

Most of the recommendations of the Herbert Commission for election procedures were followed. Special rules governed the initial election. Thereafter, the act provided that the GLC would hold elections in April, and the London boroughs in May. Councillors would be elected to three-year terms. Each GLC election would precede the borough elections by a year (for example, a GLC election was held in April 1967 and borough elections were held in May 1968).* There were to be 100 councillors in the GLC, and a maximum of 60 councillors in each of the new boroughs. The total number of councillors for all of Greater London was thus substantially reduced from the previous totals of 300 county councillors and 4,000 borough councillors. The change means, of course, that most former councillors are now without council seats in the new governments. In accord with British traditions of local government, discussed earlier, there is a provision for the indirect election, by the councillors themselves, of additional members called aldermen. As is the case with other local authorities, aldermen in the GLC serve for six-year terms, and may constitute up to one-sixth of the number of elected councillors.

It was anticipated that swings of party majorities would occur, and that control of the GLC could be expected to change hands from time to time. Actual election results are described in Chapter Three.

The London Government Act followed the recommendations of the Herbert Commission in setting up a two-tier governmental structure, and giving the boroughs functions suitable to their status as large cities within the structure. In some respects the GLC was made stronger than had been envisaged by the Herbert Commission. As we have noted, the GLC, through the ILEA, was granted all au-

---

* The intention of the London Government Act of 1963 was that ultimately the GLC and borough elections would be held the same day, but this could not be done until electoral boundaries were redrawn. Meanwhile the Labor Government decided to postpone the 1967 borough elections by one year. In the three GLC elections held so far, councillors have been elected on a borough basis, since existing parliamentary constituencies were unsatisfactory. When parliamentary boundaries are revised (probably in time for the 1973 elections), one GLC councillor will be elected for each of 92 constituency areas. This will mean a reduction in the number of councillors. (We are indebted to Professors W. A. Robson and L. J. Sharpe for this explanation.) The 1967, 1968 and 1970 election results are reported in the final sections of Chapter Three.

MAP 4—LONDON BOROUGHS IN INNER AND OUTER LONDON

thority for education in Inner London (although, as events were to demonstrate, direct political dominance over the ILEA was not to be guaranteed if the ILEA were to have a different political majority from the GLC as a whole). The GLC was also granted strong powers with respect to highways and traffic. Moreover the GLC, with its powers over housing, redevelopment, and planning, concurrent with or supplementary to those of the boroughs, emerged with important capacities for initiating and carrying out major planning recommendations, and for moving ahead with large-scale projects.

In other ways, however, the London boroughs were made stronger than had been envisioned by the Herbert Commission. Fewer boroughs meant larger boroughs, and some of the big ones became powerful cities in their own right. Lambeth, Wandsworth, Croydon, Barnet, Southwark, and Ealing, in descending order, all had in excess of 300,000 residents when created. Several boroughs, particularly Westminster, Camden, and Kensington and Chelsea, and the City of London, each had in excess of 20 million pounds sterling in ratable value.[9]

The boroughs were placed in charge of a highly significant package of services: education (in the outer boroughs only), health, welfare, and children's services, refuse collection, sewer service, library service, rating,* and various other registration and inspection functions. The boroughs were also given major responsibilities, shared with the GLC, for housing, town planning, and park administration. More responsibilities are to be given to the boroughs within five or ten years, as the GLC and the boroughs carry out mandatory reviews to determine who should manage housing estates, parks, and other public facilities initially allocated to GLC administration after previous administration by the LCC or Middlesex County. The vitality of the boroughs will be discussed further in subsequent sections.

Table 3 shows the division of responsibilities between the boroughs and the GLC. It remains to be seen how this division of functions will work out in the long run. In many cases the allocation is quite clear, one level or the other being given full responsibility for the function in question. In some other cases, like town planning, there are inevitable friction points, and questions of the workability of the formulas allocating responsibility. In Chapter Three we discuss the methods of cooperation that have evolved for coordinating the performance of various functions by the boroughs and the GLC.

PROBLEMS OF THE TRANSITION

The governmental transition, whose tempo increased from the spring of 1964 until the formal transfer date of April 1, 1965, was

---

* The rate is roughly analogous to the property tax in the United States, but is sufficiently different in its conception and administration that it must not be too readily treated as similar. Until recently, the rate was applied only to "occupiers" of property, that is, to persons making beneficial use of the property. Consequently, vacant or unused property was not subject to rating. This is now being modified. Ratable value is based on the actual or estimated rent, with certain accompanying assumptions, rather than being a fraction of estimated sales value, as in American practice. Ratable values are generally lower than American assessments, and the tax rates, calculated as so many shillings and pence—newpence after 1971—to the pound, appear much higher to Americans. Rating practice is discussed in greater detail in the final section ("Finance") of Chapter Four.

without question the largest governmental reorganization ever undertaken within a major metropolitan area. In total, some 50,000 staff had to be redistributed—excluding teachers, residential staff, and manual workers.

In order to ensure smooth handling of the innumerable details of the changeover, a plan for coexisting governments was evolved. Elections of new GLC councillors and new London Borough councillors, respectively, were held in April and May of 1964, a full year in advance of the formal changeover. Councillors and aldermen from the affected local governments remained in office until the formal transfer date. Meanwhile the new councillors established committees and selected their senior staff personnel. Council members from the old governments met with their counterparts from the new ones and formed interim joint committees to oversee the transfer of functions, property, and personnel. Staff officers from the new and the old governments also made similar preparations. Nevertheless, there was an enormous amount of work to do in an eleven-month period. In many cases councillors and senior staff of the new governments were already officers of the old governments. The burden of work involved in closing down the old units and preparing for new ones—to say nothing of the continuing need to make day-to-day decisions—was often extremely heavy, particularly during the final months of the transition period. Fortunately, Sir William Hart, the former clerk (chief administrative officer) of the LCC, also became the first clerk of the GLC and was thus able to oversee the transfer from both vantage points.

The equitable transfer of personnel was a particularly important question. The uncertainty of many individuals about their futures made for poor morale. It sometimes proved difficult to fill interim and presumably temporary positions in the LCC and the old boroughs. Inevitably some employees faced dismissal or reduction in rank, as the new governments were considerably less numerous than the old governments. For example, some former clerks (the chief administrators) were faced with the prospect of becoming assistant clerks in the new governments. A London Government Staff Commission was created by the Ministry of Housing and Local Government to suggest procedures that would best safeguard staff interests. This commission drew up regulations that guaranteed to any former employee a position comparable with that of his previous

Table 3

The Initial Division of Functions Between the Greater London Council and the New London Boroughs

Functions	London Borough Councils	Greater London Council
Personal Health, Welfare, and Children's Services	All except ambulance service	Ambulance service
Education	Twenty outer boroughs have full responsibility	Full responsibility in the Inner London Education Area (the old LCC area), subject to review within a five-year period
Housing	Primary responsibility, except for GLC powers	Overspill housing outside GL; GLC permitted to build houses within GL with permission of borough or of the Minister; continue LCC housing program (with program for transferring to boroughs to be submitted by GLC before April 1, 1970)
Town Planning	Some responsibility for preparing development plan, within framework of GL development plan; most of the authority for granting planning applications; primary responsibility for land purchase and development	Preparation of overall development plan for GL; authority for approving certain planning applications (e.g., high buildings, very large projects, historic sites); large-scale development projects and projects straddling borough boundaries
Traffic and Highways	Highway authorities for other than trunk or metropolitan roads; off-street car parking	Highway authority for all main roads (though trunk roads are the Ministry of Transport's responsibility); traffic management taken over from Ministry of Transport; licensing of motor vehicles and drivers; metered parking
Fire Service		Full responsibility

Service		
Refuse Service	Refuse collection	Refuse disposal
Sewer Service	Responsible for sewers other than main sewers, and for some local disposal plants	Main sewerage authority (except area served by West Kent Main Sewerage Board) responsible for main sewers and principal sewage disposal plants
Parks and Open Space	Provision of parks and open space within the borough	Initial responsibility within former London and Middlesex counties, with program for transferring parks serving immediate localities to the new boroughs to be submitted within five-year period (may be extended to ten years)
Libraries	Full responsibility	
Intelligence Department (Research and Statistics)		Full responsibility, including definition of the function and the placement within the GLC
"Rating" (assessment and levying of taxes)	Full responsibility as rating authorities	May raise revenue by "precepting" on the rating authorities
Control of Building Construction	Twenty outer boroughs have responsibility	Full responsibility within Inner London, but may delegate functions to the boroughs
Miscellaneous	Cemeteries and crematoria	Courts
	Registration of births, deaths, marriages	Land drainage, Thames flood protection
	Swimming pools, washhouses	Licensing places of public entertainment; betting tracks
	Varied inspection services, such as those related to health	Management of Royal Festival Hall and other facilities
	Street markets and slaughterhouses	Provision of supplies services
	Street cleaning	Provision of scientific services
	Handling elections to both GLC and borough councils	

Table 3 (*Continued*)

Functions	Special Agencies and Boards
Police	Except for City of London, which retains its own police force, the Metropolitan Police under the Home Office (a central government department) will continue to serve all of the GLC area and certain areas on the periphery
Water Supply	Remains the responsibility of the Metropolitan Water Board for the first several years; is reported that the central government will probably introduce legislation to transfer this function to the GLC
Hospital and Maternity Home Administration	Responsibility of regional hospital boards (under central government)
Electricity and Gas Supply	Responsibility of electricity and gas boards (under central government)
Public Transport	Underground and buses were initially the responsibility of the London Transport Board, under the Ministry of Transport; commuter railroads and the rest of Britain's railway system are under British Rail, a public corporation, under the Ministry of Transport; buses and Underground subsequently transferred effective January 1, 1970 to a new public corporation, named London Transport Executive, under the control of the GLC

SOURCE: Summarized from the London Government Act of 1963.

position, and compensation payable if this condition could not be satisfied. This guarantee led to some unanticipated moves by the old governments in raising the salaries of their staff members so that they would automatically receive at least these amounts in the new governmental posts.

It was also essential that a very large number of ongoing programs and countless units or parcels of public property be smoothly transferred (including the handling of complex legal formalities effecting the transfers), despite the fact that the long-range allocations had not been completed. Some responsibilities for programs and properties were assigned for only a few years, pending further review and final policy determination. The GLC, for example, took over most of the parks, housing, and other facilities from the LCC, in order to provide interim management, but it was expected that within a few years many or most of these would be given to various Inner London boroughs.

One of the most hotly debated problems of the changeover was the naming of the new boroughs. In all but one case, the new boroughs represented an amalgamation of two or more local governmental units. It was often difficult to reach agreement on names for the boroughs and upon sites for borough halls. The Minister of Housing and Local Government had ruled against the acceptability of joint names, finally allowing only one exception, Kensington and Chelsea.

Extraordinary as the changeover has been—at least from the vantage point of the student of metropolitan affairs—informed commentators report that by and large Londoners themselves were not particularly aware that so momentous a transition was under way. This suggests the comparative remoteness of local government from most of the citizens of this great metropolis.

CHAPTER III

FIRST YEARS UNDER THE NEW GOVERNMENT

Despite the complexity of the new structure and the difficulties of the changeover, local government in Greater London has settled into its new pattern and moved ahead. The Greater London Council (GLC) provides a resourceful metropolitan-wide government which may be expected to develop and to employ its specialized and in-depth capabilities (for example, broad policy planning and intelligence).* Each of the London boroughs, in turn, is a medium-sized city capable of effectively providing a sensible cluster of vital functions. In the words of Sir William Hart in 1968: "the new system is working, and working a great deal more smoothly than at times many feared might be the case. This has been brought about by a remarkable degree of cooperation between the GLC and the London Borough councils." [1]

There are already encouraging signs that the system called for by the London Government Act of 1963 is also proving flexible. No one supposed that the structure proposed was perfect, yet no one could be sure that cooperation would be forthcoming and that successive accommodations could be worked out. In fact, the representatives of the various governmental units have evolved mechanisms for cooperation, and have succeeded in initiating change. This chapter describes the GLC, the boroughs, and their relationships. It

---

* "Intelligence" is treated as a separate function—a centralized research and statistics operation—especially set out by the London Government Act of 1963, and will be discussed at greater length later.

also reviews GLC-borough working arrangements for planning, housing, and transport, and reports on the 1967, 1968, and 1970 elections.

THE GREATER LONDON COUNCIL

The GLC is composed of 100 elected councillors, and 16 aldermen who are elected by the councillors. It meets every other week, and is presided over by its chairman, who is elected by the council. Members are seated strictly according to party, with committee chairmen in the front rows and "back benchers" in the remaining seats—all arrayed in a most impressive council chamber. A GLC meeting looks like a small parliament at work. The agenda is formal and traditional. A question period is followed by committee reports and recommendations. Action by the council is largely to approve these recommendations after they have been discussed and amendments considered. Because party discipline is strictly enforced, the majority party can virtually always count on a known bloc of votes. Thus what happens in the council meeting takes on a symbolic and formal character: the verbal encounters are lively, but the opposition can only delay, and question committee proposals carefully. The majority party is clearly the government. The minority parties merely constitute the opposition.

A dozen or so council committees constitute the key working units. (The exact number and their names have been subject to change during recent years.) Pivotal committee chairmanships go to senior council members in the majority party. The committees are manned primarily by council members (each committee having both majority and minority party representation), although in certain instances additional committee members may be co-opted from outside the council. The committees provide continuing bridges between the legislative-policy functions of the elected council and the direct administrative operations of the various departments.

There has been a tendency to form and make use of committees for coordinating and controlling governmental functions. For example, the General Purposes Committee was created several years ago to assume responsibility for overall policy. It has included the chairmen of the other standing committees and two representatives from the ILEA. The Policy Steering Committee was formed in 1968; it was renamed Policy and Resources Committee and given the added responsibility for the annual budget in the late spring of 1970. The Finance and Supplies Committee is responsible for financial administration; the Establishment Committee, for personnel administration.

The other standing committees include the following (with shifts from time to time): Arts and Recreation; Housing; New and Expanding Towns; Planning and Transportation; Public Services; Strategic Planning (responsible for the Greater London development plan); and Thamesmead (responsible for a very large development, virtually a new town, on the southern bank of the Thames). The chief technical officer provides essential liaison between a given committee and the corresponding functional department. He furnishes information and staff assistance to the committee, and in turn transmits to the department policy guidance from the committee.

In one sense, the ILEA serves as the council's Education Committee for Inner London; but since the ILEA has substantial autonomy, it must also be treated as a semi-independent unit and is discussed below. A number of supporting service departments— architecture, central purchasing, engineering, law, and medical service, to name a few—serve various main functional departments and hence bear no simple one-to-one relation to the council committees. The architect to the council, for example, serves many departments and has close relations with several committees.

The decentralization of executive responsibilities to the many committees sometimes results in friction or lack of coordination in the handling of specific problems. Until recently the only overall administrative (and in a sense, executive) coordination was through the office and person of the Clerk to the Council. But this post was anomalous: although the clerk was responsible for coordinating the work of the many chief officers and their departments, he was viewed only as the first officer among equals; his authority was heavily dependent upon his personal influence. As the result of a report by the Maud Committee on the Management of Local Government, and a report to the GLC's Establishment Committee, by the management consultants, Cooper Brothers and Company, the GLC decided to provide the clerk with greater coordinating authority over the other chief officers. In November of 1967, the GLC approved a redefinition of the position, which was to be titled the Director General and Clerk to the Greater London Council. The holder of this office was to

Be the principal adviser on matters of general policy, and responsible for ensuring consistency of departmental proposals with Council policy and of securing managerial effectiveness of its officers; . . . be the head of the Council's service, the leader of the team of chief officers, and the chief executive; be responsible for seeing to the preparation and keeping up to date of a long-term assessment of resources and commitments actual or tentative, for securing coordinated advice on the forward planning of objectives and services necessary to enable members to decide the Council's policy and programme, and for seeing to the due implementation of the Council's programme; and shall report concurrently on all proposals affecting resources, the Council's programme or policy.[2]

The new title and functions were assumed by Sir William Hart, and also became the basis for a careful search for a successor, since Hart was shortly to retire. Mr. Arthur Peterson was appointed to the post in February 1968 and took office on June 1. His qualifications included considerable administrative experience in the central government's civil service, his most recent position having been deputy secretary in the Department of Economic Affairs. He hoped to strengthen the capacity of the chief officers, operating in a coordinated way, to bear the detailed operations of the GLC's services and thus help the elected council members to focus on policy determination.[3]

In an innovative move, the Herbert Commission recommended an intelligence department, which was envisaged as serving not only the GLC but the central government, the boroughs, and the general public. This would be a first-rate urban research agency responsible for continuing studies of Greater London and for the periodic open publication of statistics (by no means an intelligence agency in any cloak-and-dagger sense). The commission stressed that "the first prerequisite for a policy for Greater London is accurate and up-to-date knowledge of needs. . . . To this central intelligence department all the other departments should be able to turn for information and to it they should address requests for research and advice."[4] After considerable discussion, it was decided to place the new organization in the clerk's office rather than give it departmental status. As the Research and Intelligence Unit, it began operation in February 1966 under its director, statistician Bernard Benjamin.

The unit gradually expanded, although financial constraints have prevented all of the growth originally envisaged. With a staff of 50 and recommended expenditures for 1968–1969 of 170,000 pounds (of which 70,000 is for research on behalf of London boroughs), the unit has had a broad range of projects underway. These were organized within three professional sectors: intelligence systems for GLC services; intelligence and research for London boroughs; and research generally. The director and his staff carry on research within the unit, often on behalf of other departments of the GLC or the boroughs; contract for research to be done by universities or others; and advise on and coordinate statistical standards, survey procedures and standards, and information interchange within the GLC.

In an interview in 1968, Dr. Benjamin, as director, saw the unit as having a strategic research role and as providing definitive statistics on trends and forecasts for Greater London. He also saw the unit as assembling and analyzing technical and objective data, and was concerned with ways of giving such data maximum relevance for policy-making. But he had reservations about how far the unit should move in the direction of policy recommendation.[5]

A new Planning and Transportation Department merged the former Planning Department and the Highways and Transportation Department on October 1, 1969. The Research and Intelligence Unit was relocated in this department. Dr. Benjamin has since left. The Research and Intelligence Unit will serve the Planning and Transportation Department, other GLC departments, the London boroughs, and the general public interests in coordinating and disseminating research and statistical information for Greater London. It is reported that the unit "will now command a staff of some 200 people, mainly professional, and will clearly be in a better position to carry out a properly integrated program of research and intelligence service for the whole of London." [6] Nevertheless, it now seems fair to conclude that the original concept of a central intelligence department has been lost.

THE NEW LONDON BOROUGHS

The newly fashioned London boroughs, as already noted, are medium-sized cities in their own right. Viewed in national perspective, only Birmingham, Liverpool, Manchester, Leeds, Sheffield, and Bristol (in England and Wales) are larger than Lambeth, the largest

London borough (population 320,000 in 1966). As noted in Chapter Two, six of the London boroughs had more than 300,000 population when created; a seventh had moved into this class by 1966. Most boroughs have populations of between 200,000 and 300,000; only five boroughs and of course the uniquely small City of London (with only 4,000 population), fall below 200,000.

Furthermore, the London boroughs have fiscal resources that generally exceed those of other cities in England and Wales. For example, Westminster's total ratable value exceeds that of Manchester, Birmingham, and Liverpool. Thus Westminster, by far the richest, has 398 pounds ($955) ratable value per capita, and Camden has 137 pounds ($329) per capita, compared with Birmingham's 47 pounds ($113) per capita and Manchester's 44 pounds ($106) per capita.* Only one borough, Lewisham, has a lower per capita ratable value than Birmingham, the leading provincial city in England and Wales.

Many London boroughs have socially heterogeneous populations and remarkable diversities in land use. Several boroughs, notably Camden, Islington, Hackney, Southwark, and Lambeth, are shaped like wedges, including parts of built-up central London but also extending into the inner suburbs. Six of the outer London boroughs exceed 30 square miles in area, and only seven London boroughs are smaller than 10 square miles (the City of London, only a little over a square mile, would constitute an eighth). All of the boroughs except Harrow and the City of London are amalgamations of two or more former metropolitan boroughs or, in outer Greater London, combinations of even more diverse former units of government.† In some exceptional instances, such as Lambeth, Barking, and Redbridge, former units of government were split as well as recombined. These reconstitutions have entailed considerable adjustment.

One serious problem caused by the carving out of new boroughs relates to the use of inherited governmental office space and other facilities. As an example, take the case of Hillingdon, the most westerly of the London boroughs (which includes London's giant Heathrow airport). Hillingdon's 43 square miles are an amalgam of the

* Converted at the official exchange rate of one pound to $2.40, unless before December 1967, when the rate was $2.80.

† See the discussion of governmental structure in Chapter Two.

former Uxbridge metropolitan borough and the three separate urban districts of Hayes and Harlington, Ruislip-Northwood, and Yiewsley and West Drayton. An entirely new borough government had to be formed, by consolidating diverse operating systems and records, shuffling or locating new staff, and making the best possible use of existing space. The result has been the physical separation of various operating departments in different government buildings. The town planning department and parts of building control, for example, have been the only borough functions with headquarters in Northwood, and obviously coordination with the architects department and other departments located at some distance in other centers has proved difficult. Communication by mail has often supplanted personal contact. A new main civic center in Uxbridge is on the drawing boards, however, and assuming adequate funding (a restraining difficulty at this point in Britain's history) most departments should be centrally located by 1972.

Twenty-four of the new London borough councils have 60 elected councillors (the maximum permitted under the London Government Act). The other boroughs have fewer elected councillors: Bexley and Harrow, 56 each; Havering, 55; Merton and Richmond-upon-Thames, 54 each; Sutton, 51; Barking, 49; and Waltham Forest, 48. Aldermen, who account for up to one-sixth the number of councillors, are in turn elected by the councillors and serve on an equal basis. All 12 of the Inner London boroughs have 70 council members each and the 19 Outer London boroughs average 67 council members each, ranging from 57 to 70.[7] The London borough councils meet less often than the GLC. Typically, a borough council meets about once every six weeks. The Camden Borough Council, as an example, meets eight times a year, but takes a break during the summer. Characteristically, committees are empowered to act in their functional spheres between council meetings.

There is no standard pattern of borough council committees. Perhaps the typical number is something over a dozen, and the range is from 10 to 18 committees per council. In turn, a larger number of subcommittees, ranging from a half dozen to about 40, also hold their own meetings. On the average, committee meetings are held every six weeks (although considerable variation prevails) and subcommittee meetings somewhat less frequently.[8]

The following description of committees of the Camden Borough

Council is illustrative, but should not be construed as typical. The Camden Borough Council had 12 committees during its first three years, but when the Conservatives swept into power in May 1968, the number was reduced to eight, each with 11 members. The Conservatives also introduced a new Policies and Resources Committee. The majority leader serves as chairman and, as with all other committees, minority party representation is ensured. Each committee has an executive committee of three members: the committee chairman, a second member from the party in power, and a third member from the minority party. This executive committee is empowered to act on behalf of the larger committee, but only if there is unanimous agreement of all three members.

It is difficult to generalize about the quality of political leadership and the caliber of professional staffs in the London boroughs. Presumably the larger governments and the reduction in number of elected offices have worked to attract councillors of greater ability. Some argue that councils might well be made smaller in the interests of efficiency, but except for the reduction of the very large councils (such as those with over 75 members) this appears unlikely.[9]

By recruiting promptly and effectively, several of the boroughs were able to begin operations with exceptionally fine professional staffs. Other boroughs moved more slowly and found only a limited number of outstanding candidates for professional positions—this is discussed further in the subsection on planning. Limited evidence suggests that creation of the new London boroughs has elicited no new wave of political excitement and ambition. More than two-thirds of the first borough councillors and close to 100 per cent of the borough aldermen had been members of the previous local councils.

Borough elections have shown no increase in voter participation, and they tend to attract a smaller proportion of eligible voters than the GLC elections. Still, it has been suggested that the early elections may not have provided a fair test of potential interest, because the citizens have not yet come to identify with their new boroughs. Especially in the first election (excepting Harrow), they were voting for councilmen in expanded and largely unknown governmental entities.[10]

It remains to be seen whether, with time, the London boroughs achieve greater recognition as local governments. As new borough civic centers are created and as boroughs come to take over an increased share of the administration of housing and of parks, borough residents may have increasing bases for identification with their boroughs. Perhaps enhanced loyalty will also follow. But for the time being, at least, the London boroughs do not appear to offer very lively alternatives to the traditional allegiance to small community units.

INTERGOVERNMENTAL RELATIONS: BOROUGH-TO-BOROUGH AND GLC-TO-BOROUGH

In contrast to earlier two-tier governments (including those of the LCC and the metropolitan boroughs) in which nearly all the most important functions had gravitated to the upper-tier government, the new GLC system allocates a bundle of important functions to the lower-tier governments, the London boroughs. This offers important opportunities for each borough to work out cooperative arrangements among its own departments (for example, health, welfare services, and schools). But it is still too early for most of the boroughs to have achieved optimal internal cooperation. Each department has been busy with its own organizational problems, establishing new procedures and consolidating these with procedures inherited from earlier constituent local units. In addition, many of the new departments have had to make do with separated and even makeshift quarters. The case of Hillingdon has already been discussed.

The 32 London boroughs are handling several important functions for the first time: this has undoubtedly made them more receptive to the idea of discussions with other boroughs, and the use of common guidelines. A leading part in inter-borough cooperation has been played by the London Boroughs Association (the LBA), founded in June 1964 as the London Boroughs Committee, and given its current name in 1966.[11] This association was patterned in part after the older Metropolitan Boroughs Standing Joint Committee, but the new organization has already demonstrated a greater vitality and acceptance than the earlier one.

Each of the London boroughs has three representatives in the association. These representatives serve, respectively, on the LBA's three main working committees—General Purpose, Works, and Social Services—one representative on each committee. A subcommittee of the General Purpose Committee deals with the contentious overlapping functions—especially planning, housing, and highways. The association and these three committees meet every six weeks. A fourth committee, Education, has members from the outer boroughs only, and meets every three months.

The chief technical officers are also organized, function by function, and provide advice to the committees. An Advisory Body of Chief Planning Officers meets monthly under the guidance of an executive committee. This advisory body advises the LBA and the Planning Committee of the LBA, when requested, and moves ahead on its own initiative on other matters. Its secretariat is provided by the City of Westminster Planning Department. Correspondingly, other functional groupings of chief officers meet periodically and are available as advisers to the LBA and its committees.[12]

The LBA performs several valuable functions. It forces the boroughs to strive for their own consensus. This makes for greater consistency of action among the boroughs, which facilitates further cooperation. The LBA also serves as a spokesman and agent for the boroughs in dealing with the GLC (and the central government). More important, the LBA provides a political base for unifying and strengthening the boroughs' collective position vis-à-vis the GLC. But membership and participation of the boroughs varies, and none of the main working committees receives 100 per cent support.

Other special-function organizations also facilitate cooperation among the boroughs. The London Boroughs Management Services Committee (carried over and expanded from an earlier Metropolitan Boroughs Operations and Methods Committee), of which 18 boroughs are members, has a director, a staff of over 150 persons, and an annual budget of some 250,000 pounds ($600,000); it is organized into several working divisions. This committee is responsible for a major five-year study of the structure and operations of the main departments of the constituent boroughs. It operates various joint computer schemes by which two or more boroughs share computer facilities. The London Boroughs Training Committee, of which most boroughs are now members, has organized social work courses, mainly for borough staff members.

Combinations of boroughs have sponsored various other joint committees. These include: the London Housing Consortium, which promotes industrialized building, and in which all boroughs participate; the Metropolitan Architecture Consortium for Education (MACE), in which a majority of the outer boroughs participate, along with the Inner London Education Authority and other local governmental units in Metropolitan London; and the Central London Planning Conference, involving the City and five boroughs. In addition, various advisory bodies and committees, covering such spheres as inter-library cooperation, common assessment bases, and cooperation among health and welfare services, have been at work, sometimes reporting through the LBA.[13] In a pattern with many variants, a particular borough assumes responsibility on behalf of other boroughs for maintaining central records or a central referral service. Some selected examples, with the responsible boroughs, are: records of admission of old people to special large homes, in Camden Borough; central registry of prosecutions under food and drug acts, in Lambeth Borough; and central registry of prosecutions under weights and measures acts, in the City of London. The GLC has entered into various cooperative arrangements with the boroughs to allow it to continue certain record-keeping functions that were previously performed by the LCC, and are performed more efficiently by a central agency than when dispersed among the boroughs. For example, the GLC maintains a central index of mentally disturbed persons.[14]

While most of the functional allocations to the London boroughs and to the GLC have proved reasonably clear-cut, it was inevitable that in some spheres, particularly where functions were shared, or where the GLC was authorized to set forth broad guiding policy within which the boroughs had to fit, there would be uncertainty and contention during the early years of GLC-borough relations. As one key participant-commentator has been led to conclude: "The actual distribution of functions made by the London Government Act of 1963 may not be perfect. There are points where the lines of demarcation are not clear enough or where they are not drawn at the most convenient places." [15]

The adaptations and adjustments continue. Since 1965, the GLC has sought strengthened or expanded powers, which, if granted, might have been at borough expense. The boroughs have agreed to some claims and have resisted others. The Ministry of Housing and Local Government, as arbitrator, has also stepped in at some points to grant some of the GLC's requests and to refuse others. The Labor government has tended to resist any material strengthening of the GLC's powers.

THE MAJOR FUNCTIONS

The establishment of satisfactory intergovernmental working relationships has been especially difficult in the functional areas of planning, housing, highways and traffic management, and education. These *jurisdictional* problems are treated in this section; the discussion of *substantive* problems and policies is generally reserved for Chapters Five and Six. In discussing GLC-borough relationships in the preparation of the Greater London development plan, however, some exception is made to incorporate very brief presentations of substantive proposals, since these provide examples of the issues on which the GLC may take different positions from those adopted by the boroughs or by the central government.

PLANNING

The London Government Act of 1963 required each borough to establish certain specified chief officer posts. A planning officer was not included among these, even though the boroughs were given authority for local planning. The responses of the boroughs to the obvious need for planning officers varied: 10 boroughs established separate planning directorships (one borough, Brent, combined planning and research); 11 appointed combined architectural and planning officers; 3 appointed combined engineering and planning officers; and in the remaining 9 boroughs, the planning officers were not listed as chief officers, but were made subordinate to borough engineers or other officers.[16]

A total of 71 chief planning officer posts, or other key planning positions, became available in the various boroughs and the GLC at the time of the reorganization.[17] The boroughs and the GLC acted with marked differences in speed to fill these openings, and offered a range of positions and salaries, the GLC and the inner boroughs tending to offer the highest salaries. These factors, combined with a shortage of competent technical officers, particularly at the middle levels, resulted in considerable unevenness among the boroughs in the quality of staff. It was apparent that the needs of the expanding number of large planning departments exceeded the pool of high caliber professional talent. With the passing years, however, both the GLC and the borough planning departments have adjusted, and these shortages of technical personnel have become less serious.

The evolving planning relationship between the GLC and the London boroughs can conveniently be portrayed by focusing on three phases: preparing the development plans (including research support); regulating actual development; and proceeding with redevelopment or other special publicly conceived projects. Main stress will be on the first two, for the political tussles about role have centered on the issues of who shall determine the general policy by which development is guided, and who shall establish the specific criteria by which proposed development is judged.

Preparing the development plans.—The London Government Act of 1963 requires the GLC to prepare a Greater London development plan which "shall lay down considerations of general policy with respect to the use of land in various parts of Greater London, including in particular guidance as to the future road system." [18] This is to be a strategic plan, stating general development policy and portraying proposed patterns in broad diagrammatic terms. This requirement reflects the Herbert Commission's recommendation that the GLC provide a broad policy framework, within which the boroughs are to prepare their own more specific development plans.* It also coincides with the national commitment in the Town and Country Planning Act of 1968 to a structure or PAG-type plan (as recommended by the Planning Advisory Group reporting to the Minister of HLG).[19] Hence, the GLC development plan has been awaited with interest as the first structure plan to be prepared.

The mandated development plan presented difficulties for the GLC in its relationship with the London boroughs. The requirement that the boroughs fit their own development plans into the framework of the GLC plan obviously forced the boroughs to limit their

---

* In November 1970, the Minister for Local Government and Development in the new Department of the Environment, responding to the outlook for extensive delay in approving the Greater London development plan, approved the boroughs' going straight to local or action area planning without preparing their own structure plans. This suggests that the Greater London development plan will need to become more detailed. It also opens up a much bigger problem of the prospects for success in a two-tiered system in which the upper tier prepares the structure or policy plan and the lower tier controls actual development. (See Peter Hall, "Planning: Working Together," *New Society*, 16:912 [November 19, 1970].)

planning activity until the GLC plan was ready. Yet several of the boroughs, being well staffed and energetic, were ready and impatient to begin work. Furthermore, much of the field research needed to support the Greater London development plan was, by the terms of the 1963 act, to be conducted by the boroughs under the guidance of the GLC's planning department. Understandably, this proved difficult and produced tension because it was almost impossible for all of the boroughs to receive prompt supervisory directions from the GLC, to carry out the work, and to get the information back to the GLC on a very tight schedule. The GLC needed considerable time to assemble its full intelligence and to complete the plan. Accordingly the GLC requested, and received, approval for postponement of the deadline for submitting its development plan to the MHLG from December 31, 1968, to July 1, 1969.

In formulating a strategic plan for Greater London, the GLC found itself in a circumscribed situation. On one side, London's future inevitably depends on trends and policies affecting all of Britain and on political decisions made by central government. At most the GLC could merely recommend that the central government reconsider certain policies. On the other side, the GLC had to contend with the independence of an array of energetic London boroughs, each with its own ideas about its population growth and development role. Furthermore, the borough plans are ultimately approved by the MHLG, with the GLC merely commenting. The lack of direct approval power by the GLC materially weakens the GLC's position as a strategic planning authority.

First drafts of a written development plan and of supporting studies were circulated by the GLC for confidential study and discussion in October 1967. Reactions were varied, and often strong. Criticisms ranged from cries that the plan was intruding into areas the boroughs considered their own, to statements that the plan was too vapid and weak. Major reworking led to a March 1969 release of the final draft text to GLC councillors, borough representatives, the press, and concerned organizations. After hearings and discussions, the development plan was formally approved by the GLC in July 1969, and submitted to the MHLG for its official approval.[20]

As part of its own review process—and particularly in recognition of the pivotal but highly controversial motorway scheme—the Secre-

57

tary of State for Local Government and Regional Planning,* Mr. Crosland, announced in the spring of 1970 that a formal panel, headed by Mr. Frank Layfield, would open an inquiry on the development plan starting in October and running for perhaps six months or more. Among other things, the inquiry panel is charged with recommending whether the motorway system should be approved or whether an alternative road system would be preferable. As the inquiry got underway and the vastness and complexity of its deliberations came to be recognized, estimates of its duration have lengthened to two years. There were 23,000 objections to the development plan. Even discounting 18,000 identical objections to the motorway scheme, there remained 5,000 to be considered, of which over half focused on roads, and the remainder on other land use proposals.†

To summarize briefly (see also Chapters Five and Six) the development plan recognizes that Greater London has been losing population in recent decades. It accepts this trend, but asserts plainly that Greater London should maintain its importance as the national capital and preserve its place as a great city. A population of 7.3 million is considered likely (down from an actual population of 7.9 million in the late 1960's but above the 7.0 million or less which might result from a continuation of present trends), and is then allocated among the boroughs as "estimates of population likely to be accommodated, 1981." An appendix provides a long tabulation showing the differences between the GLC population "estimates" and the separate borough population proposals or comments on the population estimates put forth by the GLC. In most cases, the borough proposals are higher than the GLC "estimates," so that the sum of the borough proposals (filling in "estimates" for boroughs that have not made specific proposals) would appear to be some 7.7 million, or 400,000 in excess of the GLC total estimate. At this writing it is by no means clear whether the GLC will be able to enforce a population policy,

---

* Under a merger arrangement effective 1969, the Secretary of State for Local Government and Regional Planning came to oversee both the MHLG and the Ministry of Transport. See also footnote on next page.

† The inquiry proved to be formidably legalistic and unleashed an unprecedented barrage of supporting papers. The main strategic policies became all but lost in the attempt to deal with objections of a precise nature. While the process has evoked GLC officials' responses that suggest evolving policy, it is difficult to predict how satisfactory a policy framework the resultant Greater London development plan will provide.

or whether it is realistic for some of the boroughs to assume they may be able to expand as desired. Perhaps both the GLC and the boroughs will be affected by the sometimes unforeseen influences that can make demographic projections and policies precarious.

The GLC has been far more forthright in its major highway proposals. Three ringways are proposed. The innermost, Ringway 1 (formerly also called the Motorway Box), has proved to be the most controversial proposal in the plan. It is routed to take advantage of property formerly in railroad use and other non-residential land, but nevertheless cuts surgically through many existing residential areas. The boroughs have resisted the ringway on various grounds, particularly the protection of physical amenities and the preservation of established neighborhoods. At stake is the major question of acceptance of motorcars in Inner London, and the diversion of funds that might otherwise go to improve public transport. Ringway 1 symbolizes a supremacy for the automobile. (Highway proposals are discussed further in Chapter Six.)

It is highly significant that in the continuing tussle within the GLC the Department of Highways and Transportation has gained considerable power at the expense of the Department of Planning. In the summer of 1969, this culminated in the decision to merge the two departments under the nominal arrangement of equal joint directors. This has been viewed in some quarters as a victory for the roadbuilding interests and something of a takeover by the Department of Highways and Transportation.[21] In any event, a new Department of Planning and Transportation superseded the former departments, effective October 1, 1969, under joint Directors of Planning and Transportation. (A similar national merger in 1969 put the MHLG and the Ministry of Transport under a single Secretary of State for Local Government and Regional Planning.)*

Another sphere of planning, the designation of selected town centers "of strategic importance," will undoubtedly increase tensions between the GLC and the separate boroughs. Politically, it is of course very difficult to select specific centers whose growth is to be deliberately fostered, and to state or imply that other centers, usually in

---

* More recently, in November 1970, a new Department of the Environment was created, integrating the MHLG, the Ministry of Transport, and the Ministry of Public Building and Works, under a Secretary of State for the Environment. (*British Record* [November 6, 1970], pp. 2–3).

different boroughs, are not to be encouraged to grow. We may expect that each borough will actively seek to promote its own commercial interests and will object to a GLC policy plan that limits them.

Many of the proposals in the Greater London development plan are less controversial. Indeed, some critics of the plan argue that it merely strings together a series of platitudinous proposals and projects already announced, and thus is far from being a bold and tightly conceived statement of development policy. Other observers have pointed out that the plan was intended to be a structure plan, providing a policy framework within which the boroughs could move ahead with their own projects.

Regulating development.—The London Government Act of 1963 also provided the general pattern for allocation of responsibility for administering planning controls between the GLC and the individual London boroughs. The detailed regulations promulgated by the ministry did not appear until the end of March 1965, and were modified two years later.[22] According to these, the GLC was to be the local planning authority for only limited classes of development: "Places of public assembly with a capacity of more than 2,500; university or college of advance technology development; public transport terminal; monorail or hovercraft systems; mineral development in excess of five acres." [23] In a second category, London boroughs were authorized to approve applications for certain additional classes of development, but these applications must be referred to the GLC for advisory comment. Hence the GLC has an opportunity to give direction, even though advisory. These classes of development included:

Shopping provision exceeding 250,000 square feet of floor space; buildings exceeding 150 feet in height in central London and 125 feet elsewhere; office buildings exceeding 3,000 square feet of floor space; development within 110 feet of a British Railways or a London Transport passenger station; development within 220 feet of the center line of metropolitan roads (with certain exceptions); development involving material increase in traffic; or new access to metropolitan roads; public car parks for more than 50 cars; development of greenbelt land; and buildings of architectural or historic interest.[24]

Remaining types of development, a final category, were to be directly within the purview of the London boroughs.

As might be expected, points of contention have arisen. For example, the GLC claimed the right to approve all development projects for London's Heathrow airport. The borough of Hillingdon, in which the airport is located, conceded to the GLC jurisdiction only over plans for buildings or other development clearly related to expansion of the airport. The borough held that many buildings that happened to be sited at the airport did not contribute to its expansion.

In addition, the boroughs have objected to proposed increases in GLC authority over highways (to be discussed shortly), not necessarily on grounds of illogical division of responsibility for highway construction and maintenance but on grounds of unwarranted extension of planning controls by the GLC. As noted, regulations give the GLC authority to comment on borough development within 220 feet of the center line of metropolitan roads (those managed by the GLC). The double review of developers' planning applications by both a borough and the GLC compounds difficulties where the volume of planning applications handled by the London boroughs has already proved enormous. Nearly 35,000 applications were processed in 1966, of which 29,000 were approved.[25] Apparently these difficulties are being resolved. The Ministry of Transport has proposed the creation of two classes of metropolitan roads. The GLC will have full highway authority over both classes, but it will have planning authority only over the land adjacent to one of the classes.

Redevelopment and special projects.—Under the London Government Act of 1963, the GLC was made the planning authority for development of nine comprehensive development areas in Inner London (development areas are roughly comparable to urban renewal areas in American cities). These projects had already been planned or begun by the LCC. As each project is completed, it is to be removed from the authority of the GLC and assigned to the appropriate borough. The GLC also is the responsible local planning authority for the Covent Garden redevelopment,* as the well-known major

* Originally this was to have been the responsibility of a consortium embracing the GLC, the Westminster City Council, and the Camden Borough Council. By spring and summer 1971 strong grass-roots resistance to redevelopment had emerged, and the GLC was being placed in a position that seemed unpopular and high-handed. A special inquiry was convened in the summer of 1971 to hear the many objections.

market is being moved in the early 1970's to its new Nine Elms site south of the Thames.

The Greater London development plan specifies 55 additional "future action areas," and the listing includes Covent Garden as area number 56. Under the Town and Country Planning Act of 1968, which put Planning Advisory Group (PAG) plans into operation, the Minister of HLG may direct that any areas where comprehensive development should be carried out shall be treated as "action areas." [26] Nine of the action areas are to be the planning responsibility of the GLC: Covent Garden, the Victoria Transportation Center, King's Cross–St. Pancras, three dock areas (London Docks, East India Dock, St. Katharine Dock) where former docks are becoming dysfunctional, the Thamesmead new community development on the southern bank of the Thames east of Greenwich, Hounslow Heath, and Heston airport. Forty-four areas are the responsibility of the respective boroughs. Planning responsibility for three areas—Picadilly Circus, London Bridge, and Beckton—is under discussion (per the published development plan).

All 55 action areas indicated on the diagrammatic plan and briefly described in the plan statement will require comprehensive action within the next ten years, and each will require detailed, cooperative planning and public funding. In most cases private developers will be invited to participate (as in American urban renewal), and the relations between the developer and the local authorities will have to be spelled out carefully.

Communication on planning matters among the boroughs and between the boroughs and the GLC is facilitated by various organizational devices. We have already cited the monthly meetings of the Advisory Body of Chief Planning Officers. The London Boroughs Association helped the GLC and the boroughs to establish a joint working party on planning. This working party is chaired by an Assistant Clerk to the GLC, and has a formal agenda; but membership is not fixed and votes are not recorded. The number of persons present (particularly representing the GLC Planning Department) varies, depending upon the question under consideration. The working party has discussed such matters as regulations regarding high buildings, regulations along metropolitan roads, and the boroughs' role in comprehensive development (the GLC had previously agreed to delegate limited powers, but the boroughs wanted a free hand).

By the end of 1966 the working party had produced a dozen reports and had provided mutually acceptable bases for amendments to the regulations of the various ministries, and of the GLC, under which the GLC-borough planning machinery operates.[27]

HOUSING

Like other local governments, the London boroughs serve as housing authorities, being given primary responsibility for the provision of council (public) housing within their own jurisdictions. The boroughs can, and are encouraged to, work out cooperative arrangements with other boroughs for easing housing shortages. But they can provide housing in areas outside Greater London only with the approval of the Minister of HLG. As of March 1966 the London boroughs owned and operated nearly 400,000 dwellings, and in the near future will be undertaking the construction of some 20,000 dwellings annually.[28]

The GLC's role has proved more unusual and there has been no precedent on which to rely. In 1965 the MHLG, the GLC, and London boroughs agreed to establish a standing working party on London housing. In its first report, dated January 1967, this working party sought to clarify the housing mission of the GLC, and set forth these proposed principles: the GLC should complete those LCC projects already "in the pipeline"; the GLC should be expected to rehouse people displaced by its own redevelopment or other public works; individual boroughs may request GLC assistance in dealing with their borough housing problems; and the GLC must play a responsible role in meeting the housing needs of London as a whole. This includes the provision of housing outside of Greater London, to which may be "overspilled" selected households formerly residing within Greater London, particularly households being relocated from central areas where high-density districts are being thinned out in the course of redevelopment.[29]

During the first five years of its life the GLC, by statutory provision, assumed full responsibility for housing previously managed by the LCC. In 1966 this amounted to slightly more than 200,000 dwellings within Greater London—about one-third of all council housing —and another 28,000 dwellings outside, at such scattered locations as Watford, Chigwell, and Thurrock.[30] The London Government Act of 1963 stipulated that by 1970 the GLC must submit to the Minister

63

of HLG a program for the transfer of most of its housing to appropriate London boroughs.

In late 1968, negotiations between the GLC and the London Boroughs Association led to the creation of three official working parties. Within a few weeks it was announced that they had recommended transfer of some 71,000 dwellings, and that ultimately another 190,-000 would be transferred; the GLC would turn over new housing upon its completion. The negotiations, including agreement by the ministry, have proved long and complex. Many problems remain to be worked out: what fiscal arrangements were mutually satisfactory, how many families the GLC would be able to place in housing in the outer boroughs, what rent policies the boroughs would pursue in relation to the GLC's policy, and whether the boroughs would continue the policy of building homes for low-income families.

As of the early spring of 1970, the situation was unresolved. MHLG Minister Anthony Greenwood first submitted to Parliament a recommendation that 46,000 GLC houses be transferred to the London boroughs. A few weeks later, he rescinded the recommendation on the grounds that he was not satisfied. The arrangements that had been made to transfer the housing on April 1, 1970, were therefore put aside. Mr. Greenwood then appointed Professor J. B. Cullingworth to "look into the situation." [31] It may be that only a part of the GLC housing will be transferred to the boroughs. It also seems likely that the GLC will gain enlarged rights to nominate tenants for borough housing.*

TRANSPORT

The jurisdictional responsibilities regarding highway construction, traffic management, and public transport operation have remained complex, if not snarled, even after reorganization. The Ministry of Transport retained direct responsibility for about 150 miles of trunk

* Since the text was written, J. B. Cullingworth's Report to the Minister of Housing on Proposals for the Transfer of GLC Housing to the London Boroughs (London: MHLG, October 1970) has been published. Among other conclusions, it stresses two points: that no single social policy regarding housing in Greater London has been fashioned, and that an appropriate administrative body needs to be created, capable of imposing such policy on the various local authorities in the London area. This would suggest further delay in the transfer. (See also Della Nevitt, "Tenants and Their Needs," New Society, 16:675–676 [October 15, 1970].)

roads; the GLC was placed in charge of 550 miles of metropolitan roads; and the boroughs were assigned 7,000 miles of secondary roads.

Traffic management was transferred to the GLC from the Ministry of Transport. Metered street parking spaces became a responsibility of the GLC, but offstreet car parking was turned over to the boroughs. The GLC sets speed restrictions, but GLC interest in rapid movement of through traffic sometimes conflicts with borough interest in slowing traffic down for safety and amenity reasons. The ministry controls speeds on its trunk roads.

During the first years of the new GLC-borough operation, there has been a further sorting out of functions. Responsibility for road maintenance and lighting has generally been delegated by the GLC to the boroughs. The GLC, in turn, has taken over research and purchasing on behalf of the boroughs.

GLC liaison has been undertaken with central government ministries and with other governmental units. The Transport Coordinating Council for London was set up in 1966 to facilitate joint transportation planning.[32] While this council has improved the exchange of information and the identification of problems, it has had difficulty coping with tough decisions that prove distasteful to constituent members. With the concurrence of the Ministry of Transport, the GLC has been moving toward the assumption of very wide responsibility for traffic and highways. The head of the highways department of the GLC has been redesignated Traffic Commissioner and Director of Transportation, although this has probably not led to the strong leadership sought by some. Moreover, in major policy moves affecting England and Wales generally and London specifically, the central government has been implementing the concept that local governments must take over full responsibility for transportation within their own areas. The Ministry of Transport also seeks to shift road maintenance to local governments. The Transport Act of 1968 set the blueprint for the nation as a whole. Various white papers by the central government, and particularly *Transport in London,* issued in July 1968, announced that new and strengthened responsibilities were being proposed for the GLC, and that these were being forged into law by the Transport (London) Act of 1969 especially geared to London.[33] The changes are summarized:

First, the GLC has become the overall transport planning authority for London, with authority for making long-range investment proposals. As such it has been given unprecedented responsibility for an array of transport matters, and will be required to prepare and publish transport plans from time to time (consistent with the Greater London development plan). Both the Minister of Transport and British Rail are required to take these plans into account when considering investment proposals in or affecting transport in London. A Greater London Transport Planning Group has been established under the chairmanship of the GLC's Traffic Commissioner and Director of Transportation. The group includes representatives of the GLC, the Ministry of Transport, London Transport, and British Rail. Only time will permit a proper evaluation. Initially, at least, there is still no assurance of fully coordinated planning capabilities.

Second, on January 1, 1970, the previous London Transport Board, under the Minister of Transport, was converted into a new London Transport Executive, to run the underground system and London buses, under the general political direction of the GLC. The central government assumed 90 per cent of the capital debt of the present London Transport, and the new organization is expected to pay its way in the future. Commuter railway services are operated by British Rail, but the GLC must be periodically consulted about service levels and fares. Outer buses, such as the present "green buses," are being transferred to a newly formed National Bus Company. By the end of 1970 the Minister of Transport, the GLC, and British Rail were to have reached agreement on a new financial arrangement, and by the end of 1972 they are to have worked out ways of ensuring viability for the entire transport network.

Third, the GLC's direct authority over highways was appreciably enhanced. An additional 325 miles of principal roads, managed until now by the London boroughs, have been transferred to the GLC. The Minister of Transport also has agreed that ultimately the GLC should gain jurisdiction over the ministry's trunk roads. Continuous coordination with the boroughs will bring roads in or drop them out of the "principal" category. Under the new proposals, not all the principal roads under GLC management carry development control powers over adjacent land, a limitation that recognizes the boroughs' concern that GLC control over land development not be extended. The GLC was also given increased authority over parking, consolidating powers transferred to it by both the boroughs and the Ministry of Transport. So as to organize these powers, a Joint Traffic Executive for London has been established, with responsibilities to the GLC and to the Commissioner of Metropolitan Police.[34]

EDUCATION

The London Government Act of 1963 contained divergent provisions for administering education in Inner and Outer London. In Inner London it was decided to continue the London Education Service, a service for the identical geographic area (the old LCC area) dating back to the London School Board's creation in 1870 and carried forward by the London Education Act of 1903, transferring this service to the LCC.

The 53-member Inner London Education Authority (ILEA), described earlier, was placed in charge. The ILEA works primarily through its Education Committee, which includes the 53 ILEA members and an additional 19 co-opted members "experienced in education." Technically, this is a special committee of the GLC and uses many of the GLC services, such as those of the Architects Department. It has no separate powers to raise funds, but it tells the boroughs the amounts of additional taxes it expects the boroughs to raise on its behalf. Although the ILEA appoints its own staff, it has a common policy with the GLC in recruitment and promotion.

The Education Committee depends, in turn, on three subcommittees, Finance and Administration, Further and Higher Education, and Schools. The ILEA in its administrative operations decentralizes control over schools to 10 divisions (7 equate to London boroughs, 2 include two London boroughs each, and one combines Tower Hamlets Borough and the City of London). It is also commonly understood that these divisions decentralize substantial authority to the heads of individual schools.[35] Because of its size and traditional status, the ILEA maintains special relations with the central government and its Department of Education and Science.

Under the 1963 Act the ILEA was to be reviewed within five years. This provision was repealed by the Local Government (Termination of Reviews) Act of 1967, so that the continuation of the ILEA has been assured (although clearly it remains subject to future change).

The structure of the ILEA ran distinctly counter to the hopes of the Herbert Commission and the recommendations of the Seebohm Committee, both of which argued for very close administrative cooperation among the functions of education, health, and personal services.* The ILEA has tended to provide social service staff of its own, but it has also fashioned working arrangements with the inner boroughs. For example, the medical officers of health of these boroughs also act as the ILEA's principal school medical officers. The ILEA's divisional offices have increasing contact with borough chief officers (and we have noted that most of these offices serve a borough).[36] The London Boroughs Association claimed in evidence to the Seebohm Committee that ILEA's School Care Committee and its School Care Organizers "cannot fail to some extent to duplicate the work done by borough children's services. In the interests alike of economy and of good administration, it is essential that social work with families should be centered in the Borough Welfare Services." [37] But the Seebohm Committee, after weighing the matter, concluded that the special situation within Inner London should be recognized as just that. Hence it would be wrong to attempt to force a set pattern relegating child-related social services solely to either the boroughs or the ILEA alone. Special liaison arrangements must be guaranteed, ensuring links between the inner boroughs and the ILEA in the provision of services.[38]

In sharp contrast, education was entrusted directly to the borough governments in the 20 outer London boroughs. This was a new function for most of them. The Greater London Group of the London School of Economics, in its study for the Royal Commission on Local Government in England, made this assessment in 1968:

there is a general feeling that the change has effected improvements, certainly in the field of primary and secondary education, less certainly in further and specialist education. Policy is now made by those who have personal knowledge of the area. . . . Members and officers are nearer to pupils, teachers, parents and employees: in particular, there are closer relationships between Chief Officers and head teachers.[39]

To foster inter-borough cooperation on educational matters, the outer London boroughs work through an Education Committee of the London Boroughs Association. This committee meets every three

* The Seebohm Committee had not yet reported, but it was later to have an influence on the Redcliffe-Maud Commission. See *Report of the Committee on Local Authority and Allied Personal Social Services,* Cmnd. 3703 (London: HMSO, July 1968).

months. It is served by an Advisory Body of Chief Education Officers from the same boroughs.

As might be expected, the separate borough-by-borough education responsibilities have led to considerable variations in policy. At its best, this has meant experimentation and bold strides forward. Hillingdon Borough, for example, has pioneered in the development of a closed circuit television network. Other boroughs have shown great initiative in curricular developments. At its worst, it has meant that certain boroughs have failed to promote changes vigorously, and as we shall see in Chapter Six, some of the outer boroughs have lagged in submitting reorganization schemes for introducing comprehensive schools. As expected by the Herbert Commission, the outer boroughs have provided direct opportunities for cooperative arrangements between school authorities and health and welfare agencies. The school medical services have been integrated with other social services.[40]

POLITICAL CHANGE: 1964–1970

Bitter opposition to the Herbert Commission report had come from the LCC, which feared that inclusion of Conservative boroughs in the new GLC would endanger the Labor Party's dominance over London. In the first GLC elections, however, held in May 1964, Labor was able to retain control: Labor strength in the old LCC area was sufficient to balance Conservative votes in the outer boroughs. A number of Labor leaders formerly active in the LCC were elected to the new GLC. With a turnout of 44 per cent of the electorate of 5.5 million, Labor drew 46 per cent of the votes, the Conservatives 42 per cent, and the Liberals 10 per cent.[41]

A REMARKABLE SHIFT: THE ELECTIONS OF 1967

But in April 1967, with 100 elected seats at stake, a remarkable shift occurred, and the voters converted nearly half of the seats from Labor to Conservative. In an overwhelming upset, the Conservatives obtained a new working majority of 66 (91 Conservatives and 25 Labor) against the previous Labor majority of 34 (75 Labor and 41 Conservatives), including aldermen as well as councillors.

Conservative party candidates for GLC seats outside of the former LCC boundaries were preponderantly successful in the 1967 elections. Much less predictably, most of the GLC seats within the for-

mer LCC area also fell to the Conservatives. The force of the change
in the political makeup of the GLC is emphasized in this tabulation
of majorities after the two elections:

	Greater London Council Area		Inner Boroughs		Outer Boroughs	
	1964	1967	1964	1967	1964	1967
Boroughs Having Labor Party Majority in the GLC	20	6	10	4	10	2
Boroughs Having Conservative Party Majority in the GLC	12	26	2	8	10	18
TOTAL GLC BOROUGHS	32	32	12	12	20	20

Only a core group of six contiguous East End boroughs—Islington,
Hackney, Tower Hamlets, and Southwark in Inner London, and
Newham and Barking in Outer London—retained Labor majorities
in the GLC after the 1967 election turnabout. (See Map 5B, p. 76.)

Political analysts have suggested that a low participation by Labor
supporters was important, but that the widespread dissatisfaction
with the Labor government's national income policy—including
wage freezes—may have been even more significant. The Conservative sweep was clearly national in scope, and only three county councils—in areas that still had large coal-mining populations and were
the last strongholds of the Labor Party—of the total of 58 county
councils in England and Wales remained in Labor hands.[42]

The Conservatives proposed several programs in the course of
their campaigning. Once elected, the government moved ahead to
implement them. The heavy Conservative majority in the GLC permitted them to pursue their programs, and they even had sufficient
seats on the ILEA to make their views operative there. The Conservatives claimed all of the eight vacant aldermanic seats and
elected their own representatives, bringing their total number in
the council to 91, as compared with Labor's 25. The first reported
division (vote) in the new GLC was 83 to 23, indicating the way
the votes were likely to run for the next two years. Despite token
debate, the Conservatives have had the votes to put their programs
through.

Mr. Desmond Plummer, the new Conservative leader, and his party colleagues argued that a proportion of publicly operated housing—perhaps up to 10 per cent or so—should be made available for purchase by qualified tenants. They proceeded with this idea, but the program does not seem to have been especially successful, in part because the Labor government restricted sales to a small number per year.

The Conservatives made a case for a strong traffic commissioner, but were less inclined than the Labor Party to favor the possible absorption of London Transport. Nevertheless, the transfer of London Transport did ultimately occur after agreements that the central government would write off much of London Transport's capital costs. A major conflict over rents also arose, the Conservative-controlled GLC seeking to boost council housing rents to 90 per cent of market level, but the Labor Minister of MHLG permitting only a 10 shilling per week increase. On these and some other issues, a powerful GLC, with its Conservative mandate, sometimes collided with a national Labor government.

The subject of comprehensive schools also provided a lively issue. The Labor Party had been pushing vigorously for a great increase in the number of comprehensive schools—secondary schools that serve a wide range of student abilities and interests (roughly the equivalent of the American high school) in contrast to separate grammar schools for the academic elite and other schools for the less promising. Many of the comprehensive schools became coeducational, but some were developed on traditional non-coeducational terms. The Conservatives are committed to permitting each local education authority to decide its own policy, thus presumably slowing down this conversion to comprehensive schools and retaining a greater proportion of grammar schools. The newly elected ILEA proceeded to carry out its program, but this is, of course, also subject to successful negotiations with the central government, which until the June 1970 elections, was pursuing a Labor-dominated policy with respect to education.

THE BOROUGH ELECTIONS OF 1968

During the year between the GLC elections of April 1967 and the London borough elections of May 1968, the dominant Conservative majority in the GLC was offset by continuing Labor majorities in

20 out of 32 London Borough Councils. Of the 12 inner boroughs, 10 had clear Labor majorities; of the outer boroughs, 10 had Conservative majorities and 10 had Labor majorities carried over from the initial 1964 elections.

The borough elections in May 1968 were part of a national Conservative sweep. Labor lost seats in former strongholds throughout Britain in what has been called the worst debacle for the Labor Party in 65 years. Outside of London, for example, Labor lost every single seat in Birmingham, Salford, and Leicester. Glasgow voters reversed the customary Labor majority in their council for the first time since 1934.[43] Within the London boroughs, the Conservatives not only won the expected seats, but also made dramatic gains at the expense of Labor. Only four London boroughs held on to Labor majorities: Southwark and Tower Hamlets in Inner London, and Barking and Newham among the outer boroughs. Amazingly enough, Hackney and Islington boroughs, each holding a Labor majority in their GLC representation following the April 1967 elections, were swamped in the May 1968 Conservative upsurge. Before the 1968 elections there was not a single Conservative councillor on the Hackney Borough Council, but in 1968 the Conservatives won 30 seats. These, together with two Liberal seats, put an end to a Labor domination, since Labor won only 31 seats. The story of Labor's rout in the Borough of Islington is even more remarkable:[44]

Parties Represented in the Islington Borough Council	Before the 1968 Election	After the 1968 Election
Labor	65	15
Conservative	0	47
Independent	0	3
TOTAL COUNCILLORS	65	65

The net effect was to put 28 of the 32 London boroughs into the hands of Conservative coalition majorities.

This second trouncing of Labor candidates provided the Conservatives with full opportunities for cooperation between the GLC and the London boroughs, since now, after the year when the two were out of phase, party platforms could be worked toward on both tiers. The swing also gave Conservative leaders confidence of the support of the local electorate and buoyed them in their conviction that the time was imminent for a national shift. In the meantime, as noted, a heavily dominant Conservative bloc in London had to deal with a Labor-led central government.

THE GLC ELECTIONS OF 1970

Even though 1964 witnessed a complete sweep for Labor, and 1967 an equally complete sweep for the Conservatives, in both of those years the GLC and the ILEA stayed together in their political majorities. But in the elections of April 1970, political control of the ILEA and of the GLC as a whole parted company for the first time. Inner London and hence the ILEA returned to the Labor camp while, in contrast, the GLC as a whole, weighted by the overwhelmingly Conservative majority in outer London, remained Conservative.

Between 1967 and 1970 Labor picked up 15 councillor seats in Inner London, giving it a majority of 20 seats. In the outer boroughs there was no change in representation. The 1967 GLC Conservative majority of 64 councillors was reduced to a majority of 30 in 1970 (65 Conservative councillors and 35 Labor councillors). The situation can be summarized as follows:[45]

| | 12 Inner Boroughs | | | | 20 Outer Boroughs | | | |
| | Borough Majorities | | Councillor Seats | | Borough Majorities | | Councillor Seats | |
	1967	1970	1967	1970	1967	1970	1967	1970
Labor	4	8	15	30	2	2	5	5
Conservatives	8	4	25	10	18	18	55	55
TOTALS	12	12	40	40	20	20	60	60

Including aldermen, the new Conservative voting majority in the GLC stood at 36, down from 66 after the 1967 election.

The important change, of course, was Labor's recapture of the ILEA. While Labor had a strong majority of GLC councillors in the Inner London boroughs, Labor's majority on the ILEA was held to 11 seats more than its combined opponents. This reflects the carryover of borough representatives, who were overwhelmingly Conservatives, at least until the 1971 borough elections. Here is the breakdown of ILEA membership following the 1970 elections:[46]

	Total ILEA Membership	GLC Councillor Representatives	London Borough Representatives
Labor	32	30	2
Conservatives	20	10	10
Other	1	0	1
TOTALS	53	40	13

So in the few short years since the GLC and the ILEA came into being, their political fortunes have changed remarkably. And national political swings also bring different partisan power combinations. Thus with the June 1970 national elections, the central government and the GLC ended in the same political camp, and the ILEA remained the only Labor stronghold. The implications of this for educational policy in Inner London are dealt with in Chapter Six.

POLITICAL PARTICIPATION IN GREATER LONDON

The new governmental system introduced for Greater London obviously permits striking shifts in political dominance, balance, and mix in comparatively short time spans. Starting as overwhelmingly Labor in the GLC and the London borough elections of 1964, in 1967 and 1968 the voters decided to support Conservative candidates, and in 1970 finally swung back to an intermediate position. Perhaps this final pattern is the more characteristic, for it gives dominance to Labor in the 12 inner boroughs and dominance to the Conservatives in the 20 outer ones. The outer boroughs carry the greater political weight in the GLC, for their combined councillors account for three-fifths of the total.

At least three component sets of factors may be identified in analyzing the votes in GLC and London borough elections. First is the national political climate. London elections account for one-sixth of the total votes of England and Wales, and reflect national concerns and political attitudes toward the parties' respective national programs. Second, central city-suburban differences that characterize voter behavior in the United States are also found in Greater London. The 1970 GLC elections brought this distinction out more pointedly than the earlier ones did. Third, London local government is organized on a formally partisan basis to a degree quite without direct counterpart in the United States. Majority and mi-

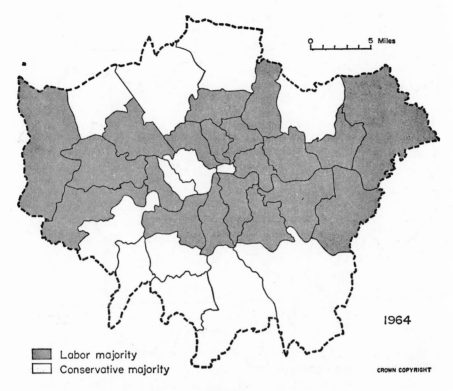

MAP 5A—POLITICAL MAJORITIES IN THE GREATER LONDON COUNCIL, BY LONDON BOROUGHS

nority party leaders have their distinct roles, and voting tends to follow party lines to a remarkable degree.

Both the GLC and the borough governments appear generally to remain rather distant from the voters. Certainly voting participation has remained fairly light, even more so for the borough elections than for the GLC elections. The turnout is also lighter within Inner London than in Outer London. Here are the percentages of voters participating in five successive elections:[47]

	GLC Election April 1964	Borough Elections May 1964	GLC Election April 1967	Borough Elections May 1968	GLC Election April 1970
Inner London	37.7	27.1	34.4	29.5	32.4
Outer London	48.3	40.8	45.4	39.6	36.6
TOTAL GLC AREA	44.2	35.7	41.1	35.8	35.0

75

Labor majority
Conservative majority

1967

CROWN COPYRIGHT

MAP 5B

The participation drop in the 1970 GLC election is noteworthy, particularly in the Outer London boroughs. It seemed as if the voters in most boroughs throughout the GLC had not been convinced that their vote was particularly important in the main GLC elections in early April 1970. But in Hammersmith Borough, where the death of a candidate delayed the election until late that same month, 45 per cent voted, the highest participation of any London borough. Somehow this one election attracted unusual interest, with the prospect of winning for Labor. Thus aroused, the voters proceeded to accomplish exactly that.[48]

In general, we may conclude that voting for GLC or London borough councillors has limited appeal. Just as the LCC never seemed to pull any considerable vote, neither, now, does the GLC, although in proportionate terms, it is similar to the national average vote in county boroughs. The GLC, it seems, is not close to the people and does not strike them as important. A 1966 survey somewhat discon-

Labor majority
Conservative majority

1970

MAP 5c

certingly showed that even two years after the first GLC elections, a full one-third of those questioned did not know what the initials GLC stood for, and 49 out of every 50 respondents could not name any of their GLC councillors.[49]

The GLC may be doing an excellent job of preparing information about its services and its functioning. For example, it has taken the initiative in organizing large meetings to get citizen reactions to the Greater London development plan and to other programs. But these succeed mainly in attracting those who strongly object to particular schemes, such as the motorway proposals. It is proving singularly difficult to make County Hall and the various borough halls as readily accessible to the average citizen as the Herbert Commission had hoped they would be.*

* Radio London was added as a new local BBC service during October 1970, and it is possible that this may contribute to greater civic awareness.

CHAPTER IV

LONDON'S ENVIRONS:
PLANNING FOR THE LARGER REGION

Formation of the GLC by the London Government Act recognized an expanded but unified London urban area by increasing Greater London's boundaries to 616 square miles, with a population of 7.9 million. But this encompassed only the built-up portion within the Metropolitan Greenbelt as belonging to London; in fact, as we have seen, Metropolitan London is growing vigorously beyond the Greenbelt into a large regional area in South East England. Greater affluence, increasing reliance on automobiles and road transport, and the appeal of the house-with-garden have combined to reinforce this outward growth into an expanding suburban commuter and employment zone.

This metropolitan regional spread is familiar to Americans, for similar patterns of physical growth prevail in the United States. But there are two distinctive features in the London situation. First, expanding Metropolitan London is very large, not only absolutely but relatively; Metropolitan London and South East England (however defined) have retained their overwhelming dominance in England and Wales. (See, for example, the trends shown in the Appendix, Tables II and III.) Second, the British central government is far more heavily committed to planning than is government in the United States.

In such a situation it becomes difficult to delineate the responsibilities of the central government, regional agencies, and local government. While the central government has not developed an overall national plan for integrating economic and physical development, it has succeeded in formulating patches of policy, and in particular, has assumed responsibility for review and approval of all development plans prepared by local governments. Obviously, political attitudes toward the role of the central government vary. Some officials and planners would prefer less planning by the central government, but many look to it to provide a complete and consistent development policy for the guidance of local governments.

In such a context, it becomes imperative both to distinguish between and to interrelate the natural extension of local government for Metropolitan London, on one hand, and regional government from-the-top-down on the other. With respect to planning, the organizational problem is to find the proper balance between regional plans that grow out of cooperation among local governments, and regional plans imposed by the central government as a part of its planning for the entire country.

This chapter describes a series of significant planning studies for South East England, which affect London and its relationship to the rest of Great Britain. It is organized into four sections. The first section deals with the work of the Standing Conference on London and South East Regional Planning during the period 1962 to 1968. The conference is a consultative and advisory organization with which local planning authorities in the South East have voluntarily aligned themselves. The second section deals with *The South East Study,* a report published in 1964 by the Ministry of Housing and Local Government, which makes physical development policy recommendations for South East England. The third section reports on the South East Economic Planning Council's 1967 report, *A Strategy for the South East.* This planning council is one of a set of regional councils appointed by the central government and tied into national planning efforts. Finally, a fourth section reports briefly on the work of a planning team based within the Ministry of Housing and Local Government (while co-opting some additional experts), which since 1968 has been preparing further reports on the large region around London.

In sum, Chapter Four focuses on the organizations active in planning for the South East, and merely outlines the kind of plans they

79

have been producing. Chapter Five deals more specifically with the problems and the substantive proposals involved in guiding the growth of Metropolitan London.

THE STANDING CONFERENCE ON LONDON
AND SOUTH EAST REGIONAL PLANNING

It is important to note that the Standing Conference is not the equivalent of a metropolitan regional government.[1] It is a voluntary association of local governments in South East England, serving as a forum for study and discussion to develop a common understanding of the regional aspects of the planning problems of its member authorities. In a loose sense, it parallels the councils of governments (COGs) that have proliferated in the United States.

A planning organization of local governments known as the Standing Conference on London Regional Planning was active in the London area in the late 1930's. It was on behalf of this body that Professor Abercrombie was commissioned to produce the Greater London Plan. The present organization, which was constituted in 1962 with the same name, originally included those local planning authorities whose areas lay wholly or partly within the area of the Greater London Plan. At first there were 13 member authorities, growing to 19 by the middle of 1964, when membership was extended to cover the London commuter area.

With the reorganization of local government in Greater London, the number of member authorities declined, because the GLC absorbed several county borough councils and the Middlesex County Council. When the central government delineated the South East Economic Planning Region in 1965, the conference extended its area to coincide. Several new members were added in 1966, the name of the organization was changed, and membership now comprises 24 constituent authorities and the London Boroughs Committee.* The conference area now includes 17 million residents distributed over 10,560 square miles. (The South East Economic Planning Region is shown on Map 1, p. 2.)

* These member authorities are: the Greater London Council; the county councils of Bedfordshire, Berkshire, Buckinghamshire, Essex, Hampshire, Isle of Wight, Kent, Oxfordshire, Surrey, East Sussex and West Sussex; and the county borough councils of Bournemouth, Brighton, Canterbury, Eastbourne, Hastings, Luton, Oxford, Portsmouth, Reading, Southampton and Southend-on-Sea.

Each member authority may have from one to three representatives, except the GLC, which may have up to six representatives. These make up the membership of the conference. Representatives of the authorities usually include the chairmen of their planning committees plus other senior council members. The conference must meet as a formal organization at least twice a year, and is presided over by an annually elected chairman who is not necessarily a representative from one of the authorities. In practice, the original chairman has been reelected each year, thus helping to give continuity to the organization.

At its meetings the conference receives and debates reports submitted to it by two panels of officials of its member authorities. One of these is a technical panel composed of the planning officers of member authorities, which usually meets monthly and does its work through a number of sub-panels and working parties, and maintains day-to-day contact with the conference organization by means of a liaison officer appointed from each local planning department. The other is an administrative panel consisting of the clerks of the constituent councils, charged with the duties of coordinating major policies, ensuring that a wide variety of interests are consulted, and giving broad direction to the conference's work. The conference is served by a small full-time secretariat, whose administrative and professional staffs are formally borrowed from the GLC. The secretariat is responsible for the agendas and reports for panel, sub-panel, and working party meetings, for the subsequent reports of the panels to the conference, and for the general management of the conference's affairs. The cost of the conference is met by member authorities in proportion to the total ratable value of their areas. The GLC meets the costs initially, and subsequently recovers the appropriate amounts from its fellow members.

The conference's constitution gives the following orders of reference of the organization: "(a) to keep under review the principal planning issues affecting the area and to assemble, assess, and disseminate planning information for the area; (b) to make recommendations to the constituent authorities with a view to establishing a joint policy; (c) to coordinate the subsequent action taken; and (d) for these purposes to consult the appropriate Government Departments and other authorities and bodies concerned." [2]

The conference has facilitated the exchange of views among repre-

81

sentatives of its member units, and, in particular, between the GLC and its neighboring local governments. It is also recognized as a valuable liaison agent and spokesman on behalf of the local governments in the South East Region in many dealings with the Ministry of Housing and Local Government and other departments. Inevitably there is a built-in provincialism, but the organization has undoubtedly provided an exposure to regional context and encouraged a breadth of outlook. Through the work of its secretariat and panels, the conference has been able to supply information on trends and prospects affecting Metropolitan London and South East England. These have been available to its member authorities and to a larger circle of political leaders and public officials. During the period from 1963 to 1968, the conference prepared an impressive set of reports summarizing trends affecting London and the South East, and commented on other reports or proposals (for example, the *South East Study* and the third London airport).

Beginning in 1966, the conference recognized the need to formulate policies and plans for the long-term future of its area. It began publishing a series of reports by its technical panel. These dealt with the principles that should underlie any long-term planning strategy, and examined broad alternative policies for future development of the area. The conference asked its member authorities to comment on three sketch maps showing ways of accommodating urban growth in the South East to the end of the century: by relying on "major growth concentrations lying generally close to London," by directing "a much larger proportion of total growth . . . away from London," and by locating urban groupings outside London and making them "slightly looser than those outlined in the other two maps." [3] The areas suggested for growth were similar to those later put forward by the Economic Planning Council (see pages 86–89).

In the final report of the series, *The South East: A Framework for Regional Planning,* published in 1968, the conference urged member authorities to express their preferences concerning development in the South East, but said that it would be inappropriate to prepare a detailed regional plan.[4] The primary reason given was that a traditional master plan would be an unsatisfactory approach to the task of guiding the growth of such a large and complex region. As an alternative, "a process is proposed whereby studies over the whole field would provide a continuously growing body of information about life in the region as it evolves, of assumptions about future possibilities, and of economic, social, and physical objectives. Within this, day-to-day decisions concerning the region's development can be taken." [5] The participation of the conference and its secretariat in the joint planning study initiated by the central government in the spring of 1968 will be described in the final section of this chapter.

"THE SOUTH EAST STUDY"

In the early 1960's, the Ministry of Housing and Local Government assumed a direct responsibility for planning for a large region around London, and in March 1964 published *The South East Study*.[6] This followed the earlier publication of regional plans for Central Scotland and for North East England, on the initiative of the central government. Use of the term "study," rather than "plan," coupled with a request by the ministry for reactions to a set of policy proposals, implied that this was only a preliminary analysis. But simultaneously the ministry issued a white paper, *South East England,* declaring government support for the *Study's* major policy proposals.[7] This gave the impression that the proposals were not tentative and subject to further discussion, but were final statements of policy. These ambiguous moves caused some confusion and resentment.

The *Study's* most important substantive contribution was its recognition of the inevitability of continued growth in the London Region, and of the likelihood of strong trends toward physical dispersal within the region. For more than two decades the nearly sacred pronouncements of the Barlow Commission (reporting in 1940) and the Abercrombie Plan for Greater London (1944–1945) had been the basis for public policy—blending an assumption that there would be little population growth in Britain with the edict that London must not be permitted to grow. *The South East Study* realistically faced the twin facts that population in Britain was growing and that the London Metropolitan Region provides so advantageous and attractive a setting that it would be both ineffective and unwise to seek to prevent it from growing. The likely magnitude of population growth of the South East Study Region for the period 1961–1981 was put at 3.5 million—an estimated 2.4 million natural increase and a 1.1 million net immigration. It was also forecast that there would be no increase in resident population within the Greater London Conurbation and that the entire increase would be in the outer parts of the London Metropolitan Region and in the rest of South East England. (See the Appendix, Table III.)

The *Study* painstakingly stressed future uncertainties. It granted that social and technological changes could have unforseen impact, and admitted that the scale and timing of public expenditures on housing, on transportation, and on other facilities would depend heavily on national capacity and priorities. But the *Study* suggested that if anything, the amount of growth anticipated might have been underestimated. Whatever the growth, *The South East Study* concluded that it must be coped with and guided, insofar as possible.

Given the prospect of vigorous growth around Metropolitan London, the challenge was to plan how it might best be distributed. The recommended strategic policy was to channel growth into selected areas throughout the South East, and to continue thinning out congested central London. Three major outlying developments were proposed, creating new or greatly expanded cities in the vicinity of Southampton-Portsmouth (subsequently encouraged to develop); Bletchley (subsequently promoted, named Milton Keynes); and Newbury (subsequently dropped). Various new towns on a smaller scale were advocated. (See Map 6; also the discussion on pp. 105–108.) Improved transport, mainly radial between the growing outer residential areas and the centrally concentrated areas of employment, was proposed, accompanied by warnings about the heavy cost involved in its construction.

The report drew varied reactions, including the criticisms that it was too inclined to extrapolate trends toward sustained growth around London, and that it demonstrated central government's unwillingness to take the tough position of asserting that Metropolitan London should not be permitted to grow further. Critics noted that the major new "planned" developments would only accommodate about one-third of the total growth anticipated in the *Study*. The other two-thirds was to be accommodated by normal processes of development, for which local planning authorities were given no guidance in the *Study*. Hence, as one critic put it, the *Study* was only a "billeting order" and not a plan. It dealt more pointedly with population projections than with the physical plan for coping with and guiding growth. Transportation was also generally given less

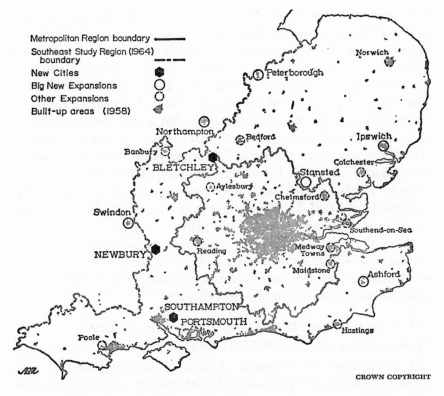

Metropolitan Region boundary
Southeast Study Region (1964) boundary
New Cities
Big New Expansions
Other Expansions
Built-up areas (1958)

Norwich
Peterborough
Northampton
Bedford
Ipswich
Banbury
BLETCHLEY
Colchester
Stansted
Aylesbury
Chelmsford
Swindon
Southend-on-Sea
NEWBURY
Reading
Medway Towns
Maidstone
Ashford
SOUTHAMPTON
PORTSMOUTH
Poole
Hastings

CROWN COPYRIGHT

MAP 6—AREAS PROPOSED FOR EXPANSION IN "THE SOUTH EAST STUDY"

attention than it warranted. Nor was the need for a set of strengthened outlying regional centers dealt with fully, despite the proposals for the planned development of three large cities.

As noted, many in British planning circles expressed the hope that central government would strengthen its activity in national and regional planning, in order to provide a consistent policy framework into which local plans could be fitted. One criticism of *The South East Study* has been the failure of its proposals to relate to any national plan for development. Specifically, it did not sufficiently lower its own growth projections to conform with what some judged to be national development policy, even if only implicitly.

But the report did help clear the air, and it was recognized as being far more candid than the previous periodic reaffirmations of metropolitan containment. It was the first statement by a central government ministry to challenge head-on the legacy of Barlow

85

Commission policy. Thus, *The South East Study* opened the door to a realistic appraisal of the forces at work, and the direction and magnitude of likely population and employment growth, and to a full discussion of methods of channeling that growth into a desirable pattern. It showed the physical planning implications of the anticipated pace of growth, thereby providing a basis for more thorough examination of the public investment that might be required, together with a realistic appraisal of what resources could be allocated. The *Study* was a step toward coordinating public investment in the South East with public investment in other sections of the country, some of which urgently need boosts to alleviate their economically depressed condition. In this sense it might be said to be an integral component of a prospective national plan.

When the Labor Government came to power in 1964 it initiated a review of *The South East Study*. This was never published, but revised figures from it were circulated to planning authorities. (This will be discussed further in the next chapter.)

THE SOUTH EAST ECONOMIC PLANNING COUNCIL: "STRATEGY FOR THE SOUTH EAST"

A Department of Economic Affairs, primarily concerned with economic planning at the national level, was set up within the central government in October 1964. Until its subsequent abolition in 1969, the department worked closely with the Treasury and other government departments, and relied upon various consultative bodies, including the National Economic Development Council (NEDC, sometimes called "Neddy"). It published *The National Plan* in September 1965.[8]

The Department of Economic Affairs, through its Regional Policy Division, was also responsible for economic policy and planning at the regional level.[9] To aid in carrying out this responsibility, in 1965 the government established a regional economic council and board for each of eight regions in England, and one each for Wales, Scotland, and Northern Ireland. The territory covered in *The South East Study* was split into two economic regions, the South East Region and the East Anglia Region. (The small county of Dorset was to be part of the South West Region.)

The South East Economic Planning Region, with 17 million residents, is by far the largest of the economic regions. It includes over one-third of the population of England and Wales. The economic council serving this region, the South East Economic Planning Council, was for several years appointed by the Secretary of State for Economic Affairs; since 1969, responsibility has been shifted mainly to the MHLG. The council is a policy-recommending body, advisory in character, and without executive powers. Its 37 part-time members are chosen to represent a range of experience, and it has been chaired to date by Sir Maurice Hackett.

Supporting and paralleling the council is an economic planning board. Its members are all civil servants in the central government, whose positions entitle them to membership. Each of these officials represents the department in which he serves as regional officer for the South East. The board is chaired by an official from the Department of Economic Affairs. This board serves as a coordinating device, involves and commits the various departments, and mobilizes their resources and powers.

In November 1967, the council published *A Strategy for the South East*.[10] This was a significant departure from previous reports by other regional economic planning councils, for the document recommended a schematic strategic physical plan for the region. The report accepted the inevitability of considerable population and economic growth in the outer areas of Metropolitan London. It then urged that highest priority be given the development of the Southampton-Portsmouth area, the Milton Keynes area (incorporating Bletchley), and the Ipswich-Colchester area. These new development points, along with a number of other outer growth points, would provide a counter-attraction to central London, promoting outward growth toward them. The in-between zones would be preserved as country and Greenbelt by the imposition of very strong planning controls. (See also Map 7, p. 108.)

Reactions to the report came promptly. A conference in London in January 1968, sponsored by the Town and Country Planning Association, provided a forum for criticism and defense.[11] However guarded the reactions may have been, they indicated a jurisdictional challenge. The bluntest criticism held that the South East Economic Planning Council failed to provide the generalized economic development policy recommendations expected by the town planners,

87

but instead invaded the physical planning sphere with its strategic plan for new development.*

A representative of the Standing Conference on London and South East Regional Planning argued that in contrast to the Standing Conference's own slower paced examination of possible alternative regional plans, the council had moved too quickly to recommend one particular scheme. In the words of Gerald Smart (County Planning Officer, Hampshire), the council's strategy

might perhaps be better regarded as a hypothesis—a supposition which should be explored as part, and only part, of the search for the best set of planning policies, economic and physical, for the region. Other hypotheses have been put forward by the Standing Conference; there are probably further alternatives too, and I do not think anyone, including the Council, can fairly be asked just now to make a final decision on what our objectives should be to the end of the century. . . . Given two or three years of intensive effort, we could be very much further advanced, and decisions could probably be justified.[12]

An active member of the South East Economic Planning Council, Peter Hall, argued spiritedly in support of the council; explaining that it had in fact studied alternatives, citing particularly those also considered in the Washington Year 2000 Plan (where a finger-plan alternative was favored and selected).[13] He then stated that the three alternate schemes put forward for discussion by the Standing Conference were, in contrast to the strategy proposed by the South East Economic Planning Council, based heavily on additional motorways for which he doubted that near-term funding was possible.[14]

First in its *Strategy* report, and then more pointedly in its subsequent written evidence to the Hunt Committee (charged with examining "gray areas" outside of designated development areas in which the rate of economic growth may give cause for concern),[15] the South East Economic Planning Council called attention to the vital economic importance of the South East and questioned the wisdom of continuing to divert away industrial expansion. The council raised an extremely important question: whether, in the interests of national economic expansion and of the promotion of exports, it might not be important to encourage rather than limit the growth of science-based and other growth industries in the South

* Interestingly, the title given the diagrammatic scheme in the report merely uses the word "strategy," rather than "strategic plan."

88

East, if that is where functional ties offer the greatest site advantages.

The next chapter explores further the substantive proposals by the South East Economic Planning Council, and compares them with the proposals of *The South East Study*. But quite apart from the substantive matters recommended and the issues at stake, several strands of controversy persisted as to the roles to be played by the central government and its ministries, the regional councils, voluntary associations like the Standing Conference, and local governmental units. A news item in May 1968, for example, was headlined "[county] councils want planners to stick to economy," and reported that "after some blunt speaking at a meeting last November . . . local authority representatives made it clear that they were responsible for physical planning, and were not prepared to have their authority usurped by the economic planners." [16] Divergent styles of planning were at stake, so that no easy reconciliation emerged.

A few members of several regional economic planning councils in Britain (although not the South East) have complained and even resigned because they thought central government was neither giving real responsibilities to the regional economic planning councils nor taking them seriously.

ATTEMPTED SYNTHESIS: THE JOINT PLANNING TEAM'S STRATEGIC PLAN

In the late spring of 1968 a new planning study was commissioned jointly by the central government, the South East Economic Planning Council, and the Standing Conference on London and South East Regional Planning (representing the local planning authorities). This two-year study was undertaken by a team of about 40 planners, geographers, economists, and sociologists drawn from governmental departments and local planning authorities. It was under the technical direction of Wilfred Burns, Chief Planner of the Ministry of Housing and Local Government. Overall guidance was provided by a steering committee chaired by the Permanent Secretary, MHLG, and composed of senior officials of the commissioning bodies.

The planning team was given broad terms of reference: ". . . it should arrive at recommendations for the future development of the [South East] Region which will be broadly acceptable to the authorities who will have to apply them—the government and local planning authorities." [17] The aim was to produce a draft of a report and plan by the spring of 1970. A progress report was released in early 1970.[18] A final report, *Strategic Plan for the South East,* was released in June 1970. Three volumes of studies were published in the spring of 1970, and publication of the two final volumes is pending.[19]

The planning team had been expected to consider all of the approaches already discussed in this chapter: testing the assumptions and policy recommendations put forward in *The South East Study,* examining the feasibility and desirability of the proposals embodied in *A Strategy for the South East,* and reviewing the substantive alternatives and methodological approaches suggested by reports of the Standing Conference.

The status and sponsorship of the planning team eased its access to various ministries or agencies of the central government. It could also distribute interim reports, through the Standing Conference, to the two dozen local planning authorities in the region under study and to procure their reactions and ideas. The team, it is reported, emphasized methods by which central government and local authorities could implement policy, once recommended.

The team devoted much of its effort to pulling together analyses of major development trends in the South East Region and of its principal problems. As a way of pushing on into the future, provisional objectives were identified and two hypothetical population distributions for the year 1991 were formulated and evaluated— Hypothesis 1991A and Hypothesis 1991B.

Hypothesis 1991A, derived from the South East Economic Planning Council's *A Strategy for the South East,* assumed the stabilization of Greater London's population at 7.3 million, and

accommodation of as much population and employment as possible in new cities and other large new counter magnet developments 40 to 80 miles away from London, notably at Milton Keynes (in association with Northampton and Wellingborough), South Hampshire, and South Essex, together with some expansion of Ipswich; accommodation of the rest of the region's population and employment growth, so far as possible, in sectors along the main radial communication routes between London and the more distant new developments; and limitations of such growth in the "green" areas between the proposed radial sectors.[20]

This hypothesis assumed a striking redistribution of population to outer edges of the South East Region and spilling over beyond it, and less vigorous growth closer in to Greater London within the London Metropolitan Region itself.

In contrast, Hypothesis 1991B projected "greater emphasis on development closer in to London, i.e., emphasizing the London Metropolitan Region, where it appeared additional employment might become more readily available than in some of the more remote growth points envisaged in [Hypothesis] A." [21] Hypothesis 1991B also concentrated "more growth . . . in the OMA [outer metropolitan area], notably in the Reading-Aldershot area, South Essex, North Kent, and also, unlike [Hypothesis] A, on the Essex-Hertfordshire border." [22] The second hypothesis assumed that the population of Greater London would continue to fall, reaching to about 7 million by 1991, and that a flow of population to parts of the Metropolitan Region just beyond the Metropolitan Greenbelt could be anticipated. It is as though Hypothesis B represented a rather natural trend, whereas Hypothesis A would depend upon the effectiveness of public policy in guiding growth outward to a limited number of major centers beyond the Metropolitan Region.

Early in its deliberations the planning team decided that a conventional physical plan seemed inappropriate for so complex a region with so uncertain a future. But they did agree on a final series of objectives and a recommended regional strategy, after evaluating Hypotheses A and B against the provisional objectives. The main features of the regional strategy proposed in *Strategic Plan for the South East* are:

The development of a limited number of major growth areas at varying distances from London, using existing or planned urban settlements as bases for growth. . .

Redevelopment and rehabilitation in London. . . .

The expansion of a number of medium-sized employment centers which have potential for growth, together with relatively small scale development in other parts of the region. . . .

In the countryside, the preservation of extensive areas of open country. . .

A regional road and rail network intended to provide for traffic between the more important centers of population and activity in the South East and between the South East and the rest of the country.[23]

The heart of the strategy is the first feature—placing stress on a limited number of major growth areas. Such strategy assumes benefits from various economies of agglomeration and from the preservation of open countryside. It also permits emphasis on a balance, for each center and its hinterland, between resident population and employment opportunities. The team recommended the following major-growth areas (with estimated population for each at the end of the century): South Hampshire (approaching 1.4 million); Milton Keynes-Northampton-Wellingborough (about 0.8 million); Reading-Wokingham-Aldershot-Basingstoke (between 1.0 and 1.2 million); South Essex (about 1.0 million); and the Crawley area (about 0.5 million).[24] Seven further medium-growth areas were also recommended. Four of the five major-growth areas were singled out for the highest priority of development (Reading was the exception). One medium-growth area, Harlow, was also scheduled for intensive development.

As of this writing, there is no firm indication as to the probable response of the central government. Nor can we evaluate with any certainty the impact of the report on the local planning authorities in the region, or on the art of metropolitan regional planning. Tentatively, it appears that the planning process uniquely involved representatives from the local planning authorities at all stages, while also working toward cooperation on the part of several central government departments.* We may hope for some continuing joint central-local machinery for keeping the strategy under review, and for ensuring effective implementation. It remains to be seen whether this plan provides a convincing and authoritative strategic lead that can rally the many governmental units in guiding the growth of the vast South East Region around Greater London. Or will it be but one more in a long series of plans?

This chapter has reviewed a variety of approaches to the task of promoting regional intelligence and policy formulation for the large region dominated by London. Taken together, the approaches suggest a political pragmatism, one approach following another without any overall design or theory. It is likely, in fact, that discussion of the

---

* A further response has been to initiate a Strategic Plan for North West England, presumably with a similar pattern of participation between central and local governments.

"best" form of regional government for Britain will remain just that. Cogent arguments can be made for representative regional government with elected officials. At the moment, however, it appears that a working arrangement bringing together the main interested ministries of central government, the affected regional council, and the various local authorities (however much they may rely on an association like the Standing Conference) is the more likely pattern.

CHAPTER V

GUIDING LONDON'S GROWTH: CONTAINMENT AND DISPERSAL

A MERICANS have long tended to value growth and even to measure progress by it. Accordingly, the question of limiting the overall size of any specific metropolitan area is seldom seriously raised in the United States. To be sure, it is recognized that such growth as may occur should receive some guidance. But few serious and effective metropolitan planning mechanisms have been developed.

Fortunately, the United States has been blessed with many highly competitive metropolitan areas. The growth of older metropolitan areas in the Northeast has been countered by growth in many other parts of the nation, especially the West and Southwest. This growth has occurred largely in the absence of conscious deliberate attempts to direct it. Neither our national government nor our state governments have yet established urbanization policies—that is, policies that would deliberately foster the growth of certain regions and restrain the growth of others.

The situation is very different in Great Britain. For more than 40 years there has been outspoken concern that the London region was likely to grow too vigorously for the social and economic well-being of Britain. Ever since the recommendations of the Barlow Commission (reporting in 1940) and the Abercrombie Plan for Greater London (1944), it has been central government policy that London's growth should be deliberately held back and that the growth of other relatively depressed regions should be stimulated. Further, it became an underlying policy that central London in particular should be decongested and that the growth of outer portions of the London Metropolitan Region should be planned carefully. To this end, the new towns concept was introduced as a deliberate planning approach. Moreover, other means were sought for promoting compact, balanced settlement, and the creation of a major Metropolitan Greenbelt. Significantly, the principal responsibility for these approaches lay with the central government. The local governments generally carried out their own planning and development within the broader policy framework provided by central government legislation and administration.

The "system" developed for planning London is distinctively British. It should not be assumed that their concern with metropolitan growth—or their arrangements for controlling it—can be directly carried over to the United States. But the United States may have been unduly slow to realize the potential significance of urbanization policy. In time we will have to consider seriously the relationship between policy set forth by the national government and by the states on the one hand, and development policy as put forward by metropolitan governments on the other. We have lacked both of these levels of firm policy, more by default than by deliberate choice.

Consequently this chapter picks up various lines of thought from earlier chapters, with the intent of focusing on the major substantive policies relating to the growth and spatial distribution of population and employment within Metropolitan London. The presentation is organized into four sections: a review of overall growth policies; approaches to holding down employment concentration in central London; approaches to orderly and compact settlement in outer parts of Metropolitan London; and efforts to foster counter-growth in other regions of Britain. Various other problems impinging on London—transportation, housing, education, the assimilation of minority groups, crime, and public finance—will be discussed in Chapter Six.

OVERALL POLICIES ON GROWTH

A highly influential package of plans and policies for guiding the growth and reconstruction of Greater London was put together during the closing years of World War II. Two main advisory plans dealt with the County of London and with Greater London. Significantly, both were prepared under planning teams led by Patrick Abercrombie. Authorities were faced with the immediate need to rebuild heavily bombed-out districts of London. Also to be faced over a longer period was the challenge of achieving a balanced and orderly development of Greater London.

These plans and subsequent development policy assumed that there would be little new overall population growth in Greater London; rigorous control of physical development could follow as desirable and feasible. Behind the plans lay a judgment that London's growth should be discouraged in the interest of helping ensure the economic growth of other regions. Thus in the late 1940's, an assumption that growth pressures would be small was combined with a deliberate policy of restraining growth. These merged to provide a planning doctrine blessed by central government and accepted by countless officials and planners for the next decade or two.[1]

But several changes in the 1950's and the early 1960's impinged on the bases for this doctrine of containment. Birthrates went up and the British population grew, a growth development that was quite unanticipated by the earlier demographic forecasts, which had served as basis for the advisory plans. London proved far more attractive to various growth activities than had been envisaged—particularly headquarters offices, specialized services, and such manufacturing as electronic and electrical goods. London continued to play a vital role in finance, and was involved in strengthened ties with the European economy. In the face of these forces, it became increasingly unrealistic to assume that the plans for London could continue to be based on a policy of containment.

Then in the mid-1960's came the MHLG's *South East Study* and the South East Economic Planning Council's *Strategy for the South East*. Both examined the presuppositions of the earlier advisory plans. The *Study* concluded that considerable growth in London was inevitable, as well as probably important for the overall economic health of the country. Thus it was the government's challenge to recognize the prospects for growth and to guide this growth, rather than continuing to act as though the growth could be stopped. The *Strategy* report built upon the *Study* report and proposed a rough, sketch-like scheme that could accommodate the growth. Both reports recognized the desirability of outer population concentrations in South East England as positive ways of clustering development and

96

building urbanized centers that could complement and hold their own with respect to the traditional metropolitan center in London proper.

Significantly, the *Strategy* report was prepared by an Economic Planning Council with loyalty to the South East, as well as responsibility for advising the central government. This meant that the council was in a position to promote the South East's cause in competition with promotional efforts that might be put forward by other regions. With various regions arguing their cases, some response, however minimal, was called for by the central government. Clearly, the government comes under diverse and heavy pressures from the various regions.

As Maurice Hackett, the Planning Council's chairman, stated in his forward to the *Strategy* report: "We are not putting forward expansionist plans for the development of the South East at the expense of other regions; this report is a sober assessment of what needs to be done if the region is to continue to make its major contribution to the country's economy. Entry into the Common Market could well increase the importance of this contribution." [2] The report goes on with this summary of its general approach:

We are all proud of London's position not only as our capital but as a unique international centre for commerce and finance, as a world-wide tourist attraction, and as a centre for the arts, education, religion, and science. It is of very great importance for the nation's prosperity that it should continue to be so. Our plans for the future must enable London to work as efficiently as possible.

To this end, the growth of [Greater] London must be contained. Firm controls must be exercised to relieve traffic congestion, to reduce the difficulties and excessive costs of business firms, and to make life as pleasant as possible for the individual Londoner. . . . Continued efforts must be made to prevent unnecessary concentration of activities in London, particularly in the central area. . . . We fully endorse the concept of holding the resident population of Greater London at or under 8 million. . . .

The rest of the region should be able to accommodate the greater part of its natural population increase, in addition to housing much of London's overspill. . . . The most promising method of achieving an ordered development of the South East is to develop city regions around the periphery of the region . . . that can provide cultural, entertainment, and shopping facilities that go some way to counterbalance the attractions of London.[3]

During the mid- and latter 1960's, an evolving set of trend summaries, policy explorations, and position papers was issued by the
Standing Conference on London and South East Planning. In seeking to articulate development objectives for the South East Region
and in putting forth tentative alternative sketch plans, the conference was also contributing to the broader framework for the region.
Within the context of these various streams of reports the GLC, acting through its Strategic Planning Committee and its town planning
technical staff, produced its 1969 development plan.

The GLC's development plan, in addition to a detailed analytic
volume, *Report of Studies* (July 1969), consists of two main reports:
Greater London Development Plan: Statement (July 1969) and *Tomorrow's London: a Background to the Greater London Development Plan* (October 1969). The latter report, intended as a popular
summary, in fact introduced some modifications in outlook. We report below the growth-containment policies put forward in these two
volumes.

To a degree, the *Statement* can be read as all things to all people.
First it assures the reader that the council intends to do everything
possible to "maintain London's position as the capital of the nation
and one of the world's great cities." Next it accepts the prospect of
considerable population decline, while nevertheless asserting that beyond a certain point continued decline could be detrimental to the
national interest. The report then accepts a population of 7.3 million
as a desirable target, below the actual population of 7.8 million at
the time the development plan was prepared. Critiques of the plan
have questioned the seeming arbitrariness of the 7.3 million population target. Even the detailed tables of the supporting analytic report
fail to indicate what alternatives were considered and why this particular figure was chosen.

The report stresses that the envisioned decline, and the consequent
"profound change within London, will be matched by rapid growth
in the parts of the South East Region beyond its boundaries." It con-
cludes with this not entirely clear pronouncement: "The whole of
Greater London must now participate much more closely in the new
patterns of regional activity." [4]

Tomorrow's London, a sweeping and eloquently phrased supplementary report, accepts the current annual net population loss of
some 90,000 persons for Greater London, but questions whether any

single population figure can sensibly be projected as a target. The report states:

So there can be no fixed population target. What we are doing, realistically, is to allow for a lower figure than today's—but without accepting that the outward movement need go on at the same very high rate which it has reached in the last few years. . . .

The aim is not to have the largest population in the world—we cheerfully cede this distinction to New York, Tokyo, or São Paulo. Our aim is to maintain London's place in the esteem of mankind. We must compare ourselves with our rivals not on the question of size, but on beauty and amenity. This is why we concentrate on the quality of the environment and the smooth functioning of our great city, not on the numbers of its inhabitants. Our task is to create an acceptable environment for our people, and allow London to function, and if we cannot do this adequately for seven million, we will have to accept an even smaller population.[5]

Within the space of several years we have thus seen an important movement away from containment as a principle for organizing Metropolitan London and a shift toward an acceptance of growth, along with an increasing concern for maintaining a viable economy and ensuring workability and livability.*

DISPERSING EMPLOYMENT FROM CENTRAL LONDON

It has long been known that some regions of the United Kingdom, notably Scotland, Wales, Northern Ireland, and Northern England,† have encountered serious economic difficulties—especially reflected in increasingly high unemployment rates—requiring direct positive relief. Central government thus adopted the policy of allocating resources to these troubled regions, and preventing undue growth in

---

* The Greater London development plan inquiry, despite its emphasis on detail, did bring out a major policy difference between the GLC with its concern for restricting the uncontrolled dispersal of employment and population out of Greater London, and the Town and Country Planning Association (with its support of even greater dispersal). GLC officials fear that Greater London will increasingly face the same situation as the largest American metropolitan areas, that is, vigorous suburbanization selectively pulling the middle-class households away from the inner city, leaving it with an uneasy mix of persons who are preponderantly poor, plus a far lesser number of well-to-do.

† The national plan deals with all these parts of the United Kingdom. We have tended, however, to focus primarily on England, since the approaches to regional development outside of England are complicated by governmental arrangements that differ from the English system.

prosperous areas, particularly London. Thus a system of industrial development controls was devised immediately following World War II, with the Board of Trade given administrative responsibility. Their intent was to steer new industrial construction away from London into regions needing increased employment. Any manufacturing firm wishing to build new facilities in excess of a certain square footage in the London area had to apply for an industrial development certificate (IDC). The exact cut-off figure has varied: from 1945 to 1948, IDC's were needed for facilities over 10,000 square feet; from 1948 to 1965, for those over 5,000 square feet; and from 1965 to 1966, for those over 1,000 square feet. From 1966 to 1971, the cut-off was relaxed to 3,000 square feet.

By and large, the Board of Trade has administered the IDC's as firmly as could be expected in a democratic society. Certificates have been refused for manufacturing expansions in Greater London if the board thought they could be better located elsewhere. Between 1962 and 1966, one-fifth of the space applied for in Greater London was refused. Thus 4.4 million square feet of industrial floor space was forced elsewhere.[6] Nevertheless, the growth of manufacturing has not been generally discouraged in the outer parts of Metropolitan London, beyond Greater London.

These controls dealt with manufacturing expansion, but they failed to cope with the remarkable rise in the kind of service activities normally conducted in offices. It was not until 1956 that the problem was formally recognized. By then nearly 42 million square feet of post-World War II office space had been created. A serious loophole in the controls had permitted construction of any new building containing up to 110 per cent of the volume of the building replaced, without requiring a special permit. Old buildings often had high ceilings and proportionately large volumes. This allowed new buildings, with their lower ceilings and more efficient layout, to provide floor space and employment proportionately greater than the nominal 10 per cent increase in volume permitted.

By the mid-1960's it became clear that London's overwhelming predominance in new office construction called for government action. Metropolitan London's 65 million square feet of new postwar offices accounted for four-fifths of all new office space in England and Wales. And for the period 1951 to 1964, central London was reported to have had an increase of nearly 200,000 office jobs.[7] (As is pointed out below, this estimate was later determined to have been too high; nevertheless in 1964 it was being accepted by the central government.)

In 1963 an early attempt was made to limit the growth of new office construction, with the creation of the Location of Offices Bureau, operated directly by the central government with the purpose of inducing firms to move voluntarily out of central London. An extensive advertising campaign was carried on and a consulting service offered. These stressed the advantages of dispersion and provided specific advice on relocation. The bureau claims to have helped relocate over 700 concerns involving 55,000 jobs during the first five years.[8]

But sterner measures were deemed necessary. The government therefore enacted the Offices and Industrial Development Act of 1965. The act required that any developer seeking to build 3,000 square feet or more of office space within 50 miles of Charing Cross, and 10,000 square feet or more of space elsewhere in South East England, East Anglia, and the Midlands, had first to secure an office development permit from the Board of Trade. This approval was in addition to the customary planning approval from the local authority.* The limitations imposed by this act have contributed to a considerable slowing down in office construction in central London. But a great volume of construction—amounting in 1966 to 16 million square feet in Greater London—had already been approved; consequently the full effect of the limitations was slow in coming. One analyst, writing in 1964, predicted that control of industrial and office space could not be expected to prevent more than a fraction of the potential employment increase. As causes of the probable failure he pointed to loopholes in the controls, possibilities for increasing employment without recourse to new space, and the tendency to con-

* There have been variations over time in the geographic areas to which the 3,000 square foot and the 10,000 square foot cutoffs for controls have applied, and we shall not try to report these in detail. Because of economic and fiscal difficulties, the more stringent 3,000 square foot figure was extended to the entire South East and the Midlands in 1966. But in July 1967, this lower limit was retained only for Metropolitan London, as described in the text. ("New Economic Measures," *British Record* [July 26, 1966]; *A Strategy for the South East: A First Report by the South East Economic Planning Council* [London: HMSO, 1967], p. 52; Central Office of Information, *Regional Development in Britain* [London: HMSO, 1968], pp. 16–17.)

centrate the controls in central London, whereas much of the significant pressure for development affected the outer parts of Metropolitan London.[9]

The central government has declared its determination to disperse governmental offices away from central London where possible. But the continuing overall growth of the total governmental establishment, including headquarters for the nationalization of various major functions, has tended to offset steps toward dispersal. About 100,000 civil servants of the central government remain in Inner London and about half that number in Outer London. There has been dispersal, however, because more than twice as many now work outside London as in London. Since 1963 some 15,000 civil servants have moved away from the capital, and another 3,000 to Outer London. In addition a number of new offices have been established outside of London: the Post Office Giro offices in Bootle with some 3,000 staff, Land Commission offices distributed in various cities, and a half-dozen major Inland Revenue offices with over 2,000 staff due to be operating outside of London by the mid-1970's.[10]

As noted, concern over the estimates available in 1964 moved the government to enact legislation restricting construction of new office space. But analysis of the 1961 census data, published in 1966, showed that the earlier estimates had greatly exaggerated the actual increase in office jobs.* Consequently the South East Economic Council concluded in its *Strategy* report that, although office development controls were still needed, particularly in Inner London, construction of office centers in Outer London and in the South East Region should be encouraged. Moreover, limited office building should be permitted, even in central London, where there was need for modernization, or for accommodation of international firms whose location in London would benefit the British economy.

In its development plan, the GLC has moved still further from the governmental expressions of alarm prevalent in 1964 and 1965. The plan suggests, in fact, the possibility of an appreciable future decline in economic activity and employment. The forecast indicates that by 1981 the resident labor force in Greater London could fall by 700,-

* One estimate is that the increase in employment from 1951 to 1961 amounted to only 74,000, instead of the 150,000 previously estimated. The South East Economic Planning Council in its 1967 *Strategy* reported the 1951–1961 increase as 56,000 (p. 48).

000. Some of this drop may be considered desirable, because it will avert excessive commuting and congestion, but too great a drop could be detrimental to the national interest. The plan suggests that it is important to ensure "that the manpower becomes available where it is most needed, under conditions which allow it to produce its greatest output." [11] The plan stresses London's invisible exports produced by banking, insurance, and other services. It recognizes London's pivotal role in tourism, Britain's fourth largest industry. In addition, it stresses the urgent need for modernization of facilities—increased hotel capacity, a modern conference center, a first-class exhibition center—and recognizes that construction to meet this need should be permitted, even in central London.

In an important new policy proposal, the development plan asserts the GLC's willingness to cooperate with the boroughs in developing "criteria of selectivity" for picking businesses and activities that deserve central locations. The GLC hopes that by relying upon the plan's policy structure and by applying the proposed criteria of selectivity it can initiate a type of planning control that would prove more effective than the present system of office development permits operated by the Board of Trade.

In addition to controls which limit and guide the location of new construction, the GLC and the London boroughs administer land-use controls designed to ensure appropriate site development, to prevent undue physical massing of buildings, and to eradicate nuisance uses. Supported strongly by the MHLG, the LCC developed and firmly administered floor-area ratio controls and daylighting controls to regulate the sheer density and spacing of office buildings. The GLC and the boroughs, like the preceding governments, have sought to control the location of office construction. Within their financial limitations, the LCC, and subsequently the GLC, have actively bought up industrial firms in order to get them out of districts where industry was unwanted, and to make land available for other uses, including parks, schools, and other community facilities.

The United States has much to learn from these various controls, and more, perhaps, from the British government's determination to maintain a firm, guiding hand. Both central and local governments have followed deliberate programs to lessen the concentration of employment in central London and to foster moves to other parts of Britain or to Outer London. Firms have been compelled to expand

103

in backward regions rather than in London. Government offices have been moved to these regions, but it has been much more difficult to force or stimulate existing private plants to move their entire operations. It is doubtful whether—in programs to divert activities to outer parts of the London Region—there has been a sufficiently forceful policy on creating new regional centers of the scale that Londoners will need in the coming decades. Both the South East Economic Council's *Strategy* and the Greater London development plan seek to foster such centers, but it is too early to know how effective the proposals will be.

PLANNED GROWTH OF OUTER LONDON

The *Greater London Plan, 1944,* prepared by Sir Patrick Abercrombie in the final years of World War II and accepted as general policy by the central government, laid down the major guidelines for two decades of planning. The principal features of the 1944 plan were thinning out and rebuilding of central London, creating and preserving a Metropolitan Greenbelt around the main portion of the conurbation, and founding planned new towns beyond the Greenbelt. Much of this has been accomplished. Many of the central residential districts have been rebuilt, although lack of funds has prevented a more sweeping attack on the slums. The Metropolitan Greenbelt with its 840 square miles was officially created; the possibility of adding another 1,200 square miles has been under consideration for several years. (See Map 2, p. 3.)

Eight new towns around London, developed by public corporations, are now maturing, ranging from advanced phases of development to virtual completion. From about 100,000 residents at the time of their designation in the late 1940's, these eight new towns had grown to a total population of about 460,000 by the end of 1969. They have thus passed the original goal of 450,000 residents, although the goal was subsequently shifted upwards to about 515,000, with "ultimate" capacity for further natural increase to 680,000. These eight new towns provide total employment for over 235,000 persons, including 100,000 in new factories and about 14,000 in new commercial offices. The towns have 2,000 new shops and 225 new schools.[12]

The planned expansion of a number of outlying towns is also in progress. As of June 1969, some 31 such schemes were completed, underway, or agreed upon, and several additional smaller schemes were also underway. For these schemes serving Greater London, 37,-000 new houses, out of a total of 86,800 to be built, had been completed by 1969.[13] "Exporting" authorities (the GLC and formerly the LCC) make agreements with "receiving" authorities (the towns being expanded) for the orderly transfer of households. Financial responsibility is shared by the central government, the exporting authority, and the receiving authority.

To date, the population accommodated in the eight London new towns approximates that proposed in the 1944 plan. The population drawn to the planned additions to existing towns is very much less than was anticipated in the Greater London Plan, but a larger population than was anticipated is moving voluntarily or is resulting from natural increase. As has been noted, suburbanization is proving far more important than was contemplated by the plan.

DEVELOPMENT OF THE SOUTH EAST REGION

The South East Study (March 1964) forecast that the South East Region would grow by 3.5 million between 1961 and 1981. One million persons could be expected to move out of Greater London. This net out-migration would just balance a similar natural increase. Consequently, Greater London's population would remain stable, and the anticipated South East Region increase of 3.5 million would have to be accommodated outside of Greater London.

The *Study* proposed that about 1.2 million of the increase be accommodated by planned developments. The *Study* accepted the primary aim of decentralizing some office employment completely out of the South East Region. It also recognized the desirability of dispersing office employment to selected new or expanded cities or towns away from central London but clearly within the London Metropolitan Region. Three new or expanded cities were proposed, each to accommodate 150,000 to 250,000 residents. They were to be located in the vicinity of Southampton-Portsmouth (77 miles southwest of central London), Bletchley (about 45 miles northwest), and Newbury (about 55 miles due west). Other important city expansion schemes were contemplated, with Northampton (northwest), Stansted (northeast, adjoining a site proposed in 1967 for a new London

105

airport and then rejected in 1968 after public protests), Ipswich (northeast), Ashford (southeast), and Swindon (west) proposed as desirable.* The possibility of expanding some of the eight new towns beyond their original planned size of approximately 65,000 was also suggested, and this was subsequently done. (See Map 6, p. 85.)

Two modifications were announced as a result of further ministerial reviews of *The South East Study*'s proposals.[14] The reviews suggested that a larger proportion of the new growth than had been originally recommended should be within 40 miles of London. Correspondingly, a somewhat smaller proportion of the total new housing would be provided by planned growth, and more by the "normal" processes of development. Thus planned growth might provide only one-fourth of all new housing instead of the one-third originally contemplated.

Nearly four years elapsed between the release of *The South East Study* (March 1964) and the appearance of the South East Economic Council's *A Strategy for the South East* (November 1967). The council dealt with a smaller geographic region, excluding East Anglia and Dorset. Thus the council's region of 17 million residents was about 1.5 million smaller than the one on which the South East Study was based. For this and other reasons it is difficult to compare the planning projections of the two reports with precision. In broad terms, however, the report by the council envisioned less future population growth in the South East, because of a drop in net migration and some continued decline in the birthrate. The council also calculated that earlier reports of an alarming growth in employment in central London were erroneous and that, judging from better 1961 Census figures and more recent estimates, employment growth was tapering off. It also showed that demographic projections for the region in-

---

* Various studies were subsequently commissioned by the Ministry of Housing and Local Government in collaboration with the affected local governments. To probe the possibility of a new city of 250,000 in South Hampshire in the vicinity of Portsmouth or Southampton, Colin Buchanan and Partners were retained, in association with Economic Consultants Ltd. To examine the prospects for development in the vicinity of Swindon (northwest of Newbury), Llewelyn-Davies, Weeks, and Partners were commissioned. Their report proposed that a new city with an eventual population of about 400,000 and a population of 250,000 by 1981 be built near Swindon. Further studies of smaller expansions or developments were also set in motion.

cluded a sizable future drop in the population of active working age and stressed the economic contribution of the region to the national economy. The report concluded, as we noted in Chapter Four, that it would be a mistake to contain prospective population growth unduly, and expressed concern that too much effort might be made to divert the liveliest growth-type economic activities to other regions, and that national interests could be harmed.

The *Strategy* report generally supported the pattern of new and expanded cities that was loosely proposed in the 1964 *Study*. The South East Economic Planning Council built upon the earlier recommendations for new urban growth points by fitting them into its own proposed plan for growth sectors—finger-like radial growth extensions running out from the Metropolitan Greenbelt along major transportation lines, as shown in Map 7. The council recommended the highest priorities for development of the Southampton-Portsmouth area; of the Milton Keynes area (incorporating Bletchley), with related developments at Northampton, Peterborough, and possibly Bedford; and of the Ipswich-Colchester area.* It judged Ashford to be less urgent, despite the earlier arguments that Ashford would be near the British end of a new Channel Tunnel. The central government during 1967 and 1968 approved four major development schemes:[15]

	From Central London	1966 Population	Planned Intake, 1964–1981
Milton Keynes	45 miles northwest	40,000	70,000
Peterborough	80 miles north	78,000	70,000
Northampton	65 miles northwest	122,000	70,000
Ipswich	75 miles northeast	121,000	70,000

In 1968 the central government announced that more detailed plans were being prepared for the Portsmouth-Southampton area, 70 miles southwest of London. Planned intake—referring to the planned movement of Londoners to these cities—would probably be held at 60,000 or so. With 850,000 population in 1966, the area was already the most rapidly growing in Britain, and it seemed unwise to try to accommodate any greater growth rate. The government also decided

* The Ipswich expansion scheme was later abandoned.

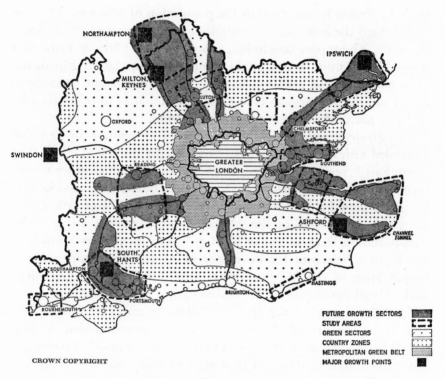

NORTHAMPTON

IPSWICH

MILTON KEYNES

LUTON

OXFORD

CHELMSFORD

SWINDON

READING

GREATER LONDON

SOUTHEND

ASHFORD

CHANNEL TUNNEL

SOUTH HANTS

SOUTHAMPTON

HASTINGS

BOURNEMOUTH

PORTSMOUTH

BRIGHTON

FUTURE GROWTH SECTORS
STUDY AREAS
GREEN SECTORS
COUNTRY ZONES
METROPOLITAN GREEN BELT
MAJOR GROWTH POINTS

CROWN COPYRIGHT

MAP 7—DEVELOPMENT STRATEGY PROPOSED BY THE SOUTH EAST ECONOMIC
PLANNING COUNCIL

that Ashford, 55 miles southeast of London, should be disapproved as a new town, and that the less ambitious scheme already underway to take in an additional 15,000 Londoners should suffice. Prolonged negotiations between the GLC and the local authorities for the expansion of Swindon collapsed in 1969.

The South East Study had proposed, and the Milner Holland report, *Housing in Greater London* (1965), had reaffirmed the need for 350,000 families to be relocated ("overspilled," to follow British usage) outside of Greater London during the 18- to 20-year period ending in 1981. This would represent about one million people. It now appears that new-town and expanded-city schemes will accommodate the planned transfer of about three-quarters of a million persons. A less predictable number of persons—perhaps 350,000—are likely to move voluntarily to the outer suburbs, to other parts of the

108

South East Region, and to other regions, particularly East Anglia and the Midlands.

ENCOURAGING DEVELOPMENT IN OTHER REGIONS

In Britain one speaks of the "Home Counties" around London and refers to the other regions as "the provinces," thus symbolizing the historical split that has persisted. Strong counter-pulls must be generated to offset London's greater attraction for growth and its real or presumed advantages. It is not enough to tell industry that it must move out of London: industry must be drawn to other centers that promise to evolve into thriving, modernized communities, and that can offer the services and physical amenities required to make them fully competitive. Obviously, it is a particular challenge to generate the quality of change in "the provinces" that will in turn abet further growth, since growth itself can be a major factor in promoting even more growth.

Various measures are being taken to promote the growth and prosperity of these other regions. For some English regions, studies or programs diagnosing the major problems and outlining the directions of development to be promoted have already been published: for the North East (1963), the West Midlands (1965), the North West (1965), the North (1966), the East Midlands (1966), the South West (1967), and the West Midlands (1967).[16]

As one example, we may examine briefly the situation in the current Northern Region (combining the former North East Region and the counties of Cumberland and Westmorland). This region comprises the five most northerly counties in England, with an area of nearly 7,500 square miles and a population of 3.3 million. The population is concentrated in a northeast coastal strip about 40 miles long and extending about 20 miles inland. The region lies generally more than four hours travel time from London, while Edinburgh and Glasgow, more remote in straight-line distances, are nevertheless within three hours of London, because of better services.

Unfortunately, the economy of the Northern Region has been based on sectors—coal mining, shipbuilding and repair, iron and steel production—that have been contracting. Moreover, the region has been relatively under-represented in growth industries. As of 1963 a comparison of the Northern Region with the South East Region and with Great Britain was indeed discouraging.[17]

109

Region	Manufacturing Employment (in per cent)	
	In "Expanding" Industries	In "Contracting" Industries
Northern Region	21.0	17.6
South East Region	39.1	7.0
GREAT BRITAIN, TOTAL	28.6	11.0

Understandably, this has given the Northern Region a less-than-average national increase in total employment during the postwar years, and has resulted in higher rates of unemployment.[18]

Region	Percentage Increase in Employment, 1953–1963	Average Unemployment Rate, 1953–1963
Northern Region	2.8	2.7
South East Region	14.8	1.1
GREAT BRITAIN, TOTAL	9.1	1.7

Thus, the Northern Region experienced the highest average rate of unemployment in England, although the rates for Northern Ireland, Scotland, and Wales have been even higher.

Correspondingly, the urbanized areas of the Northern Region— which is generally characterized by scenic and mountainous terrain —have suffered from a lack of the kind of modernization that would normally encourage vigorous economic growth. Road improvement has lagged, rebuilding of obsolete central areas is overdue, new housing is needed, and the sordid remnants of former industrial activity remain to blight the landscape. It has generally been impossible to focus fiscal resources in selected centers to spark a stronger spirit of reconstruction and generate a climate of optimism about growth potential.

In the past several years, however, the central government has reasserted its determination to promote economic development in the region and to improve general environmental conditions.[19] A summary of the program, as released by official sources in 1965, provides a sense of the action envisioned:

The programme emphasised that the area's overriding need was economic diversification, coupled with measures to remove the scars left by earlier industrial expansion, and to improve public services and the general quality of life. This demanded faster progress, especially in the spheres

110

of road construction, airport development, housebuilding, urban development and redevelopment, and the provision of facilities for industrial training and retraining. It was envisaged that the additional public service investment which the programme entailed would be concentrated within a 'growth zone' consisting roughly of Tyneside, Teesside, and that part of County Durham which lies between the Great North Road and the Coast.[20]

Considerable progress can be reported, even in the short time since 1963 when the development program was published.[21] Nearly 200 new industrial firms have been attracted, and the range of industries expanded. The unemployment rate has shown a significant decline. The region's electronic firms have formed a consortium, determined to provide the best possible service and to negotiate effectively with the government for contracts. Government centers for training or retraining workers are being expanded, and new craft skills are being taught in six-month stints, greatly speeding up what formerly was a much longer retraining process. The prospects for tapping offshore oil and gas reserves in the North Sea, while spelling further competition for the coal-producing areas, promise particular economic benefits for the Northern Region.

Governmental resources are being directed to the region. Virtually the entire region has been designated a development area, making it eligible for special considerations. The pace of road construction has been accelerated, a road tunnel under the Tyne completed, airports expanded, and rail services improved. Three ports, at Newcastle, Teesside, and Sunderland, have undergone modernization and can now handle large ships. Several new towns (Peterlee, Newton Aycliffe, and Washington), and town expansion schemes (Killingworth and Cramlington) are in process or being promoted. The government is providing grants of up to 85 per cent of the costs of eliminating derelict sites—the slag heaps and decrepit industrial structures that have so long contributed to the atmosphere of blight and stagnation. Other subsidies are available to encourage plant modernization. Controls on location of industry and offices help redirect employment from Greater London.

But much remains to be accomplished. The continuing decline of the coal industry produces pockets of serious unemployment. Indeed, conditions vary from one local community to another. Thus improved overall regional unemployment trends may still mask sub-

111

regional difficulties. The region is also far from doing away with the stereotyped image that suggests it is to be avoided by firms concerned with a fine community environment for their employees. The lure and advantages of Metropolitan London and the South East remain, and placing the Northern Region on competitive terms will call for sustained leadership and the determination to allocate scarce resources. Moreover, it is very difficult to get political agreement to concentrate development resources in only a few selected places— like the Northern Region—when other large sections of the nation also seem to qualify as development areas.

CHAPTER VI

PROBLEMS CONFRONTING
METROPOLITAN LONDON

LONDON FACES all the multiplying problems of an aging city. It has to grapple with congestion afflicting the center and the transportation channels leading to the center. It also has to keep its outer development under control, although, as we have already seen, much of this is beyond the power of the GLC, and involves the broader South East Region. Rebuilding from the bomb damage of World War II absorbed tremendous resources during the first two decades after V-Day. Moving ahead with the Metropolitan Greenbelt and with the impressive set of new towns (although both projects were outside of the jurisdiction of London local government) demanded high priorities in the late 1940's and on into the 1950's. Generally speaking, and despite exceedingly limited fiscal resources, priorities stressed the rebuilding of inner areas and the improvement of educational, medical, and social services.

The deliberate allocation of construction funds to housing, schools, hospitals, playgrounds, and varied community facilities, has slighted other improvements, notably in transportation. Without doubt, the most glaring contrast between contemporary American metropolitan communities and Greater London is the virtual absence of motorways (freeways) within London proper. But the relentless rise in automobile use is now catching up with London. Modernization of the transportation system, without destroying the very features that have made London so distinctive as a world metropolis, is a formidable challenge.

Earlier concerns for controlling London's growth have receded with the emerging prospect that Greater London will continue losing population, but new concerns rise to replace them. For example, London is destined to play an increasingly significant role in the new European political economy. Furthermore London is struggling to enhance its accommodations for the unprecedentedly huge volumes of tourists, who are now recognized as an essential feature of the British economy. Finally London must continue to adapt to changing times, remain fully competitive, and meet rising expectations for improved housing and services. To promote these necessary changes and yet preserve the best of London's unique character is a major task of the future.

Chapter Six continues our look at the ways in which the reorganized GLC and London borough system are responding to a welter of urban problems. In particular, the chapter deals with efforts to improve the transportation system, provide adequate housing, meet changing educational needs, assimilate minority-group persons who have immigrated to Britain, fight crime, and provide an adequate and equitable fiscal base. These problems resemble those in most American metropolitan settings. But the approaches, priorities, and basic financial framework for solutions may have distinctive features, reflecting British values and institutional arrangements.

TRAFFIC AND TRANSPORTATION

In many respects, London has a remarkable passenger transportation system. Its public transport is world renowned, providing a usable network of interconnected lines (underground, railroad, and bus), not to speak of an efficient and reasonably priced cab system. In carrying the heavy peak commuter loads to and from central London, public transport accommodates 90 per cent of the passengers, and only 9 per cent have to be handled by private automobile. It is reported that most, though not all, radial rail routes are crowded; these radial routes, however, help ensure the financial viability of the rail system.

Despite its success, the system is creaking at various points, and shifting demands are imposing almost unbearable strains. Efficient operation has been hampered by the fact that different parts of the system have been managed by different public agencies. Moreover, the persistence of office employment at the very center of London, combined with a continuing suburbanization of households, has introduced a much larger proportion of long commute trips and has overtaxed the radial lines into the center. Suburbanization has also greatly increased reliance on private autos in the outskirts. In the characteristic vicious cycle, this has made it increasingly difficult financially to provide adequate public transport in outlying areas of low density.

The most serious question, however, is whether the private automobile is to be invited into Inner and central London, and if so, how much is to be invested in new motorways, parking structures, and so forth. We shall return to this issue and discuss the proposals for motorways in Greater London. First, however, we shall describe the public transport system and the proposals for increasing its effectiveness.

Over 1,400,000 persons are employed in central London; between 1,200,000 and 1,300,000 of them are commuters. More than 200,000, in fact, commute from outside of Greater London on trips of 12 to 15 miles or more, and the number of these long-distance commuters has doubled in the past 10 years.[1] The peak in numbers that had to be transported in and out of central London was reached in 1962.[2] Since then the number of persons brought in by rail has held up well, but the number of passengers brought in by buses has fallen off considerably, mostly because of clogged on-street conditions, which in turn are caused by greater reliance on private cars. The fall-off in bus usage may also reflect the competitive pull of suburban jobs, and the tendency for jobs in the center to be filled by rail commuters from further out.

The capacity of the underground and commuter railroad services has slowly been increased, but it is now doubtful that much more can be done, short of providing completely new lines. The Victoria Line, the first new underground line to be built in several decades, opened in the winter of 1969, linking a growing residential sector in northeastern Greater London to Victoria Station in central London. This is being extended south under the Thames to Brixton. London Transport is seeking support for two more lines, the Fleet Line (to run from Baker Street Station, through the City, and southeast to Lewisham) and a newly proposed Wimbledon Line (from southwest to northeast), which together would provide a new "X" in London, meshing with existing lines. There was also a proposal in 1970 to

115

extend the existing Picadilly Line west from Hounslow so as to serve the Heathrow Airport.[3]

Various ways of improving the bus system are being actively explored. These include easing traffic congestion to permit better bus circulation, switching to one-operator buses to reduce costs, converting long, meandering bus lines to shorter dependable shuttle services between major centers, revising the fare structure to permit single fares or simple zone fares (made more feasible by shortened lines), providing selected major bus exchange points, and expediting the use of several transportation modes in a single trip.

Traffic congestion caused by the increased use of automobiles is London's most visible transportation problem. Automobile ownership by Londoners has doubled in recent years, and is likely to double again in the near future. By 1966, some 42 per cent of the households in Greater London had cars, and of these 6 per cent had two or more cars.[4] Car ownership in Greater London is also expected to increase rapidly from 1.4 million cars in 1966 to 2.1 million by 1981, by which time four out of five households would have cars.[5]

Numerous traffic control measures have been employed, such as one-way streets and rigid parking prohibitions. The latter are reported to have had substantial effect. These controls have now yielded almost all the improvement possible, short of new motorway and highway construction, which has been proposed in the Greater London development plan.

The proposed motorway scheme calls for three ringways to link 13 motorways or trunk highways coming into Greater London as radials. (See Map 8.) Ringway 3 is outermost, being an ellipse with a radius of 15 to 20 miles from central London. Ringway 2 is also elliptical, and has a radius of 8 to 10 miles. Ringway 1, as proposed, is a parallelogram ranging from three to five miles from the center. It is by all odds the most controversial feature of the motorway system. Once called the "motorway box," it comprises a large distributor loop around central London. While not particularly close-in by American freeway standards, it certainly cuts through portions of Inner London that up to this point would have been judged inappropriate rights of way. Construction of any motorway scheme that approaches central London as closely as Ringway 1 would have far-reaching effects.

Principal arguments for the motorway system hold that it would

116

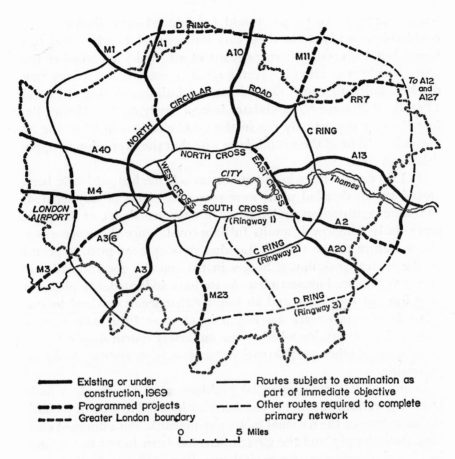

Existing or under construction, 1969
Programmed projects
Greater London boundary
Routes subject to examination as part of immediate objective
Other routes required to complete primary network

0   5 Miles

MAP 8—PROPOSED LONDON MOTORWAY SCHEME

increase transport capacity, when it is needed, to a much greater extent than would an equal investment in public transportation (either rail or the underground). Moreover, it is urged that the determination of Londoners to have and use automobiles must not be underestimated. The policy aim of the system of ringways and radial routes is to keep cars out of central London and to facilitate movement between origins and destinations in outer areas.

There are several arguments against the proposed system. It might displace as many as 25,000 households. It would have a great effect, almost certainly an adverse one, on the face of London. It is also argued that it is an illusion—as allegedly demonstrated by American experience—to assume that road improvements "solve" traffic prob-

117

lems, because more people would be deluded into thinking they could conveniently drive their cars into central London, and this would build up traffic. Perhaps worst of all, critics ask whether the system might not seriously overtax other streets whose capacity cannot be readily increased. Opposition was building during 1968 and 1969. By 1970 some 80 candidates from a newly created Homes Before Roads Party actually ran in the GLC elections in 27 of the 32 boroughs.[6] None of these candidates won, but the expression of opposition was clear.

By 1970 certain links in the motorway scheme had gradually been moved ahead: detailed plans were prepared, rights of way secured, and some construction undertaken. But the remainder of the plan, particularly Ringway 1, awaits full approval. Since the scheme is a major feature of the Greater London development plan, approval by the central government hinges in part on the government's approval of the development plan. As we have indicated, the plan was submitted in July 1969, and an inquiry that seems destined to run for as long as two years was begun in October 1970. The inquiry must seek to determine whether the motorway system should be approved, or whether an alternative transportation system would be preferable.

In any event, serious financial problems must be solved. A basic level of government support had been anticipated as part of its obligation to finance the national motorway network. But estimated costs have risen sharply, and the government has been forced to cut back its own appropriations for capital spending. This means that completion of the motorway system may take 25 years, instead of 15 as originally intended. Such a delay poses very difficult planning, acquisition, and construction problems.[7]

The motorway issue inevitably also raises questions of the relative role of public transport. The policy has been to insist that London Transport pay its own way in operating its underground trains and buses. Now that the London Transport Executive, effective January 1, 1970, has come under the general policy control of the GLC—although remaining largely independent in its day-to-day operations—this policy is open for scrutiny and possible change.

The present Conservative leadership in the GLC aims for a sufficient profit from transit operations to enable it to make needed capital improvements. The Labor Party opposition, on the other hand, supports the use of subsidies for public transport in an all-out effort to encourage the widest possible use of public transport as a positive alternative to the new motorway scheme. Labor members of the GLC are opposing fare increases proposed by London Transport, and councillors in both parties have argued in GLC meetings that they have a responsibility to weigh alternative fare levels, including even the concept of free transport. Mr. Cutler, chairman of the new Policy and Resources Committee responsible for London Transport policy, has been quoted as stating in a GLC meeting: "We can assess whether road proposals or public transport proposals will give us the greatest value and social benefit." [8]

In addition to these problems of motorway construction and public transport, the GLC faces enormous problems of controlling traffic flow and managing parking. An ingenious and rational approach to traffic control is being explored; it would charge road-use fees scaled according to the seriousness of the congestion to be relieved. At present, however, there is no assurance that it will prove technically feasible or politically acceptable. The approach would presumably depend upon the permanent installation on cars of gadgets that would automatically record the time (or distance) each car traveled in each charge zone, as a basis for billing the car owner. The drivers would be encouraged not to use high-charge roads unless the advantage was worth the added cost.

Intra-regional transportation is not all of it. Metropolitan London has also been facing enormous problems in coping with its rising volume of national and international air passengers. Heathrow, the main London airport, is badly congested. A second airport, Gatwick, has even less capacity. The central government has accepted the need for a third new airport and has been searching for the right site for several years. One site, Stansted (north and slightly east of Greater London), was selected but then withdrawn after enormous public protest. By the late spring of 1969 the Roskill Commission, appointed by the central government to advise on a fresh alternative, had narrowed the search to four possible sites; but by 1970, in a rather surprising turn of outlook, it was inquiring whether it would be more practicable to add capacity to existing airports. In December 1970, the commission recommended Cublington (a small village 45 miles northwest of London) as the new airport site. This was followed in January 1971 by the detailed report demonstrating,

119

largely on the basis of cost-benefit analyses of the alternative sites, the lowest net cost for Cublington.[9] Foulness, a site just north of the mouth of the Thames, 55 miles east of London, was shown to have much higher net costs, mainly because of the higher aggregate costs to airport users of the longer trip. A minority report by Professor Colin Buchanan favored Foulness, terming it a "disaster" to locate a major airport at Cublington.

Resistance to Cublington ran extremely high, and there was conjecture that the government, perhaps not feeling bound by a recommendation from a commission set up by a previous government, was more likely to recommend the site on reclaimed land at Foulness. As of this writing, no resolution can be reported.*

London will also be critically affected by arrangements for carrying passengers and goods across the English Channel. As of 1969 two companies were running competing hovercraft services, taking 250 passengers and 30 cars across the Channel at 70 miles per hour. Hovercraft were accounting for one-fourth of total cross-Channel surface capacity. Finally a 35-mile long railway link through the Channel Tunnel, long a dream, may become a reality by the 1980's. Current plans call for each train traversing the Tunnel to carry 300 vehicles—plus passengers—at an average speed of 60 miles per hour.†

HOUSING

Despite improvements, Greater London has been suffering from a housing shortage, from seriously deteriorating housing quality in some areas, and from rising rentals in private housing. Inner London, like metropolitan centers in the United States, attracts and holds both low-income households and special types of households— for example, elderly persons on fixed and low incomes, young childless persons and couples, and some very large families (particularly

---

* In April 1971, the government announced that the third airport would in fact be located at Foulness. This was reported as representing a "victory for environment over economics," in reversing the carefully reasoned, cost-benefit-based recommendations of the Roskill Commission.

† An information release in March 1971 stated that talks were continuing between the British and French governments and the private international group whose plans for financing and constructing the Channel Tunnel are being considered. If a favorable decision is reached, construction could begin in 1973, and the tunnel be operative in 1978. (*British Record* [March 8, 1971], p. 4.)

among immigrants). The housing shortage is the most serious problem for those who must seek rental housing at moderate costs. The hardest hit are persons with low or uncertain incomes, who are also of minority-group status, who recently arrived in London, or who have large families.

The overall quality of London's housing may be viewed in terms of its physical condition, the availability of household facilities, and overcrowding. In its 1964 report, the Milner Holland committee stressed the age of London's housing, 46 per cent having been built before 1918, and less than one-fifth since 1945.[10] The worst housing, in terms of physical dilapidation, is in sections east of central London, and in others south of the Thames.

Much London housing, and particularly the oldest housing, lacks hot water and bathtubs, and 13 per cent lacks inside water closets.[11] In addition, as documented below, the lack of plumbing facilities is seriously compounded by doubling up, that is, by two, three or more families using a dwelling originally intended for one household. In such cases, facilities that are inadequate for use by one household are even less adequate when shared by several. In addition to this serious dearth of private or exclusive facilities, overcrowding brings congestion and severely reduces privacy.

About one-quarter of all households in Greater London share dwellings and facilities. The proportion rises to well over one-half for the 850,000 households renting from private landlords. Over all, as of 1966, the following percentages of households in Greater London lacked *exclusive* use of these facilities:[12] fixed bath, 28.1 per cent; inside water closet, 26.1 per cent; hot water tap, 20.5 per cent. Households lacking exclusive combined use of all three—fixed bath, inside water closet and hot water—amounted to 34.4 per cent.

The influx of newcomers, accentuated by the arrival of thousands of immigrants during the late 1950's and early 1960's, has particularly affected certain boroughs north and west of central London. Thus, the proportions of households lacking exclusive combined use of bath, inside water closet, and hot water are unusually high in these Inner London boroughs: Islington, 67.1 per cent; Hammersmith, 57.0 per cent; and Camden, 49.8 per cent. A survey of 5,500 households in sections of Notting Hill (in Kensington and Chelsea) during the summer of 1967 showed that "less than a quarter had self-contained accommodations, a third were living at densities of more than 1.5 persons per room, and close on 60 per cent shared a lavatory (a quarter of all lavatories being used by eight or more people). And about half of all these households contained children." [13]

While the worst housing was in Inner London up until fairly recently, problems of deterioration are spreading to various areas farther out. For example, areas of overcrowding and inadequate sanitary facilities have expanded, and the Milner Holland report noted that serious housing problems are to be found in Outer London, in such localities as Hornsey (Haringey Borough) and Willesden (Brent Borough), north and northwest of Inner London.

A number of factors have contributed to the increased housing demand. As already noted, average household size has decreased. From 1951 to 1966 this trend toward smaller households—average size in Greater London dropped from 3.14 persons to 2.82—created 27,000 additional households, despite a decline in total population of about 500,000 in Greater London. Rising expectations accompanying greater affluence, have motivated people to move out of shared quarters. Rising incomes have enabled many families to pay more for housing as it has become scarce, thus pushing the average cost higher. These factors have all contributed to the serious housing squeeze on those who are unable either to compete in the housing market or to obtain council housing.

The Milner Holland report recognized that the supply of privately rented housing has been diminishing.* Much of it has been absorbed by new homeowners. Obsolete housing continues to be demolished, because it is unfit per se or because sites for new construction must be prepared. But the replacement housing tends to provide for families of higher income, rather than for the displaced families.

Traditionally, housing has absorbed a smaller average percentage of total income in Great Britain than in the United States. Coupled

* Ruth Glass argues that the Milner Holland report places too great an emphasis on reinvigorating the private market; she favors even greater reliance on publicly managed housing. Ruth Glass and John Westergaard, *London's Housing Needs: Statement of Evidence to the Committee on Housing in Greater London* (London: Center for Urban Studies, University College, 1965), especially pp. 55–60. See also Jane Morton, "Housing," *New Society*, 13:20 (January 2, 1969).

with lower average income, this of course means considerably lower average housing costs than in the United States. But as noted, housing costs have been rising, especially in London, both in absolute amounts and in proportion to incomes. Furthermore, low-income households are likely to pay much higher shares of their incomes for housing than the national average. But averages are of limited value, and for our purposes they can even be misleading. More useful are particular differentials in housing costs that can be identified as unique to Britain, and to Greater London in the late 1960's.

The most prominent differential relates to council housing, owned and operated by the local councils and providing the best housing bargains available. Not all council housing is new by any means, but it does afford self-contained units in condition far superior to that obtainable elsewhere at comparable rents. For example, 1967 rentals for council housing in Camden Borough mainly ranged from two to five pounds ($5.60 to $14.00) gross rent per week, for units of two to four rooms each.[14] Council housing, lacking the stigma attached to American public housing, provides good value for the money and a high degree of security. A large proportion of London households prefer it even over personally owned housing.[15]

Private rental housing, on the other hand, has become much more expensive in recent years, and by British standards it is now unreasonably high in many parts of London. A 1967 survey in Camden Borough showed that much of this housing was of poor quality, and much of it also subject to overcrowding. Over three-fourths of the units were not self-contained, i.e., either lacked or required sharing of a water closet, a kitchen stove or sink, or all of these. The survey provided information about prevailing rents, as summarized here:[16]

Type of Housing	Approximate Gross Median Rent per Week	Prevalent Size in Number of Rooms	Housing Units in Poor Condition of All Housing Units in Category
Unfurnished, total	£ 4 ($11.20)	2–3 rooms	57%
Self-contained	£ 7 ($19.60)		
Not Self-contained	£ 2 10s ($7.00)		
Furnished, total	£ 5 ($14.00)	1–2 rooms	83%
Self-contained	£10 ($28.00)		
Not Self-contained	£ 4 10s ($12.60)		

The Camden survey also demonstrated that low-income households now pay exorbitant rents for private rental housing. Half of all households earn less than 16 pounds net income per week, after taxes. Of the low-income families occupying furnished housing, about 65 per cent paid one-third or more of their incomes on gross rent; of the low-income families occupying unfurnished housing, about 56 per cent spent one-third or more of their incomes on gross rent.[17] The 1967 survey of Notting Hill, after reporting the high proportion of households sharing basic facilities, went on to comment: "Nor was this cheap accommodation. Nearly 70 per cent of the households were in privately rented accommodation, 43.9 per cent in furnished rooms. The median rent for a furnished room was £4 9s 2d [$12.48 per week]; for an unfurnished, £4 1s [$11.34]. Newcomers, with less than two years' residence (30 per cent of all households), and colored immigrants (23.4 per cent) paid more than this." [18] Newcomers and members of minority groups who are not yet eligible for council housing, or whose names have not been reached on the very long waiting lists for council housing, may be subjected to rent gouging.

There is also a problem in Greater London of matching the kind of housing available with the particular mix of families needing to be housed. For example, Inner London has been attracting many single persons and couples without children; they need small apartments, at a range of rent levels. Yet families with children, especially families too poor to live elsewhere, also seek housing near the center of the city. The provision of new highrise blocks of flats for such families is being seriously questioned. Thus, there has been a recent redirected effort to build in Inner London housing of relatively high density, but also offering units in two-, three-, or four-story structures, with outdoor space for most families. These newly designed housing projects should provide a welcome alternative to high-rise towers.[19]

Americans have depended predominantly upon privately built housing. The British, in contrast, have applied a considerably more socialistic or public enterprise philosophy to the housing problem. From 1945 through the early 1950's, three-fourths of all new housing in Great Britain was supplied as council housing built and managed by local authorities. This proportion later dropped to about one-half, and is expected to continue at about that level.

Within the GLC, a little over one-fifth of all housing spaces are in council housing. In Inner London, council housing makes up 27 per cent of the total; as for the rest, about one-fourth of all housing is owner-occupied and about one-half is private renter-occupied. In Outer London, council housing makes up only 18 per cent of the total available; 57 per cent is owner-occupied and only 23 per cent private, renter-occupied. In the whole of London, council housing accounts for about 40 per cent of all *rental* housing.[20] (See also the Appendix, Table IV.)

The GLC inherited some 220,000 housing units from the LCC, and the London boroughs own and manage another 380,000 units. Nevertheless it has been estimated that Greater London's housing shortage amounts to a quarter million units. In December 1965, the GLC and the London boroughs had combined waiting lists of 300,-000 households.

The central government has committed itself to sustained housing efforts nationally, and has announced increased financial support.[21] The government authorized the GLC and the London boroughs to build an additional 31,000 units per year during 1965 to 1968. The GLC completed 4,300 units in 1965 and another 5,000 in 1966; combined figures for the boroughs are not available. A considerable volume of housing is under construction, but new building has been threatened by the financial crisis gripping the nation and by the tightening of available investment funds. In early 1970, because of the government's announced cuts in capital spending, the GLC was forced to reduce its estimated annual construction of council housing units from 8,500 or 9,000 to 7,000. Moreover Camden Borough, with 10,000 on its waiting list for council housing, has had to urge families to move to other areas where they may possibly have better chances.[22]

EDUCATION

In many ways London's education problems are similar to those faced by large urban areas elsewhere in Britain and the United States. There is a search for programs relevant to the issues of these unsettling times. An especially pressing problem is confronting schools in districts where poverty and cultural deprivation are concentrated. Moreover, while London does not face race questions as widespread and intense as those on the American scene, it does have increasing numbers of "immigrant" children to educate. In physical planning terms, Inner London is faced with inadequate sites and obsolescent school plants. The urgent need for rebuilding exceeds the financial resources available. Nevertheless, the volume of new construction since World War II has been impressive.

In order to summarize the issues and approaches that seem distinctive to London, it is important to offer some background regarding British educational trends. To oversimplify, British education has tended to be more elitist in character than American education. A smaller proportion of students have gone on to university-level education, and a more deliberate process of grooming prospective university students has been institutionalized. As recently as 1958–1959 only five per cent of British young persons were entering degree courses in universities; this has since risen, but it remains far below comparable American figures.

The main educational routes have characteristically been:

1. Private or independent schools, including the bloc termed "public schools" in Britain (6 per cent of all thirteen-year olds), with students headed particularly for Oxford or Cambridge.

2. Schools with students screened on the basis of ability tests, grammar school or advanced streams within other schools (26 per cent), with students aiming for provincial universities or other possible schooling. (An increasing number are admitted to Oxford or Cambridge; more than two-thirds of the students in these two universities now come from sources other than "public schools.")

3. Early termination for those who fail to qualify for second route, secondary modern school, or other secondary school (67 per cent), with students normally leaving school at age 15 or 16.[23]

Several major changes have been undertaken in the interest of expanding and further democratizing the British educational system. Since World War II, alternatives to the traditional academically oriented grammar schools have been introduced, with main reliance on the secondary modern school. But more recently, with vigorous support from Labor Party policy, so-called comprehensive schools have been promoted, in the hope that they will largely or completely displace both grammar schools and secondary modern schools. Comprehensive schools are philosophically much closer to American junior or senior high schools, being designed to accommodate a very broad range of student abilities and interests.

Further at issue is the question of qualifying examinations, particularly the "eleven-plus" examinations. These examinations were introduced after World War II to provide a merit basis for identifying pupils with academic promise. In theory, qualification for grammar school education—generally sought by pupils and their parents as the surest route to university entry—was supposed to be divorced from the financial status or social class of a family. But after the war it was judged that the examination results could not be unraveled from a web of influences that include family status, teacher response, and other cultural considerations. So the aim of the Labor Party and the new educational philosophy was to eliminate selective bases for determining pupils' secondary school placement insofar as possible. Two new and partly conflicting criteria emerged: one would have the school serve an entire contiguous neighborhood or district, the other would permit placement to reflect pupil-parental choice.

Predictably, also mixed into all of this has been a further question regarding the separation and "streaming" of ability groups within schools. Streaming tends to persist, even in the seemingly democratized comprehensive schools. And while "eleven-plus" examinations are being abolished by all local education authorities, some criteria must inevitably be employed as a basis for placing pupils in an ability level or stream.

One further problem persists: there have characteristically been several methods by which local government authorities have provided public-fund support for students attending private schools. For some years, however, such funds have tended to be withheld, the apparent rationale being that continued public subsidy would be inconsistent with the idea of breaking down the very system that perpetuates separate and selective schools. But since the Conservative victory in June 1970, these aids have been resumed or maintained.

Recent years have also seen growing recognition that a much larger proportion of young persons, particularly in the 16 to 20 age group, should be encouraged to remain in appropriate schools. Accordingly the central government has decided that the school-leaving age should be raised, but it has had to postpone this until the required financing can be assured. This decision has also opened up important questions about the institutional patterns to be employed. The British are thus beginning to move toward counterparts to the American junior college or community college. But this

127

development is likely to be handled in British ways—by sixth-form colleges, by expanded technical schools, and so forth. In London the leaving-age practice, recent and projected, is as follows:[24]

	1968	Expected by 1975
Students Who Stay Until 16 or Older	30%	49%
Students Who Stay Until 17 or Older	15%	29%

The Inner London Education Authority (ILEA) has been converting to a greater number of comprehensive schools, thereby raising the proportion of students attending nonselective schools. But by the later 1960's selective schools were still accounting for nearly one-fifth of all secondary school admissions. In 1966 the Labor-controlled ILEA proposed the following changes in the numbers of schools:[25]

	1966	By 1970
Comprehensive Schools	77	113
Grammar Schools	72	46
Other Schools	90	46
TOTAL SECONDARY SCHOOLS	239	205

When the Conservative Party gained control of the ILEA in 1967, however, it was decided that the movement toward comprehensive schools should be slowed. Nevertheless the actual proposal made by the Conservatives in 1968, although deferring the target until 1975, recommended a preponderant conversion:[26]

	1968	By 1975
Comprehensive Schools	81	128
Grammar Schools	68	44
TOTAL, ABOVE CATEGORIES	149	172

Soon after the elections in April 1970, when Labor regained control of the ILEA, Ashley Bramall, the new ILEA leader, made it clear that the education committee would be asked to revise the 1968 plan to speed up the conversion to a fully comprehensive and non-selective secondary school system.[27]

128

The Outer London boroughs, acting independently as education authorities, have pursued a variety of approaches to the question of converting to comprehensive schools. Their activities in educational change, as of early 1970, are summarized as follows:[28]

	Number of Boroughs
Reorganization schemes implemented	5
Brent (20 comprehensive schools of 21 total)	
Enfield (20 of 29)	
Haringey (13 of 16)	
Hounslow (9 of 15)	
Waltham Forest (19 of 27)	
Reorganization schemes approved but not yet much implemented	9
Reorganization scheme under review by the Department of Education and Science (Bexley)	1
Reorganization schemes not accepted by DES, and revisions not submitted (Harrow, Hillingdon, and Sutton)	3
Reorganization schemes not yet submitted to DES (Kingston-upon-Thames, Richmond-upon-Thames)	2
TOTAL, OUTER LONDON BOROUGHS	20

While London schools have not confronted the intense problems of racial integration that face central cities in America, the schools have nevertheless been enrolling substantial numbers of immigrant children. In 1966, immigrant children amounted to 47,500 (or 12.1 per cent of the school population) in the ILEA, and to 28,300 (or 4.5 per cent) in Outer London boroughs. Of these children, 45 per cent were judged to have some problems with the use of English.[29]

MINORITY-GROUP ASSIMILATION

This leads into the fact that over the years Britain has absorbed large numbers of immigrants. Until 1962, when the Commonwealth Immigration Act took effect, persons from Commonwealth nations were granted unlimited access to Great Britain. Large numbers of young persons from the Commonwealth came to Britain for education and training. No accurate reports on this inflow and movement of Commonwealth residents were published, and to this day there is no deliberate identification of "colored" residents or immigrants, even in the census.*

It is estimated, however, that in 1951 only 0.8 per cent of the population of the Administrative County of London was colored. By 1961, the proportion had increased to 3.7 per cent, numbering about 120,000 out of 3.2 million. This proportion is small indeed, compared with the composition of central cities in most American metropolitan areas. But during the late 1950's the pace of immigration accelerated to the point where concern was being expressed publicly. In the year or so before the date set for imposition of new controls (July 1, 1962), there was a surge of immigration from those Commonwealth countries, colonies, and protectorates whose populations are recognized as preponderantly "colored." We report here the increases in the number of residents who were migrants from these areas, as the closest approximation to quantitative counts of racial minorities:[30]

Residents Born Outside British Isles	GL Conurbation April 1961	GLC Area April 1966	Increases, 1961–1966	
			Number	Per-centages
India	58,300	80,200	21,900	37.6
Cyprus	34,000	45,000	11,000	32.4
Pakistan	7,500	16,000	8,500	113.3
Other Asian and Oceania (excluding Australia and New Zealand)	13,300	20,900	7,600	57.1
Jamaica	53,400	79,300	25,900	48.5
Other British America (excluding Canada)	45,400	72,600	27,200	59.9
Nigeria	8,000	16,900	8,900	111.3
Other Africa (excluding South Africa)	12,100	25,100	13,000	107.4
Gibraltar and Malta	10,400	11,800	1,400	13.5
TOTAL, ALL CATEGORIES	242,400	367,800	125,400	51.7
As Percentages of Entire Population	3.0	4.8		

* The term "colored" is accepted usage in Britain, although it has fallen into disuse in the United States.

The figure of 367,800 migrants to Greater London expands to an estimated 515,000 residents, if children subsequently born in Britain are included.[31] In 1966 this represented 6.7 per cent of the population of Greater London, a rise from equivalent figures of 340,000 and 4.2 per cent in 1961.

Two complementary observations can be made about minorities. First, London has not yet been deluged with immigrants as have a number of metropolitan centers in other parts of the world. Second, there is, nonetheless, considerable concern that London may face serious problems of race relations in the future, and that a number of associated problems are not widely recognized.

Over the years London has absorbed residents of various minority groups. Some are ethnic or nationality groups that are not considered colored. For example, a very large number of Irish have come to live in London. Until recently, at least, the Irish exceeded the total number of the colored population. London has also provided a home for various nationalities from the Continent, including a considerable Polish population, reflecting upheavals during and following World War II.[32]

Despite their citizenship in Commonwealth countries, newcomers to England encounter a traditional society with its own distinctive outlooks and elitism. Colored newcomers not only must work their way into the normal operations of this society, but also must face more direct discrimination.[33] This takes several forms: refusing to make housing available, or charging higher rents to colored newcomers; restricting employment opportunities primarily to positions requiring lesser skills, and paying lower wages; holding attitudes that, despite public declarations to the contrary, express whites' feelings of superiority toward "colonials"; and some social discrimination challenging their presence in pubs or dancing clubs.

Greater London does not have the ghetto-like concentrations of minority groups that characterize the typical American central city, perhaps in part because the numbers and proportions of the minority population are lower. Nevertheless, there is some spatial segregation in London. In 9 of the 32 London boroughs the percentages of 1966 population from Commonwealth countries, colonies, and protectorates (including some "non-colored" population) exceeded the GLC average of 5.2 per cent by more than 1.5 times:[34]

131

	Per Cent		*Per Cent*
Islington	12.3	Lambeth	8.9
Kensington, Chelsea	11.1	Camden	8.6
Haringey	10.5	Westminster	8.6
Hackney	9.8	Hammersmith	8.1
Brent	9.4		

These London boroughs form a contiguous area, including all of the northwestern portion of Inner London, some sections (Haringey and Brent) of Outer London on the north and northwest, and one borough (Lambeth) south of the Thames and directly below central London. The occurrence of serious overcrowding and rent gouging in parts of this area has already been noted.

The three most critical problems for minorities are housing, employment, and education. But discrimination is a root factor. The broad context remains one in which many residents feel that Britain is white, and the immigrants are colored, and that the latter challenge British values. In addition to discriminatory practices affecting adult immigrants, there has been increased recognition in recent years that education and the socializing experiences of the young children may be of particular importance. The children are disadvantaged in their command of the language, and they reflect divergent cultures. The minorities most seriously affected are unquestionably the West Indians, with Africans next. In contrast, East Indians tend to have made more satisfactory adjustments, followed by Pakistanis, other Asians, and Mediterraneans (from Malta and Cyprus).

The British government has slowly, but not always wholeheartedly, moved toward anti-discrimination legislation. It has acknowledged the need for extra funds to aid local authorities with heavy concentrations of poor immigrants. The Race Relations Act of 1968 was a significant step that prohibited discrimination in employment, housing, and life insurance, among others, and extended an earlier prohibition against discrimination in public places to cover private contracts between individuals. The 1970 white paper, *The Problems of Colored School Leavers,* admits that the government could have moved in certain directions sooner, but it does not adequately address needed reforms in education.[35]

There has been a promising increase in the activity of several

formal organizations dedicated to aiding immigrants, and to edu-
cating the British public against race prejudice. Among these are
the Advisory Council for Commonwealth Immigrants, set up by the
government in 1962, and the Immigrants' Advisory Committee of
the London Council for Social Service. Several London boroughs
have established consultative committees; the former metropolitan
boroughs of Hackney and Paddington and the municipal borough
of Willesden had committees in operation for several years before
their merger with the GLC.[36] Despite these efforts, the situation continues to deteriorate in certain ways (witness the recent waves of at-
tacks by young rowdies on Pakistanis), and it is highly doubtful that
there is sufficient determination to keep ahead of growing racial
problems.

CRIME AND THE POLICE

The metropolitan police force, with direct responsibility for all
of the Greater London Area (except for the City with its own separate police force), is organized under the Home Secretary and the
Home Office of the central government. The force is not a part of
local government, was excluded from the terms of reference of the
Herbert Commission, and was not among the functions assigned to
the new Greater London Council or the London boroughs. But with
the creation of Greater London in 1965, the Metropolitan Police
District was enlarged to include all of Greater London apart from
the City (and the Temples, which in part lie outside the City). A
few portions of the district also extend outside of Greater London.[37]

The metropolitan police force is an integral part of what is, in
effect, a national police system. It is responsible for maintaining a
central registry of crimes and criminals and a central fingerprint
bureau, and for providing detective services, through what is generally known around the world as Scotland Yard. Other police forces
in Britain are required to contribute to its files, and they in turn
may make use of them. Detectives may be made available to aid
other police units if requested.

London police confront two particularly serious problems. First,
crime has been increasing significantly—by 1966, for example, indictable offenses had risen to 282,600. This was a big jump from
197,000 of five years earlier, and nearly triple the less than 100,000

comparable annual offenses in the mid-1950's. (In 1967 the total of indictable offenses dropped to 273,000, the first encouraging downturn in years, and steadied at 275,200 in 1968.)

Together with over 1,100,000 non-indictable offenses, by 1963 there was a grand total of 1,300,000 offenses. The number of indictable robberies passed 1,000 for the first time in 1962, and by 1967 it had risen to more than 2,000. Holding ominous implications for the future is the fact that cases in which firearms were carried has been rising noticeably. In 1968 it was up to 15 per cent of all robberies and assaults with intent to rob, a leap from 11 per cent in 1967. This is still, of course, very small by American standards. The proportion of indictable crimes solved dropped from 30 per cent in 1957 to 21 per cent in 1965. This percentage rose to 24 per cent in 1967 and to 25 per cent in 1968. In recent years violence against persons has not increased proportionately as much as crimes against property.[38]

The second police problem is that of recruiting and holding a fully staffed force. At the end of 1968 the authorized strength of the metropolitan police was 26,046, up only moderately, considering the marked rise in crime, from the 19,600 authorized at the end of World War II. At that earlier date, however, the force actually comprised 14,100 persons. By 1948 it had risen to only 15,600, and by 1962 it numbered 17,800 persons, short about 2,400. At the end of 1968, the actual strength had risen to 20,539; this was 5,507, or 21 per cent, under strength.[39] The situation had become so grave by 1965 that the Home Office took several strong measures. An intensive recruiting campaign was undertaken, with more advertising and stepped-up training. Pay was increased. The use of police cars and two-way pocket radios was increased. Consultations concerning the recruiting crisis have continued between the Home Office and the Police Federation, a union representing over 99 per cent of the force below the rank of superintendent. The results have been moderately encouraging. In every year recently, from about 3,500 completed applications some 1,100 new policemen have been trained and admitted to the force.[40] Civilian manpower has also increased even more rapidly, with the trend toward civilians taking over some jobs previously handled by police officers, thus further freeing the latter for other functions.

Like cities in the United States, London has been having more political demonstrations than formerly. They are similar even to the causes—a major concern being the Vietnam war. The Metropolitan Police have gained a reputation for successfully handling large crowds. Their method depends largely on deploying very large numbers of police, on the traditional lack of firearms, and on firm and patient cordoning and crowd dispersal. One of the largest recent demonstrations occurred in October 1968, when a crowd of 100,000 was forecast to protest the Vietnam situation. The police used approximately 9,000 officers, who channeled and controlled a crowd actually estimated at 25,000 to 30,000. In general, the London police act with civility and restraint, although it would undoubtedly be inaccurate to assume that they are without their occasional biases and antagonisms. To date, however, the Metropolitan Police have not had to cope with the full-scale riots that have erupted in several American cities.

One important function of the Metropolitan Police is traffic control. In a major step toward better traffic management, the Metropolitan Police and the GLC created the Joint Traffic Executive for Greater London in 1968. This body is headed by a pair of technical officers from the two parent organizations, and is expected "to agree [on] priorities for joint action in highway and traffic matters, to ensure that traffic regulations and orders are capable of economic enforcement, to increase the speed of executive decision and, generally, to promote good order and efficiency in the use of the roads of Greater London." [41] Computer-controlled traffic signal coordination for the West End, the main shopping, governmental, and theater section within central London, were inaugurated at the beginning of 1968. They proved so successful that the numbers of foot police needed for peak-period traffic control were greatly reduced and traffic conditions improved. The Joint Traffic Executive has also been coordinating the expansion of the parking control program initiated by the GLC.

FINANCE

Greater London appears to be meeting its fiscal obligations without the sense of crisis and despair that afflicts many large American metropolitan areas. But British circumstances are so overwhelmingly different from those in the United States that generalizations are unwise and direct comparisons difficult. Among the many features that distinguish British and local finance from American are: the sharply different character of Britain's local tax structure (as compared with the property tax); heavy British reliance on firm guidance from the central government; a general expectation, although not happy acceptance, that taxes will be high; the low levels of Britain's municipal pay scales; different values, reflected in the prevalent socialization of services in Britain; and different service-level expectations, i.e., an acceptance of less affluence in general, but combined with insistence on high standards for certain services and amenities.

All governmental costs are rising: construction costs have gone up sharply, wages have tended to climb, and stabilization attempts have not been successful. Moreover, subtly but inevitably, popular expectations of service levels, welfare payments, and so on, have been elevated. Greater London has better financial resources than the rest of England and Wales and the Herbert Commission reported that it also tends to use these resources fully in its attempts to meet residents' needs. In 1959–1960, for example, the average of rates levied in the Greater London area as a whole was almost identical with the average for all of England and Wales.[42]

Fiscal powers and resources of the London boroughs are generally similar to those of other local governments in England and Wales. They rely on three main sources of income: about two-fifths comes from local rates (taxes); about one-fifth from housing rents, interest, and other local income; and about two-fifths from central government grants.[43] The GLC is different in one important respect: it cannot directly levy and collect rates. It must precept on the London boroughs and the City; that is, it reports to the lower-tier units the tax it expects to be earmarked for its use. In turn, these units collect these additional levies and turn them over to the GLC. As of the 1969–1970 fiscal year, the GLC budget for noncapital expenditures called for 48 per cent of its income to come from precepts on the borough councils; 39 per cent from rents, loan repayments, and other income; and 13 per cent from Exchequer grants.[44]

Rates.—Although rates in England and Wales are, in principle, roughly parallel to American property taxes, they have several very different features. The rate is a tax only on "occupiers" (persons having exclusive right of possession and making some beneficial use of

136

the property), so that owners of property in disuse are not liable for rates or, under the provisions of 1967 legislation, are liable only for a fraction of full rates. Agricultural land and buildings are exempt, and there are also exemptions for churches and for certain charitable and nonprofit organizations. No rates are payable on Crown property, but in lieu payments are made by the central government. The ratable value of property is its actual or estimated annual rent, assuming that the tenant pays the rates and pays for repairs and insurance. This clearly differs from the American practice of assessing taxable value as a fraction of estimated market (sales) value. Since 1948 the ratable values have been set and periodically revised by valuation officers of the Board of Inland Revenue, with complaints heard by local valuation courts, and appeals by the Land Tribunal.

In principle rates are reimbursement for local services; consequently the exact configuration of rates applied within a local district depends on the package of services being delivered. As in the United States, special rates are layered, to give the total rate levied. Rate rebates are available for households with small incomes. All residential rate payers get the benefit of slightly lower levies than those applied to commercial and industrial properties. The differences are made up by the central government in the so-called "domestic element" of its grant-system.

Central government support.—The British government formerly provided support to local governments for many specified services (such as education, roads, health and welfare) but these aids have been almost completely replaced by general support funds, termed rate support grants. The latter provide a basic and general-purpose supplement to the funds local authorities collect in rates. Rate support grants payable to the London borough councils have three elements: the needs element takes into account such matters as population, school-age children, persons over 65, and road mileage; the resources element is paid only those local authorities whose ratable (per capita) resources are below the average; and the domestic element reimburses local authorities for the rate rebate they are required to give householders. These rate support grants are in effect unconditional block grants, although the central government may reduce a particular grant if a local authority fails to maintain reasonable standards of efficiency and progress.[45]

Equalization formulas.—In addition to the broad supplemental support schemes in effect throughout England and Wales, special fiscal adjustments or equalizations occurred in Metropolitan London. For an interim period of eight years following the reorganization of the London government, certain allocations of rates are being made from boroughs within the GLC to Essex, Surrey, and Kent. These were the Home Counties that lost large urbanized areas containing heavy concentrations of ratable value to the newly formed GLC. This allocation provides these counties needed fiscal relief, partially compensating for the loss and helping them through the period of adjustment.

Before the reorganization of London's government, there had been a form of rate equalization within the LCC area. And for four years following 1965 an Inner London Rate Equalization Scheme was in operation. According to this formula, the total amount of Exchequer rate support grants paid to the individual boroughs in Inner London was pooled and then redistributed so that the boroughs could have similar total rates. In other words, the boroughs whose resources were high relative to need, received less than the boroughs whose resources were relatively low. The very rich borough of Westminster, for example, received only about 6 pence on the pound of ratable value, while Southwark, with low ratable resources, received 6s(shillings) 9d(pence), or 14 times the level of Westminster's support. As a result, the total rates of both boroughs were similar: Westminster's was 9s 7d on the pound (48 per cent of ratable value), and Southwark's was 11s 6d (57 per cent of ratable value). The rates of all the other Inner London boroughs lay between these two figures, except for the City of London, whose very high property base gave it a general rate of only 9s 1d (45 per cent of ratable value).[46]

Soon after the new London government was created, the London Boroughs Association, in cooperation with the GLC, commissioned a broad study of needed rate equalization in both the Inner and Outer London boroughs. Proposals by Professor A. R. Ilersic for a new equalization scheme were published by December 1967, and the first installment of a proposed four-year transition to the new formula went into effect in April 1968, having received formal provisional acceptance by the Minister of Housing and Local Government and the local authorities. (Mr. Greenwood, the Minister, made it clear that he was prepared to consider recommendations for modification based on experience.)[47]

Two important features are incorporated into this latest equalization plan. First, a resource pool is formed, using a levy of two shillings per pound of ratable value (that is, 10 per cent) paid by each London borough. This is redistributed to boroughs by a formula measuring relative resources and needs. It was estimated that this would result in the net transfer of some 4.3 million pounds ($10.3 million) from wealthier boroughs in Inner London to certain relatively poorer Outer London boroughs. Second, the GLC's own share of support funds from the central government will rise, as payments that would otherwise go directly to wealthy Inner London boroughs are shunted to the GLC to enable it to meet pressing central city problems for which it is responsible.

The following example shows how equalization worked for two London boroughs at opposite extremes of affluence in fiscal year 1968–1969:[48]

	Rich Borough: Kensington and Chelsea		Poor Borough: Hackney	
	On the Pound	Per Cent	On the Pound	Per Cent
Required for Borough Purposes	3s 2d	16	10s 2d	51
Precepted by GLC, Metropolitan Police, and Others	8s 1d	40	8s 2d	41
Subtotal, Rates Needed	11s 3d	56	18s 4d	92
Rate Support Grant (from central government)	− 2s 5d	−12	− 4s 7d	−23
Subtotal, Rates Less Rate Support Grants	8s 10d	44	13s 9d	69
London Rate Equalization Scheme (either payment + or receipt −)	+ 1s 5d	+ 7	− 1s 6d	− 8
Rates Finally Levied	10s 3d	51	12s 3d	61

Kensington and Chelsea collected 10s 3d on the pound. Only 3s 2d of this, or less than one-third, went to the borough for its own use. The remainder went to other boroughs, to the GLC, and to the

Metropolitan Police. But of the 12s 3d rate collected by Hackney, a full 10s 2d, or about five-sixths, is available for its own use, and most of the rates needed for the GLC and the Metropolitan Police come from the central government and the interborough pool.

Like the United States, Great Britain is continually searching for ways of equalizing the property tax burden. In a major move, the General Rate Act of 1967 authorized local governments to levy half-rates on the owners of empty properties, who previously paid no rates on vacancies. The argument was that this would encourage owners to seek productive use of their properties, and that this would more equitably spread the assessment base and thus provide some relief to property occupiers. Not all local authorities rushed to take advantage of the new legislation. Some decided that the effort of administering the additional levy would largely offset the monetary increment, particularly since the additional income might lessen the rate support grants from the central government. In the Greater London area, by 1968, 19 boroughs and the City of London had chosen to levy rates on empty premises. Perhaps not surprisingly these included the very boroughs that were already better off with respect to rate resources.[49]

SUMMING UP

Chapter Six has reviewed major problems with which the responsible governments in the London region have had to cope. We have seen the efforts to accommodate the automobile, while also maintaining one of the world's outstanding—but troubled—transit systems. We have seen the perpetual and discouraging struggle for adequate, fairly priced housing. The search for the best national educational policy has been described, as well as closely related efforts by responsible local authorities within Greater London to provide acceptable levels of educational service, to reduce class barriers to education, and to overcome schooling difficulties found in districts with low-income families or ethnic and racial minorities. The challenges of combating increasing crime levels, and of maintaining a fully manned and effective police force have been outlined. Finally, the fiscal problems of the GLC and the London boroughs were reviewed, along with the efforts to achieve a reasonably equitable tax system, using various equalizing measures.

Some of the most discouraging of these problems reflect the obsolescence of physical plant that characterizes the worst sections of London, and the dearth of available fiscal resources. Family income remains low and the housing situation is critical. Ethnic and racial problems are growing, but are not severe by American standards; the absolute numbers and the concentrations of minorities are much smaller in London. Minorities tend to be found in greater numbers in the outer portions of Greater London (such as Haringey and Brent) where physical obsolescence is less serious than in the central areas. Britain's sense of fair play notwithstanding, discriminatory practices are widespread, contributing to the immigrants' already disadvantaged situation.

Despite all these problems, there has been a persistent and encouraging effort to improve conditions, and to channel resources to areas needing help. This in part reflects British socialism. It is also in the tradition of the LCC, which in its own impersonal way struggled for years to provide good services for Londoners. One is left with a distinct sense that the GLC and the boroughs valiantly carry on this struggle to serve a significantly expanded clientele of Greater Londoners.

OTHER BRITISH
REORGANIZATION PROPOSALS:
A COMPARATIVE ANALYSIS

W E ARE PRIMARILY concerned with the organization and functioning of Metropolitan London. Up to this point the previous chapters have described in considerable detail the Greater London reorganization proposals and implementation during the 1960's. But
the London reorganization is only part of a much broader effort to
modernize local government throughout Great Britain. As was suggested in Chapter Two, it seems appropriate to ask whether the main
concepts that underlie the Greater London reorganization have
proven sufficiently valid to guide and be used in subsequent reorganization proposals for other British metropolitan areas. If they
have not been carried over to other reorganization schemes, we may
then ask what alternative ideas have been substituted. Accordingly,
Chapter Seven considers several reports of British commissions that
studied and made recommendations for other areas in England,
Scotland, and Wales, so that we may determine the extent to which
the Greater London reorganization has served as a model.

First the principal recommendations of the Royal Commission on
Local Government in England (the Redcliffe-Maud Commission)
are examined, along with the government's responses. Clearly the
commission's recommendations have general significance for other
metropolitan regions in England, and are also relevant to our own
London study. The commission studied the reorganization of

Greater London, and its recommendations inevitably imply a certain acceptance or rejection of the principles upon which London's reorganization was based, although its direct charge was to deal with England outside of Greater London. In addition, of course, the commission looked into the developing outer fringe of Metropolitan London, beyond the jurisdiction of the GLC.

Second, and more briefly, we examine the recommendations of the Royal Commission on Local Government in Scotland (the Wheatley Commission). The Wheatley Commission dealt with a much smaller and more sparsely settled population than that studied by the Redcliffe-Maud Commission. It did, however, consider the problems of two major metropolitan regions, the large Glasgow area and the smaller Edinburgh area. It is instructive to compare the recommendations of these two roughly parallel commissions, because they reached divergent conclusions. These differences are only partly explained by the variations in the social geography of the areas studied.

Third, Chapter Seven reports on the move to reorganize local government in Wales, resulting from a 1967 white paper. The white paper, in turn, was a response to a 1963 report of the Local Government Commission for Wales. Another in-put was a 1970 white paper for South Wales. Although no major metropolitan region is involved, as in England and Scotland, it is useful to examine the work on Wales because it provides still further evidence of British thinking about local governmental reorganization.

THE REDCLIFFE-MAUD COMMISSION: UNITARY GOVERNMENT, IN MOST AREAS

In 1966 the eleven-member commission was charged with reviewing the structure of local government in England outside Greater London, and making recommendations for its reorganization.* The report of the commission, issued in 1969, comprises three main volumes and a short summary volume.[1] Volume one presents the

---

* This commission has also been termed the Maud Commission (the chairman was Sir John Maud when appointed). We refer to it as the Redcliffe-Maud Commission, because the chairman was named Lord Redcliffe-Maud before publication of the commission report. This terminology helps distinguish the Royal Commission from the earlier Maud Committee on the Management of Local Government, also chaired by Sir John Maud.

majority report, with which ten of the members concurred (with minor reservations). Volume two contains the lengthy dissenting views of commission member Derek Senior. Research appendixes fill the third volume.

The commission majority and Senior largely agree on the shortcomings and problems of English local government. Four basic faults are cited:[2]

1. "Local government areas do not fit the pattern of life and work in modern England." The gap will widen as the pace of social, economic and technological change quickens.

2. "The fragmentation of England" into 124 independent governmental units—79 county boroughs and 45 counties—"has made the proper planning of development and transportation impossible." * As a result there has often been hostility between the county boroughs and the counties; this has made it harder to consider difficult questions on their own merits.

3. "The division of responsibility within each county between the county council and a number of county district councils, together with the position of county boroughs as islands in the counties, means that services which should be in the hands of one authority are split among several.† This greatly complicates the work of meeting comprehensively the different needs of families and individuals."

4. "Many local authorities are too small, in size and revenue," and in consequence lack highly qualified manpower to do their work efficiently.

The commission suggests that as a result of these basic faults, local government seems irrelevant and impotent to residents. Parliament and the central government doubt the ability of local government to conduct local affairs. Moreover, owing to the variety and number

* Counties are the normal government units into which most of England is divided. County boroughs are the governments of those major cities that have been granted a county-municipal status so that they are outside the control of any county. County boroughs, while smaller and generally urban, thus parallel counties, and are roughly equivalent to consolidated city-county governments in the United States. Counties tend to have smaller lower-tier units, such as urban and rural districts. In contrast, county boroughs are unitary governments with no lower-tier units.

† At present England has 1,086 county district councils: 227 are noncounty borough councils, 449 are urban district councils, and 410 are rural district councils.

of local governments, the latter cannot act effectively in dealing with the central government.[3]

The majority members and Senior agree on certain ideas: that town and country are interdependent, that local government must enable citizens and political leaders to have a sense of common purpose, and that local authorities must be large enough to attract the resources and skilled manpower they need. Both emphasize that "all services concerned with the physical environment (planning, transportation, and major development) must be in the hands of one authority," and the majority report declares that all "personal services (education, personal social services, health, and housing), being closely linked in operation and effect, must also be in the hands of one authority, as strongly recommended by the recent report of the Seebohm Committee." [4]

The majority report recommends a *two-tier* governmental formula for each of the three largest metropolitan areas, and a unitary *single-tier* system for the rest of England. Thus two-tier governments would be provided in West Midlands (the Birmingham area), SELNEC (the Manchester area, the term being an acronym for South East Lancashire and North East Cheshire), and Merseyside (the Liverpool area). In 1968 these areas had populations of 3.6 million, 3.1 million, and 2.2 million, respectively. Each would have a metropolitan authority as the upper tier, and sets of seven, four, and nine metropolitan districts, respectively, to be the lower-tier governments. (See Table 4.)

For the most part, physical environmental services would be allocated to the upper tier, and personal services to the lower tier. Main services at the metropolitan level would include: police, fire, water supply, main sewerage and refuse collection, registration, and licensing. Planning powers stronger than those possessed by the GLC would be given to the metropolitan authorities. Housing policy and certain supplementary building powers would be assigned to the metropolitan level, and building and management aspects of housing given to the district level. (Table 5 lists this division between tiers in some detail.)

The commission majority recommends 58 single-tier governments in the remainder of England, arguing that the benefits of unitary government outweigh its disadvantages. It recommends that the

Table 4

The Size of the Lower-Tier Units: Redcliffe-Maud Commission Recommendations and the Greater London Reorganization[a]

	Total Metropolitan Population[a]	Number of Lower-Tier Authorities	Population of Lower-Tier Authorities[a]			
			Largest	Smallest	Median	Mean
Greater London						
Herbert Commission (Population figures, 1959)	8,438,190	52[b]	(Croydon) 249,000	(Barnes-Richmond) 81,210	166,750	165,360
Actual Reorganization (Population figures, 1966)	7,671,220	33[b]	(Croydon) 322,570	(Kingston-upon-Thames) 142,010[c]	239,780[c]	239,570[c]
Manchester (SELNEC)						
Commission Majority	3,232,000	9	979,000	176,000	286,000	282,000[d]
Mr. Senior's Dissent	3,122,000	12	867,000	108,000	215,000	205,000[d]
Birmingham (West Midlands)						
Commission Majority	3,014,000	7	1,314,000	200,000	295,000	283,000[d]
Mr. Longland's Dissent	3,014,000	4	1,314,000	200,000	302,000[d]	567,000[d]
Mr. Senior's Dissent	3,611,000	12	1,044,000	104,000	247,000	233,000[d]
Liverpool (Merseyside)						
Commission Majority	2,063,000	4	936,000	274,000	298,000[d]	376,000[d]
Mr. Longland's Dissent	2,063,000	3	1,234,000	274,000	415,000[d]	415,000[d]
Mr. Senior's Dissent	2,235,000	8	757,000	108,000	192,000	211,000[d]

[a] 1968 unless otherwise noted.
[b] Including City of London.
[c] Excluding City of London.
[d] Excluding largest authority.

SOURCES: Author's calculations are based on data in *Report of the Royal Commission on Local Government in Greater London, 1957–1960*, Cmnd. 1164 (London: HMSO, October 1960), pp. 233–236; *1966 Annual Abstract of London Statistics* (London: Greater London Council), Table 15, p. 10; *Royal Commission on Local Government in England, 1966–1969, Vol. I, Report*, Cmnd. 4040 (London: HMSO, 1969), Tables 1, 2(a), 2(b) and 3(b), pp. 304–309, 313.

Table 5

Allocation of Services in Large Metropolitan Areas: Redcliffe-Maud Commission Proposal

Metropolitan Authorities	*Metropolitan District Councils*

1. Planning
Building regulations
Transportation
Intelligence
 	
2. Housing
  (a) metropolitan housing policy
  (b) building in the interest of the entire metropolitan area
  (c) building to ensure fulfilment of planning policies
  (d) policy for selection of tenants
  (e) metropolitan rent policy
 	
3. Water supply
Main sewerage
Sewage disposal
Refuse disposal
Clean air, metropolitan priorities
 	
4. Arts, entertainment, sports, parks, and recreation (in the interest of whole metropolitan area)
Nomination of members to authorities for national parks
 	
5. Police
Fire
Ambulance
 	
6. Coordination of investment in metropolitan area
	1. Education
	Libraries
	Youth employment
	
	2. Personal social services
	Personal health services
	
	3. Housing (within framework of metropolitan policy)
	  (a) building (except as allocated to metropolitan authority)
	  (b) house management
	  (c) all other housing powers
	
	4. Local sewers and drains
	Refuse collection
	Clean air, local action and enforcement in accordance with metropolitan priorities
	Cemeteries and crematoria
	Coast protection
	
	5. Arts, entertainment, sports, parks, and recreation (in the interest of individual districts)
	
	6. Food and drugs
	Weights and measures
	Consumer protection
	Shops Act
	Licensing of places of public entertainment
	Registration of births, deaths and marriages
	Registration of electors
	
	7. All other local government functions
	
	8. Rating

SOURCE: *Local Government Reform: Short Version of the Report of the Royal Commission on Local Government in England*, Cmnd. 4039 (London: HMSO, June 1969), p. 18.

unitary local authorities should have a population range of 250,000 to one million, and that the "new local government pattern should so far as possible stem from the existing one." [5] It follows, of course, that some large metropolitan areas would be given new single-tier governments. Consequently this challenges by implication the validity of the two-tier pattern of government already put into effect in Greater London, and recommended for the three next largest metropolitan areas.*

In addition to the proposed unitary governments, the majority would provide for eight provinces. These entities would settle "provincial strategy and planning framework within which the main authorities [both two-tier and unitary] must operate," while collaborating with the central government in the development of each province. Finally, the commission calls for many local (neighborhood) councils, although no exact number is suggested, "elected to represent and communicate the wishes of cities, towns, and villages in all matters of special concern to the inhabitants," having the right to be consulted by the local authority within which each falls, but having only options to perform certain local services, subject to the agreement of the principal authority.[6] Such local councils are not recommended for the two-tier governments.

Thus what at first appeared to be clearly either a two-tier or a single-tier pattern is modified to provide an added provincial level, however amorphous. Moreover the single-tier governments are to be supplemented by voluntary local councils. This suggests that single-tier government may not in itself be sufficient, for it requires both the coordinating guidance of the province and the grass-roots base of the local council.

Derek Senior is not as interested in population size as are the other commissioners. He insists that the recommended patterns of local government must respect the social geography of settlement patterns produced by a motor-age society. For most of England he recommends:

---

* The largest conurbation broken up into single-tier governments by the majority was West Yorkshire around Leeds and Bradford. This was made into a single region of 2.1 million by Senior's proposal. Other metropolitan areas treated in single-tier fashion by the majority report, in approximate order of size, were: Tyneside (Newcastle-upon-Tyne), Sheffield, Nottingham, Bristol, Coventry, Teesside (Middlesbrough), Stoke-on-Trent and Leicester.

a predominantly two-level system of service-running local government, comprising 35 directly elected regional authorities, responsible for the planning-transportation-development complex of functions (including water supply, sewerage, refuse disposal, and other technical services) for capital investment programming, and for police, fire, and education; and 148 directly elected district authorities responsible for the health service, the personal social services, housing management, consumer protection, and all other functions involving personal contacts with the citizen.[7]

The modal number of Senior's districts per regional authority would be 3, the median 4, and the mean 4.7. (The last figure is pulled up by the Manchester and Birmingham regions, each of which would be given 12 districts.) Senior finds only four exceptions to the need for two-tier government. Around Cambridge, Peterborough, Leicester, and Lincoln his criteria can be satisfied by single all-purpose authorities.

Senior also recommends five provincial councils, whose members would be nominated by local authorities, but appointed by the central government. These provincial councils would be responsible for long-term strategic planning, and for communicating provincial "needs and aspirations" to the central government. He also proposes directly elected common councils at the grass-roots level, each to serve "as a sounding board for community opinion on all matters affecting the local environment." [8] These councils have no part in the statutory duties of local government.

A comparison of the contrasting views emphasizes the commission majority's strong belief in the effectiveness and simplicity of single-tier local government. The majority hold these advantages to outweigh a significant disadvantage: the size of unitary authorities is not functionally related to the service to be performed. In contrast, Senior relies on two-tier governments of greater complexity, particularly where, as in planning and housing matters, the upper-tier authorities are to formulate policy and the lower-tier authorities to administer the programs.

As might be expected, responses to these proposals during the ensuing debates have been quite varied. Although the unitary governments appeal to some observers, in general they are widely opposed. The two-tier governments seem attractive in principle, but become more questionable as specific schemes are put forth. Inevitably, there are strong objections to specific units and boundaries.

Consequently this major effort to establish new units of local government has elicited many reservations and fears. What is remarkable, especially in comparison with the American local government scene, is that the proposals have been issued and carry great authority. Moreover they had been in the process of full hearing and political implementation until the change of government in June 1970.

The recommendations of the Redcliffe-Maud Commission that apply to the region surrounding London are of particular interest. The commission majority and Senior offer strikingly different suggestions for the reorganization of local government in the vicinity of London. The majority recommendation favors the creation of eight unitary authorities around Greater London—seven would border on Greater London and an eighth, the middle part of Buckinghamshire, would come within about two miles of it. These proposed new units are listed below, along with population, area and the identification numbers assigned in the report:[9]

Name (Present County)	1968 Population	Square Miles
48. Mid-Buckinghamshire	323,000	420
49. Luton and West Hertfordshire	707,000	358
50. East Hertfordshire	665,000	615
51. Essex	865,000	832
52. Reading and Berkshire	794,000	879
53. West Surrey	819,000	590
54. East Surrey	419,000	292
55. West Kent	872,000	755

No super organization of these units is proposed or discussed. The eight authorities, plus Greater London and eight more authorities, ranging from Northampton and Oxford (on the north and northwest) to Southampton and Dover (on the south coast of England), would comprise a South East province. The province would have a population of 9.3 million, excluding Greater London, or 17.1 million with London.

On the other hand, Senior explicitly states that the region around London has unique planning problems and therefore deserves special regional arrangements. Merely to propose a large, rather amorphous provincial authority would be insufficient. He judges it necessary to await the proposals of the South East Study Team before deciding precisely which strategic planning authority and which implementing or executive authority would be most appropriate. Meanwhile, to promote the idea of a regional planning authority, he designates a "metropolitan planning area" as its maximum domain.[10] This area would comprise the following five upper-tier regional authorities and their constituent lower-tier districts:[11]

Region and District	Name (Administrative Center)	1968 Population	Square Miles
Region 27	St. Albans	1,325,000	895
27(a)	St. Albans	247,000	138
27(b)	Watford	319,000	111
27(c)	Luton	227,000	118
27(d)	Letchworth	179,000	169
27(e)	Harlow	353,000	359
Region 28	Chelmsford	843,000	764
28(a)	Chelmsford	239,000	529
28(b)	Southend-on-Sea	299,000	98
28(c)	Basildon	305,000	137
Region 29	Reading	921,000	928
29(a)	Reading	386,000	597
29(b)	High Wycombe	230,000	188
29(c)	Slough	305,000	143
Region 30	Guildford	1,439,000	1,206
30(a)	Guildford	262,000	263
30(b)	Aldershot	335,000	333
30(c)	Staines	310,000	119
30(d)	Reigate	312,000	196
30(e)	Crawley	220,000	295
Region 31	Maidstone	893,000	812
31(a)	Maidstone	179,000	263
31(b)	Tunbridge Wells	202,000	286
31(c)	Dartford	206,000	86
31(d)	Rochester-Gillingham-Chatham	306,000	177

To recapitulate, the commission majority proposes creation of eight new unitary local authorities, averaging 685,000 in present population and ranging from 323,000 to 872,000. The commission does not suggest any special arrangement for metropolitan regional government, other than a very large South East province. Senior proposes 5 upper-tier regional authorities averaging nearly 1.1 million, and 20 lower-tier districts averaging 270,000. Additionally, he recommends an "appropriate planning authority" for this large region, as well as a very much larger province. The planning authority would include at most 13.2 million, while his proposed province would include 20 million. Although the planning authority is Senior's idea, it could be superimposed on either the majority's or Senior's set of local authorities.

THE WHEATLEY COMMISSION: TWO-TIER GOVERNMENT, WITH LARGE REGIONS

The Royal Commission on Local Government in Scotland, chaired by Lord Wheatley, produced a virtually unanimous report. All nine members generally concurred in its recommendations.[12] One note of dissent and two notes of reservation involved three commission members. The dissent is explained below.

Scotland has long been caught between its dependence on British government and its striving for autonomy. The Scottish nationalists call for complete independence from Britain. A certain administrative decentralization of the Scottish Office in Edinburgh is, of course, already in effect. Moreover, because Scotland is relatively small, with only 5.2 million residents in 1968 (5.6 million projected for 1980), a decentralization of power from the British central government could place certain political and administrative powers at an all-Scotland level. That is, Scotland could operate as a single strong region. But its terms of reference prohibited the Wheatley Commission from grappling with these larger issues. Instead, it was expected merely to examine the structure of local government.[13]

First, Scotland's geography deserves consideration. The thinly settled Highlands, together with the island groups to the north and west, account for nearly half of Scotland's land area but contain only about one-quarter of a million population, at a density of only 19 persons per square mile. Glasgow and its metropolitan region, with only about 10 per cent of Scotland's land area, contain half of Scotland's population—about 2.5 million. The Edinburgh metropolitan region contains a population of something over a million. Together the two major metropolitan regions account for about seven-tenths of Scotland's population.

The commission faced the formidable task of recommending a local governmental system that could accommodate these extremes of heavy urban concentration and sparse settlement. Accordingly the commission considered but rejected a pattern of unitary, all-purpose authorities as not fitting ". . . the geographical and social facts of Scotland. Any all-purpose system for Scotland would be bound to fall between two stools. Authorities would either be too small for the large-scale services, or too big for the local services." [14] Instead, the Wheatley Commission recommends a two-tier system, with 37 *lower-tiered* districts being given relatively unimportant functions—strictly local planning, refuse collection, regulation and licensing, building control, etc.—and seven *upper-tiered* regions being given the major functions. The proposed allocation appears to pay little attention to the principles developed by the Redcliffe-Maud and Herbert Commissions. (The full breakdown of functions is shown in Table 6.)

Critical analysis of the recommendations for Scotland may appropriately start with the fact that a two-tiered system has been applied to both metropolitan and non-metropolitan areas. Such insistence on symmetry poses certain questions.[15] It also suggests separate comparisons with the counterpart English proposals for the large metropolitan areas, and for other sections.

Of the seven proposed Scottish regions, the West Region would be the largest, with 2.5 million residents and an area of over 3,200 square miles. Within this region, Glasgow (1,186,000 population, 150 square miles) would constitute but a single district. The region would include 10 other districts with a median population of 120,-000, ranging from 52,000 (Lanark) to 200,000 (Paisley).[16] The South East Region would be next largest, with a population of 1,087,000. The main lower-tier district would be Edinburgh, with a population of 489,000. Five other districts would have a median population of 125,000, ranging from 88,000 (West Lothian) to 152,000 (Mid- and East Lothian).

The most significant feature of these recommendations for the two chief metropolitan areas is allocation of the principal functions to the upper-tier regions. Thus the upper tier would get major planning, transportation, water supply, and sewerage functions; the per-

Table 6

Allocation of Services in Scotland: Wheatley Commission Proposal

Regional Authorities	District Authorities
Major planning and related services	Local planning and related services
Industrial development	Assistance to industry
Transportation and roads	Redevelopment
Water, sewerage	Control of the countryside
Redevelopment, new towns, control of the countryside	
Tourism	Building control
Personal social services	
Education	
Social work	
Health	
Housing	Housing improvement
Protective services	Civil defense (local aspects)
Police	
Fire	
Civil defense	
Weights and measures and consumer protection	Regulation and licensing
Refuse disposal	Licensing courts
Coast protection	Environmental functions: refuse collection, food and drugs, etc.
Parks and recreation[a]	Parks and recreation[a]
Museums and art galleries[a]	Museums and art galleries[a]
Registration of births, deaths, and marriages	Libraries
Registration of electors	Administration of justice

[a] Function exercised concurrently by the two tiers.

SOURCE: *Scotland: Local Government Reform: Short Version of the Report of the Royal Commission on Local Government in Scotland*, Cmnd. 4150-I (Edinburgh: HMSO, 1969), pp. 11–12.

sonal social services (education, social work, and health); housing; and selected other activities. Glasgow and Edinburgh would be stripped of their direct responsibilities for these functions, and would be relegated to relatively insignificant district status. Put another way, the main functions would be given to an expanded region, which would include central city, major suburbs and outer metropolitan sections.

The five remaining regions would average about 315,000 population. Four of the regions would average 2,900 square miles in area, and the Highlands and Islands Region would cover 14,100 square miles. The 18 districts outside of the two metropolitan regions would average 87,000 population and the ten non-metropolitan districts (excluding the eight exceptionally large Highlands districts) would average 100 square miles each.

Scotland now has over 400 separate local authorities, of five disparate types. Many of the local governments are time-honored, and the break with tradition will prove difficult. The main note of dissent, by Commissioners Anderson and Johnston, urged creation of a system of 101 lower-tier units in place of the 37 districts recommended by the commission; this would more nearly preserve a sense of local traditional community. As they state: "We have reservations about the degree of community cohesion at the proposed shire (district authority) level. Although the shires (district authorities) do meet the criteria established by our Intelligence Unit and represent a clearly discernible level of community, we doubt whether this level can command the same degree of commitment that we feel would evince itself at the level beneath." [17]

The changeover promises to be a long and complex affair. A constitutional commission (the Crowther Commission) has been "studying the relationship of the countries and regions of the U.K. to the central government at Westminster," and it appears likely that local government reform will wait upon its report.[18] Assuming clearance at that level, any reform will still require the drafting and passage of a thoroughly recast Local Government (Scotland) Act. Many other changes—as in codes, financial arrangements, and transitional mechanisms—must also be recommended and approved. Overall, however, it seems likely that the reform of Scotland's local government will move ahead more rapidly than that for England.

A PROPOSAL FOR WALES: ENLARGED COUNTIES FOR THE UPPER TIER

Wales and Monmouthshire have only 2.7 million residents and no large metropolitan areas. Cardiff, the capital of Wales and the largest county borough, has a population of less than 300,000. Two white papers form the basis of our brief report. The 1967 white paper, *Local Government in Wales*,[19] pre-dated the two royal commission reports for England and Scotland, called for a mere modification of local governmental structure, and was expressed in tentative terms, suggesting that the subsequent royal commission reports would deserve consideration. A 1970 white paper, *Local Government Reorganization in Glamorgan and Monmouthshire*,[20] responded to royal commission reports by recommending a thorough shift to a pattern in line with the Redcliffe-Maud report.

The 1967 proposals for Wales are quite different from those subsequently made for England. The 1967 white paper is based in part on the work of an Inter-Departmental Working Party, set up in 1965, which in turn reviewed earlier reports of a Local Government Commission for Wales.[21] The 1967 proposal recommended that the three metropolitan areas in South Wales be continued as county borough councils, following the British tradition of organizing large cities as separate unitary authorities. But this recommendation was reversed in the 1970 white paper. For the remainder of Wales, the 1967 proposals would reduce the number of counties to 5 from a previous 13, and would make them upper-tier authorities. The proposal would create 36 new lower-tier districts in place of an existing welter of some 200 non-county boroughs, urban districts and rural districts, and 900 parishes. The new counties would average 425,000 in population, and the new districts just under 60,000.

The new county councils "should have responsibility for the same functions as the present county councils, notably, education, personal health and welfare, child care, civil defense, town and country planning, roads, traffic management and road safety, weights and measures, animal health, composition and description of food and drugs, small holdings, and the registration of vehicles, births, and deaths."[22] The new district councils would have the same general powers now exercised by non-county boroughs, urban districts, and rural districts including housing, environmental health, hygiene, sanitary arrangements for food, parking, control of communicable disease, and so on.

The 1970 white paper deals only with Glamorgan County (South Wales) and that anomalous independent county, Monmouthshire, which is traditionally linked with Wales. These two counties contain the most concentrated population and development. The recommendations would divide the area of the two into three unitary authorities, centering on Swansea, Cardiff, and Newport. These new councils, ranging in population from 372,000 to 919,000, would collectively account for 63 per cent of Wales's total population. The white paper also proposes directly elected community councils, strictly local in scale, with limited executive functions. Like the local councils proposed by the Redcliffe-Maud Commission, however, they would mainly represent local opinion and would not qualify as full-fledged local governments.

RESPONSE FROM THE LABOR GOVERNMENT

The Redcliffe-Maud Commission was able to devote its disinterested attention to considerations of efficient provision of governmental services and democratic participation in local government. The actual changes made will result from hard political calculations and pressures.[23] It has been difficult to monitor the intricate sparring that followed publication of the commission's report and to predict the mix of the coalitions that will be needed for final political action.

The first step from Royal Commission report to legislation was taken by publication in early February 1970 of a white paper entitled *Reform of Local Government in England.* This provided a set of policy guidelines indicating the Labor government's response to the Redcliffe-Maud Commission proposals. The government accepted the gist of the commission's majority report, with the following main changes:[24]

1. Two additional metropolitan areas—in West Yorkshire in the north and Hampshire in the south—would be granted two-tier status, bringing the number of such metropolitan authorities to five. The number of unitary authorities would thus be reduced from 58 to 51, since seven of them would be absorbed by the two new metropolitan areas.

2. Education in the metropolitan areas would be given to the upper-tier authorities, rather than to the lower-tier units as recommended by the Redcliffe-Maud Commission. This would entrust education to authorities having the greatest fiscal and manpower resources.

3. Rating would also become a function of the upper-tier authorities, since the transfer of education to these authorities would place most local expenditures on their shoulders.

4. Local authorities would no longer be responsible for health functions. Removal of these functions would clear the way for a unified health service. This would be a responsibility of the central government, to be administered on the basis of health areas coterminous with the new local authorities.[25]

5. District committees would be established as a way of keeping the councilmen of unitary authorities in touch with their respective areas. Each committee would consist of a mixture of council members of the unitary authority and members of the local council. The central government would make further recommendations about the functions that might suitably be decentralized and given to district committees.

6. Various other functional arrangements would be changed. Police areas would be adjusted to coincide with proposed authorities or combinations of such authorities. Responsibility for fire service was not decided upon. The three largest metropolitan authorities and the unitary authority for Tyneside would take over as passenger transport authorities as provided in the Transport Act of 1968. Other metropolitan and unitary authorities would assume control of municipal transport in their areas.

7. The government expressed a willingness to discuss a number of questions, such as salaries and expenses of councilmen, disqualification of government employees from running for election, and the size of councils. Aldermen would no longer be members of local councils, with council membership limited to directly elected councillors. (This might also affect aldermen in the GLC and the London boroughs.)

Discussion of the Redcliffe-Maud Commission report and the government's white paper focused on the recommended pattern of unitary governments. Critics have asked why, if two-tiered government is the better form for nearly half of the British population—44 per cent for England, Scotland, and Wales combined, and 42 per cent for England alone—a single tier should be imposed on the rest of England. They have been concerned with home rule and skeptical about the protection that district committees or local councils can offer against unsympathetic decisions by a remote authority. If the Wheatley Commission, for example, has been able to recommend main functional responsibility for an upper-tier expanded county level of government and also to recommend that smaller districts be formally granted certain authority for functions appropriate to a lower-tier government, why could this not also have been the recommendation for England? Like Derek Senior, the critics have argued that the unitary authorities represent an unfortunate compromise:

they are too small for some types of planning and development questions, but also too large for personal and social services.

Defenders of the proposals have responded that the unitary authority more nearly ensures clarity of overall responsibilities, the kind of strong and definite mandate that can, along with adequate financing, best guarantee viability to a local government. They contend that divided responsibilities mean frustration, inefficiency, and a weakening of local government. This, in turn, offers a greater chance that central government will take over by default.

The white paper deferred any firm proposal regarding the provincial councils recommended by the Redcliffe-Maud Commission until it is determined what the Crowther Commission on the Constitution will say respecting the relation between regional—or in the case of Wales and Scotland, "national" councils—and British central government. Meanwhile the existing regional economic development councils will presumably continue to serve. This means, of course, that there is still no consistent national policy for government at a level between national and metropolitan or local—that is, at a *regional* level.

FRESH RESPONSES FROM
A NEW CONSERVATIVE GOVERNMENT

Clearly no British government could carry through a local government reorganizational proposal, and certainly not a comprehensive overhaul on the scale recommended by the Redcliffe-Maud Commission, in the waning months preceding a general election. Thus it became evident that the Labor Government's white paper of February 1970 could not possibly be implemented before the impending election.

Indeed, the game was changed completely when the Conservatives won the June 1970 election and formed their own new government. Peter Walker, the Conservative's spokesman in this sphere had already asserted that any reform would probably not take place before the second year of a potential Conservative Government. He explained that it would take at least a year to prepare the legislation after systematic consultation with those primarily affected.[26] As 1970 wore on, there was increasing skepticism that the actual reform would move ahead with any promptness. The most pessimistic pre-

159

dictions were that action might be postponed for several years. In any event, it appeared increasingly likely that, in seeking to accommodate the tremendous groundswell of protests to the proposed reform, the commission's recommendations and the Labor Government's white-paper responses might undergo further emasculation.

By September 1970, Mr. Walker had announced that the Conservative Government would introduce a distinctively different bill, probably in 1971–1972. Reports had it that this bill would be based on a two-tier system rather than the single-tier system proposed by the majority of the Redcliffe-Maud Commission.

In mid-February 1971 the government issued white papers outlining proposals for England and for Scotland, and a further report on Wales.[27] New local governments would take over in England and Wales on April 1, 1974, and in Scotland on April 1, 1975. In England, elections for the new councils would be held in 1973.

Many features of the reorganization remain to be worked out. Modifications in the proposals of the white paper on England could be introduced as a result of political debate. Nevertheless, the general shape of the likely future government was formally brought into the open. The government had intended to introduce the appropriate legislation in 1971–1972, but delay is quite possible.

As is outlined below, a two-tiered structure is proposed for all of England. This marks a decisive turning away from the Redcliffe-Maud Commission's majority recommendations for unitary authorities in all but the metropolitan areas. Superficially, at least, the Conservatives might even appear to have followed the path proposed by Derek Senior. This impression gains credence if one reads only the white paper for England, for its proposals seem to build on points made by the Redcliffe-Maud majority and by Senior.

The accompanying, less publicized circular and the separate map, however, throw a considerably different light on the proposals. Far from Senior's recommendations for freshly conceived local authorities with boundaries based on contemporary social geography, the circular's proposals retain most of the traditional counties as upper-tier councils, and most existing larger urban authorities as new lower-tier districts. Most county boroughs can expect to become such lower-tier districts, and in metropolitan areas the boroughs will retain a major bundle of functions.

The Conservatives thus managed to couch their proposals for

change in the general spirit of the Redcliffe-Maud Commission and the Senior recommendations, while actually preserving most of the existing local authorities.

As one might expect, the reactions have been varied, and some undoubtedly reflect partisan considerations. Certain observers argue that, despite the traditional guise, the proposed changes are far-reaching. Others consider the proposals very timid, a "sell-out" to political expediency, and an affront to the groundwork and principles developed by the royal commission. Where the metropolitan areas are concerned, the proposals come nearer to resembling the earlier recommendations. The government's proposals embody far more compromise where non-metropolitan reorganization is at stake. Is this a bold new scheme or an opportunity lost? Probably the balance points toward the latter.

ENGLAND: PROPOSALS FOR METROPOLITAN AREAS

Six metropolitan governmental systems—in addition to London— are proposed by the February 1971 white paper:

1. Merseyside: centering on Liverpool.
2. South East Lancashire and North East Cheshire (SELNEC): centering on Manchester.
3. West Midlands: centering on Birmingham, but in elongated form including Wolverhampton and Coventry.
4. West Yorkshire: Leeds, Bradford, etc.
5. South Yorkshire: centering on Sheffield.
6. Tyne and Wear area: Newcastle-upon-Tyne, Sunderland, etc.

These areas have been defined compactly and generally do not encompass the larger hinterlands making up the outer parts of these metropolitan regions.

The new upper-tier metropolitan county councils would exercise the following functions: strategic and policy aspects of planning; highways, traffic, and public transport; selected reserve housing powers; certain regulatory powers; environmental health; refuse disposal; police and fire; and other functions as shown in Table 7.

The new lower-tier metropolitan district councils, expected to average about 200,000 in population, would exercise these functions: education; personal social services; direct developmental and control aspects of planning; the main housing responsibilities; libraries; ref-

161

Table 7

Allocation of Functions in England: Conservative Government
Proposal, February 1971

A. To lower-tier district councils within metropolitan areas and to upper-tier
county councils outside of metropolitan areas

Education

Personal social services

Libraries

B. Metropolitan and non-metropolitan areas

Upper-tier councils	*Lower-tier councils*
Planning	Planning
Plan making	
Development control: strategic decisions	Most development control
Acquisition and disposal of land for planning and development purposes	Acquisition and disposal of land for planning and development purposes
Highways, traffic and transport	
Housing: certain reserve powers (e.g., for overspill)	Housing
Building regulations	Housebuilding
Weights and measures	Housing management
Food and drugs	Slum clearance
Clean air	House and area improvement
Refuse disposal	Refuse collection
Environmental health	Environmental health
Museums	Museums
Parks and open spaces	Parks and open spaces
Playing fields and swimming baths	Playing fields and swimming baths
Coast protection	Coast protection
Police	
Fire	

Notes: Functions are concurrent where listed for both tiers. Administration of water
supply, sewerage and sewage disposal to be considered in light of the report of the Central
Advisory Water Committee. Some counties will need to be amalgamated for police and
possibly for fire services.

SOURCE: *Local Government in England: Government Proposals for Reorganization,* Cmnd. 4584
(London: HMSO, February 1971). Based on Appendix, p. 16.

use collection; and, concurrently with the metropolitan county councils, certain other functions.

Personal health services are expected to be transferred to new
health authorities, when the National Health Service is reorganized.
A few functions—water supply, sewerage and sewerage disposal—

will not be allocated until the report of the Central Advisory Water Committee has been released.

Judging from such details as have been made available, it would appear that the allocation of functions within metropolitan areas closely resembles that proposed by the Redcliffe-Maud Commission, except that the February 1971 white paper divides planning and gives considerable development control and redevelopment to the district councils, gives housing overwhelmingly to the district councils, and gives certain regulatory powers (food and drugs, clean air, weights and measures) to the metropolitan councils. The white paper allocates education and personal social services to the district councils, as did the earlier commission.

ENGLAND: PROPOSALS FOR NON-METROPOLITAN AREAS

The white paper of February 1971 proposes 38 county councils, mainly corresponding to existing counties, and also incorporating county boroughs that had long enjoyed independence from county control. The new counties would be administrative counties with power over their entire territories, and the proposed structure for all of England outside of the metropolitan areas would thus be completely two-tier. The white paper also proposes about 370 district councils. These would average just under 10 per county and would probably range from 40,000 to 100,000 population. The districts have not been delineated—this will be the task of a new Local Government Boundary Commission, to be established.

The non-metropolitan county councils would be given even more power than the metropolitan county councils, for they would include education, personal social services, and libraries, in addition to the county council functions already listed for the metropolitan counties. Thus many existing county boroughs, now functioning as major independent cities, will lose education, social services and libraries when they become second-tier district councils.

But unlike the situation created if the Redcliffe-Maud majority recommendations had been carried out, most county councils would retain their essential identities, and most county boroughs and many other larger units of local government would stand a fair chance of retaining their identities, or at least of keeping a local hand in municipal affairs, even if their exact geographic boundaries were to be altered.

163

The Conservatives understandably reacted with pleasure to the new proposals. The counties, traditional strongholds for the Conservative Party, will largely be preserved and given considerable power. But it remains a pivotal question whether the Conservatives, through the counties, will in fact take over political control of the large urban areas, or whether the large urban areas with their traditional Labor Party majorities may not instead extend their political dominance over entire administrative counties.

SCOTLAND

The white paper of February 1971 dealing with Scotland proposes substantially the two-level structure that had been recommended by the Wheatley Commission. There will be minor changes in geographic coverage of a few authorities. Overall, the number of regions will increase to eight instead of seven, and the number of second-tier districts to 49 instead of 37. The exceptionally large region around Glasgow would not only be retained but also be enlarged, to more than 2.5 million residents.

The Conservatives also propose to shift some functions—notably concerning housing—to the lower-tier districts. This will put a package of interdependent sub-functions in the hands of the district authorities. Further, it would make for a distribution of functions in Scotland more nearly like that in England, although the Scottish regional authorities would likely remain stronger than the English upper-tier councils.

WALES

Proposals in February 1971 from the Welsh Office also follow the pattern proposed for England, with seven upper-tier counties and 36 lower-tier districts (varying from three to eight per county).

REVIEW: RECOMMENDED STRUCTURE
FOR LARGE METROPOLITAN AREAS

This section compares and contrasts the structure finally adopted for Greater London, and the structures recommended for large metropolitan areas in the remainder of England and in Scotland. Wales is excluded because it has no large metropolitan areas. Recommendations for smaller metropolitan areas and local government generally are discussed at the end of this chapter.

1. As with Greater London, two-tier structures are recommended for the largest metropolitan areas in England, and for the Glasgow and Edinburgh areas. Thus the general principle of two-tier local government for metropolitan areas is accepted.

2. Under the GLC reorganization, of course, no London borough of great size was created, thus following the earlier metropolitan borough pattern under the former LCC. But in the recommendations from the Redcliffe-Maud and the Wheatley Commissions, the largest cities—such as Birmingham (1,314,000), Glasgow (1,186,000), Manchester (979,000), and Leeds (840,000)—are consistently maintained *in toto,* and are shaped into new lower-tier districts, sometimes being expanded by incorporating other local authorities. Consequently some of these new districts are very large. The pattern resembles that in the first Toronto metropolitan reorganization because it respects the integrity of pre-existing central cities. These large cities would also be retained as lower-tier districts under the February 1971 proposals.

3. The outer limits of the GLC were determined primarily by the Metropolitan Greenbelt. This gives the GLC the character of an expanded city, yet truncating it so that it is without direct authority over much of the area that is now so rapidly suburbanizing outside the Metropolitan Greenbelt. As compared with London, the metropolitan governments recommended by the English and Scottish commissions include more of the outer suburban area. This provides greater opportunity for planning, but it diminishes local control and increases local fears of domination by an unsympathetic central authority. But the February 1971 white paper for England tends to hold to very compact metropolitan areas, apparently not unlike Greater London, while the white paper for Scotland retains—or even expands—the regions around Glasgow and Edinburgh.*

---

* The English white paper stated: "The boundaries of these areas should include all the main area, or areas, of continuous development and any adjacent area into which continuous development will extend. It may be right to include closely related built-up areas, too." While this was intended to restrict the new metropolitan county councils to built-up areas and did not in any event apply directly to Greater London, Desmond Plummer, Leader of the GLC, is reported to have interpreted this policy as a suggestive basis for considering expansion of the GLC boundaries to reflect the outward urbanization that has been occurring beyond the GLC. He stated that the GLC would soon call for a review of its outer boundary. (*The Times,* February 24, 1971.)

165

4. In general, the majority members of the Redcliffe-Maud commission recommend larger lower-tier authorities than the original Herbert Commission, Derek Senior, or the Wheatley Commission:[28]

Median 1959 population of boroughs recommended by the Herbert Commission	167,000
Median 1966 population of new London boroughs as actually created	240,000
Median 1968 population of new lower-tier authorities for the three largest metropolitan areas, as proposed by Derek Senior	215,000
Median 1968 population of new lower-tier authorities for three metropolitan areas, proposed by Redcliffe-Maud Commission majority; and for five metropolitan areas proposed by white papers	c. 300,000

For the Glasgow and Edinburgh regions, the Scottish commission proposes lower-tier districts averaging about 110,000, exclusive of Glasgow and Edinburgh, which would become much larger districts.

The Conservative Government proposals in the February 1971 white paper for England call for district councils of about 200,000 population, roughly the average size of the Greater London boroughs as created, and of the district councils as recommended by Senior.

5. Under the proposed Redcliffe-Maud metropolitan reorganization schemes, as well as in the one implemented in Greater London, major functional responsibilities—for education, for personal, social, and health services, for housing management and control, for rating, and so on—would remain with the lower-tier authorities. This would permit former cities and new amalgams at the metropolitan-district level to function as cities, with the upper-tier authorities taking over planning, transportation, water and sewerage, protective services, housing policy, and other selected functions. In contrast, under the Scottish reorganization scheme proposed by the Wheatley Commission, the new upper-tier authorities would assume most functions. Lower-tier governments, including the former cities of Glasgow and Edinburgh, would only have subordinate roles. Senior's minority recommendations fall, in spirit, between these two schemes, envisaging coordinate roles for the two governmental levels, and shared responsibilities for planning.

The February 1971 proposals by the Conservatives move a bit closer to the Senior recommendations, with planning and housing functions split, and with concurrent powers over some other functions. Education and personal social services would remain the most significant services allocated directly to the district councils in English metropolitan areas, but these would be allocated to the upper-tier authorities in Scotland.

6. The Herbert Commission proposes that the GLC exercise strategic policy guidance over several functions, and that the London boroughs have executive responsibility for these same functions. Senior concurred. But the English majority view and the Scottish approach lean toward a clear separation of functions, some going to upper-tier and others to lower-tier authorities. The February 1971 proposals reintroduce some shared functions, especially planning and housing, with some other lesser functions shared as well.

7. The various commissions recommend different allocations of responsibility for education. The Herbert Commission recommends policy-setting by the GLC and administration by the London boroughs. In fact, when the GLC was established, education was given to a special ILEA (for Inner London) and to the London boroughs (in Outer London). Shared educational responsibilities were thus avoided. The Redcliffe-Maud majority proposes that education, along with the personal health and social services, be allocated to the lower-tier districts. Senior proposes that education be the responsibility of the upper-tier governments, but with substantial decentralization of operating responsibility to district authorities, each being coterminous with corresponding health and welfare authorities. The 1970 white paper of the Labor Government assigns education to the upper-tier authorities. The Wheatley Commission would give education to the upper-tier regions, thus supporting the ILEA pattern, in contrast to that adopted for Outer London.

In the February 1971 white papers, the Conservatives propose different allocations for education. For the metropolitan areas in England, education would be the responsibility of the lower-tier councils, including many former cities that had been education authorities. In Scotland, the Wheatley Commission recommends that education be the responsibility of the upper-tier regional authorities, thus transferring education away from Glasgow and Edinburgh.

167

REVIEW: RECOMMENDED STRUCTURE FOR SMALLER
METROPOLITAN AREAS AND OTHER URBAN REGIONS

On leaving the largest metropolitan areas, we find the various recommendations differing sharply. The Redcliffe-Maud Commission
majority report recommends all unitary authorities, with a median
population of 447,000 and a median area of 738 square miles. Senior
recommends only four unitary authorities, with a median population
of 375,000. Even for small metropolitan areas, he recommends two-
tiered arrangements essentially like those he outlined for the large
metropolitan areas. The 1970 white paper sides with the Redcliffe-
Maud majority and recommends unitary authorities with a median
population of 429,000 and a median size of 842 square miles.

The Redcliffe-Maud Commission's emphasis on unitary government for all but the largest metropolitan areas was indeed an extremely important development in British thinking on local governmental reorganization. And, as of early 1970—following the Labor
Government's support for these unitary governments—one would
have had every reason to believe that the considerable momentum of,
and support for, two-tier local government had been significantly reduced. The Conservative Government's decision 12 months later was
momentous, for it clearly turned local reform back towards two-tier
government. Thus all of the most recent official proposals—for non-
metropolitan as well as metropolitan local government—throughout
England, Scotland, and Wales, agree firmly in preferring two-tier
local government.

CHAPTER VIII

IMPLICATIONS: WHAT DOES IT ALL MEAN?

Lonpon DESERVEDLY commands the interest of Americans. It is one of the world's great cities. It has long been intimately associated with elements of our own American heritage. It has served as a political, financial, and cultural center for a very large English-speaking portion of the world's population. Simply on its merits as a venerable and unique metropolis, it warrants our attention. In addition, the recent creation of a completely new governmental system for Greater London is of special relevance to Americans who are grappling with the enormous problems of governing their own metropolitan regions. Furthermore, other vigorous reform proposals have been emanating from Great Britain, helping broaden our outlook on possible directions for governmental reform.

It is tempting to look directly for the lessons to be learned, but trans-Atlantic borrowing, in this case, has its hazards. Despite evidence of common outlook and the overwhelming importance of what passes for a common language, Britain and the United States have deep-seated differences in underlying assumptions, and in social and institutional arrangements. These differences may, in fact, be all the more important because they are not stated explicitly. Thus it is essential to look at differences that may affect the validity of borrowing governmental concepts from the London experience. We present two brief sections, one on British government as it relates to London, and one on Metropolitan London itself, to stress distinctive features and to warn against lifting reform ideas piecemeal, and out of context.

DISTINCTIVE FEATURES OF BRITISH GOVERNMENT

Chapter Two stressed that British central government is strong and straightforward in its internal make-up, and in its dominance over local government. Above all, the British operate on the fundamental presumption that the business of government is to govern. The central government—"the Government"—attracts elected officials and administrative officers who share an elitist tradition of public service, and it commands the respect of most of the citizenry. Traditional forms and great trust pave the way for the slow but persistent engineering of change. At its best the British governmental machinery runs smoothly.

Three main characteristics of British government can be summarized as follows: First, local government in Britain is an integral part of a total governmental structure in which the dominating role of the central government is a critical feature. Second, the character and functioning of local government reflect certain distinctive features and styles associated with large elected councils and supplementary council committees. Third, reforms in local governmental structure occur mainly through Parliamentary action and on the initiative of the central government. Obviously a great deal hinges on central government policy, and on the relations between central government and local governments.

The traditions and trappings of local government in Britain may be misleading to Americans, because they provide a cloak of autonomy for the inherently subordinate status of local institutions in the overall system. Local governments in Britain can be realistically seen as decentralized administrative units that carry out the mandates of Parliament and the regulations of the departments in Whitehall; they are not really independent units of government. Local authorities have only those powers granted by the central government. Correspondingly, changes in these powers, or changes in the manner by which they are exercised, must be approved by the central government. Elaborate administrative machinery, manned by higher civil servants, hovers watchfully over local affairs.

British local governments, while lacking full cabinet structures and any office analogous to that of prime minister, maintain some of the spirit and structure of the central government. Political party influences have operated forcefully in London government—although not always so strongly in all British local government. Thus in the Greater London Council (GLC) and in each London borough a majority party bloc of council members governs, and the minority party constitutes the loyal opposition. Policies in some areas, such as education, are drawn along fairly clear party lines, from the national level to the local.

The GLC with 116 members, and the London borough councils, generally with 70 members each, rely heavily on functional committees. In the British tradition, these large councils ensure a variety of viewpoints, even to the point of representation on political party lines. They also facilitate the manning of a large number of committees by council members, thus tying the committees directly to the councils.

As was indicated in previous chapters, it is generally expected in Britain that the central government will periodically reexamine local governmental structure and legislate necessary changes. In the case of London, this reexamination has been infrequent and, in the Twentieth Century, largely ineffective. Nevertheless, the paternalistic power of the central government to reorganize local government is not just a latent possibility. Moreover when the government does move, as in the appointment of the Herbert Commission and subsequent action taken in the London Government Act of 1963, there is general acceptance of the idea that such reform is the government's prerogative. It is virtually impossible to overemphasize this feature of the British system: central government can and does act on major governmental reforms. Moreover, once legislated, they are implemented forthwith and generally accepted.

LONDON'S UNIQUENESS

London is obviously in a class by itself. Its dominant influence within Britain and its functional roles make it a unique national and world metropolis. Its venerability, historic importance, civic grandeur, and parade of pageantry cannot be matched in the United States. Like other national capitals, London draws much of its character from the fact that it harbors Whitehall, the seat of national government. The government spreads its own direct control and management over large sectors of activity and land use in the City, dominating London's local government even more, no doubt, than it dominates local government throughout the country. London is also heavily influenced by the unique character and status of the City of London as a world financial center. With its own traditional independence and dynamics, the City provides a special foundation for London's greatness; in physical, functional, and symbolic terms, much of London's eminence and distinctiveness is built around the Whitehall-City axis.

But if the central government's proximity colors London's character, so too does the sheer size and importance of the GLC as a major unit of government. County Hall is situated diagonally across the Thames from the Houses of Parliament, and for several decades (in the years of LCC occupancy as well as of the GLC) has prominently symbolized the stature of London's government. The monumental setting resembles the magnificence of Stockholm's or Oslo's city hall, rather than the characteristically much more modest American seat of municipal government.

In short, Greater London is subject to divergent pressures. Insofar as London's local government is heavily dominated by the central government, there is a tendency for it to be downgraded. The very location of the central government in the heart of London, and at many other scattered locations in London, makes for inevitable intrusion into decisions that local governments might otherwise make. Yet the unusual importance of Greater London and the stubborn seriousness of its problems have called forth unusual efforts from the local level, for London's is no ordinary local government. We shall need to consider the whole of this complicated background as we try to discover which reform ideas derived from London's experience have the greatest relevance for the metropolitan United States.

LESSONS FROM LONDON AND BRITAIN

What is to be learned from the experience of Greater London, and from subsequent reports of other review commissions dealing with the rest of England, Scotland, and Wales? What main concepts can be distilled from the detailed picture that has been presented? Several possible conclusions follow:

1. A traditional pattern gives the British central government responsibility for structural reform of local government. There is wide-

spread acceptance of the central government's initiative, of Parliament's direct legislative role, and of subsequent administrative responsibility by various central government ministries.

2. Britain's central government assumes broad and often surprisingly detailed responsibilities in overseeing local government. Detailed mandatory reviews of local plans and programs are customary. Thus local government can appropriately be viewed as an administrative agent for the central government.

3. For all its close ties to the central government, British local government deliberately encourages a broad representation of interests through the widely accepted mechanism of a large directly elected council. The council members in turn serve as members of the various standing committees that help make up the total local governmental framework. This pattern has been fully respected in proposed reorganization schemes. It may well be that the merit of large elected councils is being recognized by American political reformers, who see the advantages of winning greater representation for minority groups and for a wide range of viewpoints. These advantages can be particularly relevant in very large cities and metropolitan-wide units.

4. British local reforms that have been urged or implemented in recent years have justifiably attracted much interest in America. This is especially true of the central government's measures to bring local government organization up to date, because it bears on local government's basic capability to be efficient and responsive in carrying out its duties, including those specifically delegated to it within the total British governmental system.

The reports of the Herbert Commission and the other review bodies were requested by the central government, and were aimed toward parliamentary action and ministerial implementation. But the scope of inquiry given to these review bodies specifically excluded fundamental questions of the relationship between central and local government. It also excluded certain functions that were assumed to be the central government's responsibility.

5. The Herbert Commission's review of Greater London and other commissions' reviews of other areas have demonstrated the practicality of pragmatic, rational approaches to problems of local structure. The deliberations of these commissions diagnosed the problems, spelled out principal alternatives, and concluded with

point-by-point proposals that provided the basis for implementing legislation. These reviews have fostered discussion and debate leading to acceptance of reform, however rocky the path. The Herbert Commission report has already become a classic. It is a clearly written and inspiring document, and thus is "must" reading for anyone concerned with the reform of government in large metropolitan areas. It is also revealing to examine the way this report was translated into reality.[1]

6. Certain basic principles appear to have gained acceptance during recent British reviews:

a. New two-tiered metropolitan governments have been accepted for the largest English metropolitan areas, and one is already established for Greater London.

b. Multi-function local government is reaffirmed as preferable to heavy reliance on special-function districts (although a few special-function districts proved untouchable in the review process).

c. Fundamental to the reforms, lower-tier governments (the boroughs in the case of London) are enlarged to sizes enabling them to assume substantial responsibility, and to carry out specialized functions with economies of scale and overall efficiency. A population of 250,000 had been treated as an approximate minimum, but the Conservative Government proposals of February 1971 for England placed lower-tier units in metropolitan areas at about 200,000, and in non-metropolitan areas at about 40,000 to 100,000.

d. Divisions of functions between the tiers can be worked out, and can be further modified as the new governments learn from operating experience. (As noted, in Greater London these allocations have been undergoing some revisions.)

7. The final reorganization scheme for Greater London, proposed initially in the Herbert Commission report and implemented by the London Government Act of 1963, incorporated these main features:

a. A two-tier arrangement was created in which new London boroughs became the main governmental units responsible for the largest package of functions, and the GLC became a metropolis-wide government responsible for planning and management functions for Greater London as a whole.

b. The 32 London boroughs were mainly formed by consolidations of former local governmental units of various types. They are all now important cities in their own right, averaging about 250,000 in population. The boroughs assume major responsibilities for health, welfare, and children's services; education (in the outer boroughs only); housing (shared with the GLC); refuse collection and local sewer systems; libraries; and rating. The traditional City of London has been preserved and is treated as a special 33rd borough.

c. The GLC is a new governmental unit, yet it builds upon the precedent of the LCC and expands the latter's territorial coverage. The GLC, encompassing 8 million residents and a 616 square mile area, is given some distinctive functions: intelligence (research and statistics), fire and ambulance services, and certain others. Moreover, it has "senior" policy responsibilities with respect to functions shared with the boroughs: town planning, traffic and highways, housing, parks and open space, and sewer and refuse services.

d. Evidence suggests that the GLC capitalizes on the traditional identification of residents with "London" or "Greater London" in a broad sense. Nevertheless, in most respects the GLC is remote from the people. The boroughs, designed to be closer to the people, are generally still too new to have elicited a strong sense of civic identification. It is apparently difficult to create a balance between efficiency and citizen participation, the two criteria used by the Herbert Commission.

e. As something of a compromise, an Inner London coinciding geographically with the former Administrative County of London is preserved in several ways. First, the Inner London Education Authority (ILEA) serves as a semi-independent unit of government to run the schools there; its Education Committee, overseeing education in Inner London, is, by extension, akin to a GLC committee. Second, the GLC assumes control of building construction in Inner London, while this control goes to the boroughs in Outer London. Third, the GLC assumes somewhat greater and more direct responsibilities for certain planning matters within Inner

London, partly reflecting a carryover of former LCC projects and major new projects like Thamesmead and Covent Garden.

8. Several problems have required resolution during the few years that the Greater London governmental system has been in operation (it took over in 1965). In particular, the appropriate sharing of functions has proved difficult to resolve, and certain responsibilities have been shifted more fully either to the boroughs or to the GLC. By the terms of the London Government Act, some functional allocations were to be examined within the first five years.

9. Subsequent proposals for governmental reorganization in other parts of Britain have provided a good deal of variety and are worth considering.[2] Five basic patterns are summarized and presented in order of the increasing responsibility given the upper-tier governments:

a. Two tiers, the lower-tier units being the principal governments, and the upper-tier units being assigned coordinating and planning responsibilities. (Recommended by the Herbert Commission.)

b. Two tiers, the upper and lower tiers being coordinate, and each tier assigned significant functions. Certain functions, such as planning and housing, shared by both tiers. (Recommended by the Senior minority report for almost all areas in England, and, with altered allocations, by the Conservative white paper for England.)

c. Two tiers, with significant bundles of functions given to each tier, but shared functions being avoided whenever possible. (Recommended by the Redcliffe-Maud Commission for the largest metropolitan areas in England.)

d. Two tiers, the upper tier being very strong and exercising most functions; the lower tier preserving traditional local contacts, but handling few formally assigned functions. (Recommended by the Wheatley Commission for Scotland, and, in slightly modified form, by the Conservative white paper for Scotland.)

e. Single-tier (unitary) governments handling all functions. Optional local councils could be responsible for representing localities, and could also assume limited functions, as permitted by the principal local government. (Recommended by the Redcliffe-Maud majority report for all but the largest metropolitan areas, but repudiated by the Conservative white paper for England.)

The preceding patterns are intended as ideal types, identified as pure alternatives. But we know that in actuality most concrete governmental schemes represent composites, embodying features taken from alternative patterns. Thus the actual structure resulting from the London Government Act of 1963 probably most nearly resembles pattern (b). But it also leans toward pattern (a), particularly in the outer London boroughs, in assigning principal functions to the lower tier. Moreover, it resembles pattern (c) in avoiding shared functions, except for planning, housing and roads.

What, then, are we to make of the post-London government reform schemes? Which are most supportive of, and hence serve to validate, the Greater London structure? Which reject in principle the Greater London structure? Derek Senior's minority report, scheme (b), most closely resembles the structure of Greater London, and most consciously supports principles inherent in Greater London's organization. The Redcliffe-Maud majority recommendation for the largest English metropolitan areas, scheme (c), comes next. And of all the patterns, scheme (e) is most directly in opposition to the principles employed for Greater London. It is the recommendation by the Redcliffe-Maud majority for most of England, including some large metropolitan areas.

10. If the various royal commission reports have a crucial weakness, it lies in their apparent disregard for the politics of local government reform. We must say "apparent" because all of the commissions are inevitably concerned with the political acceptability of their major proposals. Perhaps it is unreasonable to suggest that royal commissions should consider bringing partisan politics explicitly into their deliberations, or touching on partisan concerns in developing the supporting rationale. Yet Americans seeking to learn from British experience must look beyond the high-sounding prose of the royal commission reports to learn how political support is actually mustered, as well as how political resistance can frustrate the reform effort.

We saw in Chapter Seven that the Labor Government would have supported the main features of the Redcliffe-Maud majority recommendations. For the very large metropolitan areas this would largely

have followed scheme (c), and would have remained generally supportive of the Greater London structure. For the rest of England,
and including numerous metropolitan areas, this would have tended
to follow scheme (e), and would have definitely repudiated the principles and the structure of Greater London. Significantly, the non-
metropolitan changes would have introduced major departures from
existing county lines (counties being traditionally Conservative) and
might have permitted some of the new unitary governments to be
dominated by city populations (which are traditionally Labor).

But the Conservative Government, after wresting leadership from
Labor, brought out different recommendations. For the large metropolitan areas, expanded to six, the recommendations veered toward
scheme (b), thus falling between schemes (c) and (b). These metropolitan recommendations remain generally supportive of the Greater
London pattern. Significantly, the recommendations for the rest of
English local government came close to scheme (b) in their allocation
of functions—although differing markedly from Senior's thoroughgoing *geographic* restructuring. The Conservative proposals largely
respected the identities of existing counties, most existing county boroughs, and other large local governments. As of this writing, the final
partitioning for the non-metropolitan governments is in the hands
of a yet-to-function Local Government Boundaries Commission. The
Conservatives thus catered to local governments, particularly the
county councils, which are traditionally Conservative. The recommendations will probably have the effect of subordinating some cities
to Conservative county political dominance.

For whatever reasons, the Conservatives have taken a far less bold
approach to local government reform than the earlier Labor leadership. On the other hand, it would now appear that the Conservatives
have a much greater chance of carrying the reform through than did
Labor. The so-called timidity of the Conservatives also evokes less
resistance from the grass roots than would the Labor proposal.

11. Greater London is caught up with urban development trends
and policy over a much more extended region, generally designated
as South East England. Questions of regional government and regional planning for this larger area inevitably affect the evaluation of
local problems. While there is no full-fledged regional government,
two coterminous organizations have been serving a South East Eng-

land Region that includes 17 million population, plus the GLC, 12 other county councils and 11 county borough councils.

These two are (1) the South East Economic Planning Council, appointed by the British central government; and (2) the Standing Conference on London and South East Regional Planning, a voluntary association resembling the councils of governments (COGs) in the United States. In addition, a South East Joint Planning Team—created by the central government to merge leadership and technical staffs from the MHLG, other government departments, and local planning authorities through the Standing Conference—has provided a new pattern of regional planning that may prove a prototype for other metropolitan areas.

We cannot possibly foretell the future of government and planning for the larger London region. As of this writing, it appears that the regional economic planning councils are likely to be declared redundant, and that standing conferences for regional planning will be promoted for all metropolitan areas in England. This would put British metropolitan areas closer to the COG pattern already so prevalent in the United States.

Two further observations may be in order: (a) The Standing Conference on London and South East Regional Planning, like the American COGs, is by no means an equivalent of regional government. In fact, it makes even less pretense of encompassing the full range of governmental functions than do most COGs in the United States. (b) Insofar as the central government continues to rely on a joint-team approach to regional planning, co-opting both central government and local government resources, a rather intriguing possibility is introduced, one that apparently is relatively untried in the United States. The American counterpart of the central government in such efforts would presumably be the state government. Or perhaps full intergovernmental participation by all three governmental levels—federal, state and local—could be considered.

To sum up, we have described the remarkable governmental reform effort that has been unfolding during the past 15 years in Greater London, and has also been spreading to other parts of Britain. The new Greater London governmental system may be judged generally successful. We have suggested various preconditions that helped make it possible, and in some ways also shaped the resulting structure. It now remains to discuss briefly certain questions about the new system as these bear on basic problems of metropolitan governmental reorganization, and to ask what conditions might enable cities in the United States to benefit from the London experience.

UNRESOLVED ISSUES OF HIERARCHY
AND FUNCTIONAL ALLOCATION

The spate of British local government reform proposals, and the debates they engendered, have revealed a basic conflict over the way a local governmental system should be organized. While the conflict is by no means new, the recent discussions may have brought to light some new implications for those who are concerned with reorganizing governments in metropolitan areas.

One concept calls for a strict hierarchical arrangement: The upper tier lays down policy constraints within which lower-tier units are expected to operate. Under this formula, both tiers may be concerned with similar functions (such as housing, education, or planning). The upper tier establishes policy or sets standards, and the lower tier manages or administers the functions in accordance with the policies and standards put forth by the upper tier. In metropolitan governmental situations, the upper-tier government comes to specialize in policy planning, in intelligence, and in establishing the broad framework within which the lower-tier government administers the functions in question. This idea was vigorously advocated by Derek Senior in his minority report to the Redcliffe-Maud Commission. The concept was also implicit in the Herbert Commission report, with respect to certain functions.

A conflicting view opposed such open dependence upon hierarchy, and on policy dictated by upper tiers. This view urged that shared functions be avoided, and that some functions be clearly assigned to the upper tier and other functions to the lower. The Herbert Commission report stressed that it was not recommending superordinate and subordinate governments, but merely different types of governments, complete with different functions, the differentiation taking into account matters of scale and functional coordination. And the Redcliffe-Maud Commission report urges a straightforward means of avoiding hierarchy, advocating a single-tier government for most of England.

The main function that has been caught up in this controversy is probably town planning, but the issue extends to other functions as well, including education, housing, and indeed any function where the upper-tier government is expected to establish broad policy guidelines with which lower-tier governments are to comply. The Herbert Commission, for example, proposed that the GLC establish educational standards, and that the London boroughs manage the schools within those standards.

Planning can be viewed as strictly a local government function. This has generally been the prevailing concept in the United States. But a mature planning system in a comparatively socialistic nation like Britain leans toward a greater interdependence between local and regional plans, and also, if prepared, national plans. Each governmental level becomes responsible for the shaping of plans and planning policy, on a scale and to a degree of detail commensurate with its own jurisdiction. Yet all the while, each level works within the policy guidelines established by the plans of higher governmental levels. And each, in turn, establishes the policy framework for any more local levels under it. Thus, as a general principle, any system of planning reflects and depends upon a rational governmental hierarchy.

It is therefore not surprising that the British Parliament has enacted legislation requiring structure (strategic policy) plans by counties and county boroughs, as well as by the GLC. These plans are subject to review and approval by the Ministry of Housing and Local Government. Within the policy laid down by such plans, other strictly local and more precise plans are also prepared, and these are not subject to ministry approval.

As we have noted, the Greater London development plan is a structure plan, prepared under mandate as a guide for Greater London's future, and as a framework within which London borough planning may proceed. According to the GLC, "the development plan for Greater London shall be prepared first, to form the context for the borough plans which will follow." * In his minority report,

* *Greater London Development Plan: Statement* (London: GLC, July 1969), p. 9. But in November 1970 the Minister for Local Government and Develop-

Senior pursues this idea further and recommends an even stronger requirement that the upper-tier government approve the plans of the lower-tier governments. As he explains it, under his proposal "all local plans should have to be submitted for approval (not just for comment *en passant,* as in Greater London) to the regional authority, thus ensuring that they will be designed to promote rather than undermine the purposes of the structure plan and safeguarding the regional authority's ultimate responsibility for statutory plan-making." [3]

At just this point, the rationality of a hierarchical planning system may come into sharp conflict with ideologies emphasizing local autonomy. The hierarchical planning model probably meets less resistance in Britain than in the United States, but even in Britain one finds both ambiguity and deliberate efforts to obscure the issue. Senior suggests that his colleagues on the Redcliffe-Maud Commission never moved beyond recognizing two levels of plans for their two-tier system for large metropolitan areas. They did not insist that lower-tier plans be subject to review by upper-tier governments.

In a sense, this brings us full circle, back to the hierarchical relationship between central government and local governments. We may conclude that in broad terms there is an acceptance of hierarchy in Britain—an acceptance embedded in British culture and based on shared expectations, which need not be stated explicitly. This acceptance supports higher levels of government in enunciating policies that are respected by lowel levels.

In his minority report, Derek Senior articulated a refined rationale for the principle that upper-tier metropolitan governments prepare policy plans, and then approve or disapprove of lower-tier development and control activities based on these plans. The Redcliffe-Maud majority, in contrast, played down such hierarchical relationships by allocating functions either to one tier or the other in metropolitan areas, with housing the sole exception, or by doing away with two-tiered local government entirely in non-metropolitan areas. When

---

ment approved a major change whereby the London boroughs would be able to proceed directly to their own action plans and to development control, without preparing borough structure or policy plans. This poses a further question regarding hierarchical organization: whether lower-tier authorities can successfully carry through policy established by an upper-tier authority. See the note on p. 56 for further detail and reference.

the Labor Government issued its white paper on England in February 1970, it appeared that the proposal put forward by Senior had proved unacceptable, and that this would weaken the case for its applicability in the United States. But the Conservative Government's white paper of February 1971 proposed a hierarchical approach to planning, and the sharing of several other functions between upper- and lower-tier local governments. Consequently there is perhaps still a reasonable chance that reform proposals, based on such "rational planning" approaches within a hierarchical structure, can gain political support in the United States, as they have in Britain.*

APPLICABILITY TO THE UNITED STATES

We have suggested that various preconditions paved the way for reform in Greater London and shaped the resulting structure. A number of questions have also been raised as to the existence of comparable preconditions in the United States, to help assess the possibility that ideas embodied in the Greater London experience may also prove fertile in America.

In general, we must conclude that some of the most important preconditions are not fully present in the American setting. Still, it would probably be unwise to conclude that the significant differences between Britain and the United States, and between London and large American metropolitan areas, rule out the prospects of borrowing selectively from the trans-Atlantic experience. We shall point out various differences, in cautioning against too-ready borrowing. Nevertheless these differences should not discourage imagi-

---

* Somewhat disconcertingly, a series of impressions during a several-weeks' visit to London in the summer of 1971 tend to convey a discouraging outlook regarding the prospects for "rational planning." Informed opinion seems to suggest that town planning is rather seriously bogged down between the GLC and the boroughs (with the Greater London development plan inquiry serving to caricature the serious differences). Further, it appears that regional planning for the South East is by no means assured, with vast gaps between pronouncement of policy and effective implementation; and that there is little if any evidence that central government is prepared to offer responsible national planning guidance of a coherent nature. This may reflect some partisan reaction on the part of British town planners to a Conservative Government ideologically disinclined to sponsor "Planning." Apparently Britain, like America, has its distinct ups and downs in planning. Perhaps this is for the best, as it may enable each country to sustain pluralistic sets of outlooks as to the kinds and degrees of planning needed.

native efforts to derive applicable lessons from the British experience.

In place of the essential directness and relative simplicity of a central-local relationship, the United States has a vastly more complex federal system, involving cooperative partnerships between the federal government and the various states. There are also highly varied and everchanging relationships between individual state governments and local governments, as well as emerging relationships between the federal government and local units. Roscoe C. Martin has spoken of this whole set of linkages as cooperative federalism, and has stressed how loose and flexible the patterns are.[4]

The role of the individual state government has been pivotal. Most states have been reluctant to step in forcefully to supervise urban governments, or to modernize local governmental structure in metropolitan areas. Some states, to be sure, have been strengthening their organized responsibility for guiding and supporting urban governments. Various examples come to mind: New York State, through its Urban Development Corporation and other programs; New Jersey, through its Division of Community Development; Minnesota, with its Municipal Commission; and Indiana and the Indianapolis consolidation are a few examples. Others could be cited. With a number of major changes underway in recent years, we must recognize that the mere diffusion of the most vigorous of these existing state programs to most other states would in itself comprise a remarkable development. But delaying battles will undoubtedly be fought, state-by-state, so that the prospects for change in individual states remain unclear.

The federal government, with its recognized financial resources and with its political capacity to establish policy and foster programs that some local residents may find unpopular, has been actively strengthening its direct supervision of and financial aid to urban and metropolitan areas. Moreover, the national government has been insisting that the availability of federal funds must be contingent on coordinative review by specified metropolitan agencies, or by the rapidly spreading COG-type pseudo-governments. Through such actions the federal government has already instituted what is, potentially at least, an unprecedented degree of scrutiny by a new, intermediate (metropolitan) governmental level that, with federal backing, comes to assume ever-greater hierarchical character.

Urban local governments in the United States, although potentially valuable partners in the federal system, have almost invariably tended to take a more independent stance than local governments in Britain. Indeed, some American cities have long held home-rule powers that literally give them substantial autonomy. Even lacking home-rule powers, local governments, bolstered by strong grass-roots traditions, are able to behave as though they were independent. They can try to play state and federal governments off against each other, by shopping among alternative supporting programs. They can pick specific programs from the cornucopia of federal programs and agencies, and they have certain choices in selecting state programs. They may weigh available financial support (which they seriously need) against grant or loan conditions that would make them dependent upon state or federal agencies (which they may prefer to avoid).

We have grown accustomed to the looseness and disorder of the American system. We accept a blurring of lines, and a sharing of functions on other than strict hierarchical lines. Partnerships between the federal government and the states are accepted, as well as partnerships between local governments and the two other levels. We do not ordinarily conceive of these relations as hierarchical in any rigorous sense. We accept Morton Grodzins' "marble-cake" model rather than any orderly hierarchical layering. "Intergovernmental cooperation" has become standard operating procedure, no matter how cumbersome the structure. We have been led to believe that our capacity to work cooperatively is more important than the governmental structure. Thus the Committee on Economic Development, in its recent influential report, seems very comfortable in advocating "sharing of power" approaches that presume only vague and indistinct structural arrangements.[5]

In general, we have tended to look to local areas for initiative in implementing local government reform. We expect reform somehow to spring from the grass-roots. We have tended to shun efforts to impose local governmental reform from above. More than we realize, we may be engaging in self-fulfilling prophecies of failure, by doggedly insisting on local reform referendums, which we suspect are doomed to defeat. By taking such views, we blind ourselves to the possibilities that effective formulas for change can be developed and imposed by state governments, presumably with the support of the federal government. As Professor W. A. Robson has argued:

One fundamental self-imposed obstacle to local government reorganization in the U.S. is the belief that a local government cannot be amalgamated or changed unless a referendum in favor of the change is carried out—a most unlikely event, especially in the suburbs of large cities. There is, I believe, nothing in the laws or constitutions of the states to require this, which really denies the right of the state government to reorganize the local authorities which it created or established. . . . In very few countries—especially among the Western ones—are local authorities willing to initiate reform or prepared to assent to it. Almost everywhere (except perhaps in Sweden) reorganization has been imposed by a higher level of government.[6]

Perhaps such grass-roots beliefs are, in part at least, beginning to be understood as myths. The fact is that some highly significant reorganizations of metropolitan government in the United States have been brought about by state legislative action alone. For example, Minnesota established the Metropolitan Council for the Minneapolis-St. Paul metropolitan area, Indiana established a consolidated metropolitan government for Indianapolis, and California established the Bay Conservation and Development Commission (BCDC)—all without local referenda. This contrasts with the referendum obstacles that have defeated many other American metropolitan government reform efforts to failure. The lesson to be learned is that the state legislatures have the necessary authority, and that if action is seriously sought, the state legislative route may avoid delays, defeat, and detrimental side effects.[7]

Thus we are already moving significantly toward a greater recognition of the need to strengthen the hierarchical character of our own governmental system. Cooperative federalism is all well and good, but if it perpetuates the power of existing local units to forestall reform proposals affecting the future structure of government in our ever-growing metropolitan areas, then a greater acceptance of state and federal authority to reorganize local government will be an essential way around the veto. At the same time, there is a complementary need for higher levels of government to decentralize and delegate such powers as can be relinquished to a revitalized local government.

Despite the divergences from the American setting, certain lessons from the London and British experiences come through with irresistible force. Both countries are recognizing that large metropolitan areas constitute the dominant urban form in the modern industrialized world. And on both sides of the Atlantic there is emerging recognition that this vigorous urban form urgently requires viable new versions of local government.

In Britain the need for viable governments has wisely been placed in a larger context. Thus governmental reform for local units throughout each of the three parts of Britain—England, Scotland, Wales—have been reviewed, and patterns have been recommended and debated for each. Accordingly, the reform of London's metropolitan government is seen as but a portion of the broader English local government reform effort.

A major lesson from Britain is precisely this: there is wisdom in initiating systematic large-scale reform of local government. In the United States perhaps the effort should be state-by-state, rather than relying solely on a pattern of one-metropolitan-area-at-a-time. What the British communicate by their actions is that the rationalization of local government should be the direct responsibility of a superior government. In the American context, we may readily interpret this to mean that it should be a direct responsibility of state governments, with strong federal encouragement and support.

Except for the Redcliffe-Maud majority report favoring single-tier local government, the entire British reform effort is solidly on the side of two-tier government. A new two-tier system has been in operation in Greater London for several years, and is put forward on principle by the Conservative Government for six other large metropolitan areas in England. It is urged for 28 new local governmental units in the remainder of England, and for new local governments throughout Scotland and Wales. This is impressive, across-the-board reform policy and action, backed by equally impressive and closely reasoned, exhaustive reports.

It is clear that two-tier local government has some disadvantages. These were thoroughly examined in the majority report of the Redcliffe-Maud Commission. But it is also abundantly evident that, on balance, the advantages of the two-tier organization were judged to be superior to those of a single-tier structure. Two tiers permit the differential location of functions, and otherwise facilitate employing a wide range of variations. (In general, more major functions were allocated to lower-tier units in the large metropolitan areas than in non-metropolitan areas.) The two-tier arrangement also provides for the possible retention at both levels of units that are identical with or that closely resemble preexisting local governments. In the latest Conservative recommendations for non-metropolitan England, for example, a large number of existing counties are retained as upper-tier units, but with many previously independent county boroughs also drawn in and retained at the lower-tier level.

One lesson from Britain that deserves great stress is the determination to insist upon adequate size for local governmental units. If a local government is to be viable, it must be large enough to ensure a highly competent and professional staff, and a broad political base. In accord with the determination to carry through this principle, the Greater London boroughs were created as substantial cities in their own right. The various recommendations of the other royal commissions were supportive of the same principle. It now appears that in acting on the recommendations for England, the Conservative Government has divided on this principle, carrying through the idea of large lower-tier units for the six metropolitan areas, but reverting to much smaller units—the proposed sizes ranging from about 40,000 to 100,000, although the precise determinations have not yet been made—for nonmetropolitan lower-tier governments.

Readers will quite properly draw their own conclusions. For our part, we are struck by two complementary approaches that dominate the British policy toward local government, and especially toward metropolitan area institutions. Britain accepts the responsibility of the central government to provide continuing guidance on urban matters, and to supply periodic leadership in reforming the structure of local government. The British also recognize that effective performance by local government, as a partner in the conduct of public business, requires that local units be fashioned into much larger entities (and hence fewer in number) than they have traditionally been. Moreover, the local system must be so organized that both strictly local and broader regional responsibilities can be handled.

It may seem ironic that a supposedly "tradition-laden" Britain can agree on extensive and rational reforms, recognizing the need for a governmental system that is able to cope with the realities of metropolitan life. In any event, British accomplishment contrasts sharply with our own performance. One would hope that the future will see a better showing for fundamental urban governmental reorganization in the United States, a nation that has pioneered sweeping changes in technology, and in many other spheres of human endeavor.

ADMINISTRATIVE COUNTY OF LONDON. This upper-tier authority was created in 1888 to unify London's local governmental system. It comprised the County of London, governed by the London County Council (LCC), and the City Corporation of London, a separate governmental unit. The LCC was complemented by 28 lower-tier metropolitan boroughs, created in 1899. The Administrative County of London embraced 117 square miles and a population of 4.5 million at its peak in the early 1900's. It had a population of 3 million in 1965 when it was absorbed into the Greater London Council (GLC).

ALDERMAN. Aldermen are voting members of local councils who are selected at large by the popularly elected councillors. Aldermen serve for six-year terms and may constitute up to one-sixth of the number of elected councillors. Proposals of the Redcliffe-Maud Commission (1969) would have led to the abolition of aldermen, but 1971 proposals by the Conservative Government may extend their existence. See also "Councillor."

BOARD OF TRADE. The Board of Trade is a long-established unit of central government with responsibility for commerce, industry, and overseas trade, and with central responsibility for all industries not specifically allocated to other departments. It administers controls over the location of industry and, selectively, of offices. See also "Industrial Development Certificate" and "Office Development Permit."

CENTRAL AREA. The Central Area is a statistical unit of about 8.5 square miles lying roughly within the ring formed by London's main railway stations, and containing the West End, Bloomsbury, the City of London, and other central districts. There have also been other definitions of central London, including the area known as the London Conurbation Center, 10.4 square miles, formally agreed to by the Registrar General and the Greater London Council.

CITY OF LONDON. The City is an historic area of one square mile, constitutes the City Corporation of London, and contains one of the world's major financial centers. The Corporation has its own Common

190

Council. While it is separate from the GLC, in many respects the City functions as a 33rd London borough.

COUNCILLOR. A councillor is a member of a local council. He is directly elected by the voters, either at large, as in the case of London borough council elections, or to represent a specific London borough, as in the case of the GLC elections. Councillors represent at least 86 per cent (six-sevenths) of the membership of local councils, the remaining members being the appointed aldermen. See also "Alderman."

ECONOMIC AFFAIRS, DEPARTMENT OF. The Department of Economic Affairs is a central government agency that is responsible for national economic planning and regional development, in existence from 1964 to 1970. It sponsored the National Economic Development Council (NEDC, also called "Neddy") and ten regional economic planning councils within Britain. See also "South East Region."

GREAT BRITAIN. Great Britain is the largest of the British Isles. It comprises England, Wales and Scotland. The United Kingdom includes Great Britain and Northern Ireland (Ulster).

GREATER LONDON. Greater London refers to an area of 616 square miles and nearly 8 million residents, under the control of the Greater London Council (GLC). The Council was created in 1965 by the London Government Act of 1963. See also "Greater London Conurbation."

GREATER LONDON AREA. This term refers to the review area of 840 square miles, assigned in 1957 to the Royal Commission on Local Government in Greater London (the Herbert Commission). See also "Royal Commission on Local Government in Greater London."

GREATER LONDON CONURBATION. The conurbation is a statistical area designated by the Registrar General, who is responsible for the British census. It is roughly comparable to the concept of "urbanized area," used by the U.S. Bureau of the Census. Since 1965 it has been coterminous with Greater London (616 square miles); before that it was somewhat larger (722 square miles).

GREATER LONDON COUNCIL (GLC). The new London government was created by the London Government Act of 1963, and came into being April 1, 1965. The GLC is the upper tier in a two-tiered system that also includes 32 London boroughs and the City of London. More specifically the term designates the council that governs Greater London. The GLC has 116 members, of whom 100 are directly elected councillors and 16 are indirectly elected aldermen.

GREATER LONDON TRANSPORT PLANNING GROUP. This body was established by the Transport (London) Act of 1969 to augment the GLC's role as the planning authority for transportation within Greater London. The group is chaired by the GLC's Traffic Commissioner and Director of Transportation. It includes representatives of the GLC, the Ministry of Transport, London Transport, and British Rail.

HERBERT COMMISSION. See "Royal Commission on Local Government in Greater London."

191

HOME COUNTIES. This term designates the counties around London. We use the phrase only as it was used by the Barlow Commission in its 1940 report, to include specifically the counties of Bedfordshire, Buckingham-shire, Essex, Hertfordshire, Kent, Middlesex, and Surrey.

HOME OFFICE. The Home Office is the central government department that controls the Metropolitan Police and has responsibility for a variety of domestic administrative functions not specifically assigned to other ministries.

HOUSING AND LOCAL GOVERNMENT, MINISTRY OF (MHLG). MHLG is a central government ministry that was created in 1943 as the Ministry of Town and Country Planning. After one other name change, it was given its MHLG title in 1951. It is responsible for town planning, housing, and a range of local governmental services in England and Wales. In 1970 it was absorbed by a new larger unit, the Department of the Environ-ment.

INDUSTRIAL DEVELOPMENT CERTIFICATE. The term designates a document issued by the Board of Trade, authorizing specified industrial develop-ment in a given geographic area. It must accompany any application to the local authority for planning permission.

INNER LONDON. Inner London refers to the central portion of Greater London. Before 1965 it constituted the Administrative County of London.

INNER LONDON EDUCATION AUTHORITY (ILEA). ILEA is a special govern-mental unit created by the London Government Act of 1963 to admin-ister education within Inner London. The controlling authority has 53 members, of whom 40 are the GLC councillors for the 12 Inner London boroughs. Thirteen are representatives from the Inner London borough councils and the Common Council of the City of London.

JOINT TRAFFIC EXECUTIVE FOR LONDON. This is an administrative agency established by the Transport (London) Act of 1969, and is responsible jointly to the GLC and to the Commissioner of Metropolitan Police. The executive ensures close joint working arrangements on matters of traffic and parking management.

LOCATION OF OFFICES BUREAU. Since 1963 this bureau has been operated by the central government, with the purpose of inducing firms to move voluntarily out of central London, and to relocate in outer London loca-tions, or away from London entirely.

LONDON BOROUGH. A London borough is a lower-tier unit of govern-ment created by the London Government Act of 1963. There are 32 Lon-don boroughs, plus the City of London. The latter is a special govern-ment reflecting historical differences, but is roughly equivalent to a 33rd borough. Except for the City, London boroughs range in population from 142,000 (Kingston-upon-Thames) to 320,000 (Lambeth). London boroughs are governed by elected councils ranging in size from 56 to 70 members.

LONDON BOROUGHS ASSOCIATION (LBA). The LBA was founded in 1964 and given its present name in 1966. It is the organization through which the London boroughs can coordinate their functions, as well as develop agreed-upon positions in their collective dealings with the GLC and the central government.

LONDON COUNTY COUNCIL (LCC). See "Administrative County of London."

LONDON METROPOLITAN REGION. The region is a specific statistical area designated in the late 1950's by the Ministry of Housing and Local Government to include the Greater London Conurbation, the Metropolitan Greenbelt, and additional newly developed land outside of the Greenbelt within commuting distance of central London. This region has a diameter ranging from 80 to 100 miles, embraces about 4,400 square miles, and includes a population of 13 million.

LONDON TRANSPORT BOARD OR EXECUTIVE. Both terms, London Transport Board and London Transport Executive, have been used to designate the authority established by the central government under the Ministry of Transport to operate bus and underground transit in Metropolitan London. By the Transport (London) Act of 1969, the London Transport Board under the central government surrendered its governance to a newly created London Transport Executive, now responsible to the GLC. The transfer took place in January 1970.

MAUD COMMISSION. See "Royal Commission on Local Government in England."

METROPOLITAN GREENBELT. The Greenbelt is a band of open countryside, six to ten miles in width and covering about 840 square miles, encircling Greater London. It was created mainly in the late 1940's by action of the central government, and is incorporated in local development plans.

METROPOLITAN LONDON. This generic term includes various definitions of the functionally integrated region around Greater London. See also the more precise terms "Greater London," "Greater London Area," "Greater London Conurbation," "London Metropolitan Region," and "South East Region."

METROPOLITAN POLICE. This term refers to the Metropolitan Police, who have responsibility throughout Metropolitan London (except within the City of London), and are under the Home Office of the central government. Police were excluded from the terms of reference of the Herbert Commission, and are not a function of either the GLC or the London boroughs. There is a corresponding administrative area, known as the Metropolitan Police District. Since 1965 it has been adjusted geographically virtually to coincide with Greater London.

METROPOLITAN WATER BOARD. The board is an independent agency, in operation since 1904, with sole authority for water supply in an area of nearly 600 square miles. Its operation was specifically excluded from consideration by the Herbert Commission, and it was not affected by the reorganization of Greater London government.

OFFICE DEVELOPMENT PERMIT. Permits are authorizations issued by the Board of Trade for office construction within 50 miles of central London. They must accompany applications to the local authorities for planning permissions.

OUTER LONDON. This term designates the outer portion of Greater London, the part that is outside the former Administrative County of London. Although the term is commonly used for convenience, it does not carry the official usage implicit in the term Inner London.

OUTER METROPOLITAN AREA. The London Metropolitan Region (see entry for that title), less Greater London.

OUTER SOUTH EAST. The South East Region, less the London Metropolitan Region.

OVERSPILL HOUSING. Overspill housing refers to the planned provision of new housing, usually public, in outer districts of a metropolitan area so that families may be rehoused from inner districts, if displaced by redevelopment, or if quartered in substandard housing. The central authority, the outer local authority, and the MHLG all cooperate in the administrative and fiscal arrangements.

PLANNING ADVISORY GROUP (PAG). A group appointed in 1964 by the MHLG to review national development planning. PAG-type "structure plans" based on recommendations of PAG's 1965 report, *The Future of Development Plans*, tend to be general statements of policy, rather than specific outlines.

RATE. A tax roughly analogous to the property tax in the United States, but with essential differences in concept and implication. Rating is the system for collecting this tax. See also the footnote on p. 38 and text pages 136–137.

REDCLIFFE-MAUD COMMISSION. See "Royal Commission on Local Government in England."

ROAD CLASSIFICATION.

Type of Road	*Responsible Highway Authority*
Motorways—limited access freeways or thruways (in American terms)	Ministry of Transport
Trunk roads—additional major highways, not limited access	Ministry of Transport
Metropolitan roads— principal roads	Greater London Council
Primary and secondary roads—all other roads	London boroughs

194

ROYAL COMMISSION ON LOCAL GOVERNMENT IN ENGLAND. Also known as the Redcliffe-Maud (sometimes merely Maud) Commission. It was created in 1966 to review the structure of English local government outside of Greater London, and to make recommendations for reorganization. The Redcliffe-Maud Commission reported in 1969.

ROYAL COMMISSION ON LOCAL GOVERNMENT IN GREATER LONDON. Also known as the Herbert Commission (for its chairman, then Sir Edwin Herbert), created in 1957 and charged with recommending governmental reorganization for the Greater London Area, which it did in its 1960 report. The London Government Act of 1963 followed the essence of these recommendations, and the new government came into effect in April 1965. See also "Greater London Area" and "Greater London Council."

ROYAL COMMISSION ON LOCAL GOVERNMENT IN SCOTLAND. Also known as the Wheatley Commission. It was created in 1966 and charged with reviewing the structure of Scottish local government. A published report was submitted in 1969.

SOUTH EAST ECONOMIC PLANNING COUNCIL. This body comprises some 37 members appointed by, and expected to offer advice to, the British central government. It is one of a set of such planning councils in Great Britain. See also "South East Region."

SOUTH EAST ENGLAND. South East England is a generic term embracing various specific definitions. See also "South East Region" and " 'South East Study' Region."

SOUTH EAST JOINT PLANNING TEAM. During a two-year period, 1698–1970, a technical group guided by a steering committee reviewed previous planning reports and prepared a new strategic plan. This effort was jointly commissioned by the central government, the South East Economic Planning Council, and the Standing Conference on London and South East Regional Planning.

SOUTH EAST REGION. This region is essentially synonymous with the South East Economic Planning Region, the domain of the South East Economic Planning Council. Containing more than 10,000 square miles and about 17 million residents, it includes the counties of Bedfordshire, Berkshire, Buckinghamshire, Essex, Hampshire, Hertfordshire, Kent, Greater London, Oxfordshire, Surrey, East and West Sussex, and the Isle of Wight.

Another version, only slightly different in extent, is the South East Standard Region, which merely adds Poole Municipal Borough (a city of just under 100,000 population) adjacent to and part of the Bournemouth area. In the text and tables no effort has been made to distinguish between these two versions.

"SOUTH EAST STUDY" REGION. This very large region was especially employed by the Ministry of Housing and Local Government for its 1964 report. It is no longer actively employed for statistical or policy matters.

It was an ad hoc amalgam of three former Standard Regions: Eastern, Southern, and London and South East. In addition to the South East Region defined above, it included East Anglia (to the northeast) and the county of Dorset (to the southwest). This expanded region totalled about 16,000 square miles and included 18.5 million residents.

STANDING CONFERENCE ON LONDON AND SOUTH EAST REGIONAL PLANNING. The conference is a voluntary association of local governments—the GLC, 12 county councils, 11 county borough councils, and the London Boroughs Association—embracing a region coterminous with the South East Economic Planning Region. The conference was organized in 1962, and gained its present name and geographic extent in 1966.

WHEATLEY COMMISSION. See "Royal Commission on Local Government in Scotland."

NOTES

NOTES TO FOREWORD, pp. v–viii

1. Foreword to Victor Jones, *Metropolitan Government* (Chicago: University of Chicago Press, 1942), p. ix.
2. Stanley Scott, "The Study of Urban Government: First Steps Toward an International Discipline," *Public Administration Review*, 29:550–551 (September–October 1969).

NOTES TO CHAPTER ONE, pp. 1–18

1. Ministry of Housing and Local Government, *The South East Study, 1961–1981* (London: HMSO, February 1964).
2. M. J. Wise, "The Impact of a Channel Tunnel on the Planning of South-Eastern England," *Geographical Journal*, 131:167–185 (June 1965).
3. *Report of the Royal Commission on the Distribution of the Industrial Population*, Cmd. 6153 (London: HMSO, January 1940).
4. "Britain's 'Two Nations,'" *New York Times* (April 24, 1963).
5. For a broader review of developments to 1960, see Donald L. Foley, *Controlling London's Growth: Planning the Great Wen* (Berkeley and Los Angeles: University of California Press, 1963), especially Chapter Five. Later controls on office employment will be discussed below.
6. Adapted from *Greater London Development Plan: Report of Studies* (London: GLC, July 1969), Table 3.6, p. 41.
7. *The South East Study, 1961–1981*, Table 21, pp. 138–139.
8. This point draws upon Brandon Howell's comments, based on his critical reading of the manuscript. See also the case made by the Greater London Council: *Greater London Development Plan: Statement* (London, July 1969), pp. 10–11, 18–21.
9. *Greater London Development Plan: Report of Studies*, Table 2.5, p. 14.
10. For 1951–1966: *Ibid.*, Table 2.4, p. 11. For 1966–1968: *Strategic Plan for the South East: Report by the South East Joint Planning Team* (London: HMSO, 1970), Table 2.6, p. 12.
11. *Strategic Plan for the South East*, Table 2.7, p. 12.
12. *Greater London Development Plan: Report of Studies*, Table 2.8, p. 15.
13. *Ibid.*, Table 3.52, p. 70, and Table 3.46, p. 65. Office space may not serve

as a good indicator of office employment, since office space per employee grows at an unknown rate.

14. *Ibid.*, Table 3.41, p. 61.

15. Mimeographed table. (London Transportation Board, Commercial Office, February 1963). These 1962 figures represented a peak in volume of entry, and entry figures tapered off during the next several years. See further discussion in Chapter Six.

16. Net density comparisons adapted from *County of London Plan* (prepared for the LCC; London: Macmillan, 1943), p. 156, and *Administrative County of London Development Plan, First Review 1960: County Planning Report*, Vol. 1 (London: GLC, 1960), Table 12, p. 32; and p. 174.

17. For a general account of the rationale behind new towns and for specific descriptions of the individual new towns to date, see Sir Frederick Osborn and Arnold Whittick, *The New Towns: The Answer to Megalopolis* (New York and London: McGraw-Hill, 1963).

18. Estimated as follows: 360,000 in eight London new towns (*Town and Country Planning*, 38:44 [January 1970]); 135,000 in 27 expanded towns serving Greater London (37,000 or more completed dwellings with an estimated 3.6 persons per household [*ibid.*, p. 50]); 105,000 in LCC estates beyond Greater London (Foley, *op. cit.*, footnote 58, pp. 205–206).

NOTES TO CHAPTER TWO, pp. 19–43

1. In this entire section on local government, we have drawn freely from reports of the Maud Committee, i.e., the Committee on the Management of Local Government, *Management of Local Government: Vol. I, Report of the Committee* (London: HMSO, 1967); *Vol. IV, Local Government Administration Abroad* (London: HMSO, 1967); *Vol. V, Local Government Administration in England and Wales* (London: HMSO, 1967).

2. The authoritative study extensively drawn upon in this whole section on London history is William A. Robson, *The Government and Misgovernment of London* (London: George Allen and Unwin, 2nd ed., 1948). Also *Report of the Royal Commission on Local Government in Greater London, 1957–1960*, Cmnd. 1164 (London: HMSO, October 1960), especially Chapters Two and Four.

3. *Report of the Royal Commission . . . Greater London*, pp. 39–41.

4. We have drawn extensively on Gerald Rhodes, *The Government of London: The Struggle for Reform* (London: London School of Economics and Political Science, and Weidenfeld and Nicholson, 1970). This work provides a thorough treatment of the period 1957 to 1965, focusing on the activities of the Herbert Commission and the later steps in establishing the new London government.

5. Royal Commission on Local Government in Greater London, *Minutes of Evidence, 68* (London: HMSO, 1960) paragraphs 15605, 15607, 15611, pp. 2842–2844.

6. *Report of the Royal Commission . . . Greater London*, p. 186.

7. The following sources were used extensively for information on the shift to the new governmental structure for Greater London, but are not separately footnoted in the remainder of this section: Rhodes, *op. cit.*; William A. Robson, *The World's Greatest Metropolis: Planning and Government in Greater London* (Pittsburg: Institute of Local Government, University of Pittsburg, 1963); Geoffrey Block, *Greater London Government* (London: Conservative Political

Centre, March 1964, No. 11 of the Local Government Series); David Peschek and L. J. Sharpe, "London Changes Over," *New Society*, 3:18–20 (April 9, 1964); Frank Smallwood, *Greater London: The Politics of Metropolitan Reform* (Indianapolis: Bobbs-Merrill Co., 1965); Sir William Hart, "Reorganization of London Government—Proposals and Solutions," and Donald L. Foley, "Planning Problems in the Reorganization of London," papers presented at Seminar on Problems of Metropolitan Reorganization, Centre for Urban Studies, University of Toronto, September 30, 1965. Other sources included interviews with J. D. Jones, V. P. Lipman, and C. J. Pearce, administrative officers in the Ministry of Housing and Local Government, July 1964, and discussions with Sir William Hart, clerk of the new Greater London Council, July 1964 and September–October 1965.

8. *Report of the Royal Commission . . . Greater London*, p. 207.

9. *The Times*, Supplement on London Local Government (April 1, 1965).

NOTES TO CHAPTER THREE, pp. 44–77

1. Sir William Hart, "Great Metropolitan Giant of London," *Municipal Journal*, 76:375 (February 16, 1968).

2. Greater London Council Minutes, 21 November 1967, p. 687.

3. *The Guardian* (February 21, 1968).

4. *Report of the Royal Commission on Local Government in Greater London, 1957–1960*, Cmnd. 1164 (London: HMSO, 1960), p. 199.

5. Personal interview, 1968;

6. "Research and Intelligence Unit: Reorganization," *Quarterly Bulletin of the Research and Intelligence Unit*, GLC, No. 8 (September 1969), p. 3.

7. Committee on the Management of Local Government, *Management of Local Government: Vol. V, Local Government Administration in England and Wales* (London: HMSO, 1967), p. 588.

8. *Ibid.*, pp. 588–589.

9. This point was made by Professor C. D. Foster.

10. The Greater London Group, London School of Economics, *The Lessons of the London Government Reforms* (London: HMSO, 1968. Research Studies 2, Royal Commission on Local Government in England), pp. 42–43.

11. *Ibid.*, pp. 17–18.

12. *Ibid.*, pp. 18–26.

13. *Ibid.*, pp. 18–25.

14. *Ibid.*, pp. 21–25.

15. Hart, *op. cit.*, p. 375.

16. Tabulated from a listing of planning officers in *Estates Gazette* (April 2, 1966).

17. Ministry of Housing and Local Government, *London Government Staff Commission, 1963–1965* (London: HMSO, 1966), p. 50.

18. *London Government Act of 1963*, sec. 25, paragr. 3.

19. Ministry of Housing and Local Government, Ministry of Transport, Scottish Development Department, *The Future of Development Plans: A Report by the Planning Advisory Group* (London: HMSO, 1965).

20. The following draft plans were consulted: *Greater London Development Plan: First Draft of the Written Statement* (London: GLC, October 1967); *Greater London Development Plan: Draft Studies* (London: GLC, October 1967); *Greater London Development Plan: Statement* (London: GLC, draft text, March

1969). In this chapter we have relied primarily on the March 1969 draft statement; this was the one available to GLC councillors and aldermen for their consideration and policy approval.

Later, two formal published versions appeared: *Greater London Development Plan: Statement* (London: GLC, July 1969); and *Greater London Development Plan: Report of Studies* (London: GLC, July 1969). A third published report followed, ostensibly a popular summary of the first two, but also incorporating the fresh views of David Eversley, recently appointed Chief of Strategic Planning, who had not been responsible for the work leading to the first two reports. *Tomorrow's London: A Background to the Greater London Development Plan* (London: GLC, October 1969). These are further drawn upon in a section of Chapter Five, where the broad development policy for Greater London is discussed.

21. Editorial in *Architects' Journal* (July 30, 1969).

22. MHLG, The Town and Country Planning (Local Planning Authorities in Greater London) Regulations 1965/679, and 1967/430.

23. *Ibid.* Also abstract of presentation by A. G. Powell at a Ministry of Housing and Local Government seminar, November 1966.

24. *Ibid.* (Both sources.)

25. *1966 Annual Abstract of Greater London Statistics* (London: Greater London Council, 1968), Table 146, p. 141.

26. *Greater London Development Plan: Statement*, p. 59.

27. Interviews. *The Lessons of the London Government Reforms*, pp. 28–30.

28. Of these, 336,654 were permanent dwellings and 47,242 temporary. *1966 Annual Abstract of Greater London Statistics*, Table 151, p. 145.

29. Ministry of Housing and Local Government, *The Housing Role of the Greater London Council Within London* (London: HMSO, 1967), pp. 2–4.

30. *1966 Annual Abstract of Greater London Statistics*, Tables 150–151, pp. 143, 145.

31. Jane Morton, "Greenwood's Veto," *New Society*, 15:522 (March 26, 1970). Also interview with B. H. Wilson, Town Clerk, Camden Borough, July 1968; Jane Morton, "London's Housing Transfer," *New Society*, 12:840–841 (December 5, 1968); note concerning transfer in *Housing Review*, 18:461 (March–April 1969).

32. Minister of Transport, *Transport in London*, Cmnd. 3686 (London: HMSO, July 1968), p. 7.

33. *Ibid.*, pp. 9–18.

34. "Transport Policy," *British Record* (December 26, 1968), pp. 1–2. *Financial Times* (November 28, 1968).

35. See *1969 Inner London Education Authority Guide* (London: ILEA, 1969); also article on the ILEA, *London Times* (April 9, 1970).

36. Anthea Tinker, *The Inner London Education Authority* (London: HMSO, 1968. Research Studies 8, Royal Commission on Local Government in England), pp. 9–10.

37. As quoted in the Greater London Group, *The Lessons of the London Government Reforms*, p. 9.

38. *Report of the Committee on Local Authority and Allied Personal Services*, Cmnd. 3703 (London: HMSO, July 1968), pp. 72–74.

39. Greater London Group, *The Lessons of the London Government Reforms*, p. 5.

40. *Ibid.*, p. 9.

41. *The Times* (April 13, 1967).

42. "What It's All About in Tory London," *The Economist* (April 22, 1967), pp. 324–327; Ann Corbett, "London Countdown," *New Society*, 9:81 (January 19, 1967).

43. *The Times* (May 11, 1968).

44. Derived from reports in *The Guardian* (May 10, 1968).

45. Derived from "What It's All About in Tory London," p. 326; *The Times* (April 11, 1970).

46. *The Times* (April 9, 11, and 29, 1970). Also "The Politics of London," *The Economist* (April 11, 1970), pp. 18–19.

47. *1967 Annual Abstract of Greater London Statistics* (London: GLC, 1969), Tables 1.05 and 1.09, pp. 7, 10. The 1970 figures should be regarded as provisional, being calculated from newspaper counts, borough by borough.

48. *The Times* (April 29, 1970).

49. "The Politics of London," p. 19.

NOTES TO CHAPTER FOUR, pp. 78–93

1. The principal written sources for this section are the technical reports and press notices, from December 1962 to July 1969. Interviews with Brandon Howell, Technical Secretary for the Conference, aided at earlier stages, and have been particularly helpful in contributing substantial changes to the final draft.

2. Standing Conference on London and South East Regional Planning, *Constitution and Membership* (London, June 1970).

3. Standing Conference on London and South East Regional Planning, "Planning London and the South East up to 2000 A.D." (Press notice No. 24, August 2, 1967), pp. 3–4.

4. Standing Conference on London and South East Regional Planning, *The South East: A Framework for Regional Planning*, LRP 1180 (London, 1968).

5. Standing Conference on London and South East Regional Planning, "A Venture in Partnership" (Press notice No. 29, July 17, 1968), p. 2.

6. Ministry of Housing and Local Government, *The South East Study, 1961–1981* (London: HMSO, March 1964).

7. *South East England*, Cmnd. 2308 (London: HMSO, March 1964).

8. Department of Economic Affairs, *The National Plan*, Cmnd. 2764 (London: HMSO, September 1965).

9. The following written sources regarding regional economic planning were drawn upon: "Regional Economic Planning: Statement by the First Secretary of State and Secretary of State for Economic Affairs" (London: Department of Economic Affairs, December 10, 1964); *The National Plan* (London: HMSO, September 1965), especially Chapter Eight, "Regional Planning," pp. 84–100; Peter Self, "Regional Planning in Britain," *Urban Studies*, 1:55–70 (May 1964); Benjamin Chinitz, "Regional Economic Policy in Great Britain," *Urban Affairs Quarterly*, 1:5–21 (December 1965); W. T. Rodgers, MP, Parliamentary Under Secretary, Department of Economic Affairs, "The Future of Regional Planning," *Journal of the Town Planning Institute*, 52:216–218 (June 1966); Phipps Turnbull, "Regional Economic Councils and Boards," *Journal of the Town Planning Institute*, 53:41–49 (February 1967).

10. *A Strategy for the South East: A First Report by the South East Economic Planning Council* (London: HMSO, 1967).

11. Town and Country Planning Association, *Proceedings of Conference: A*

Strategy for the South East (London: 1969). Also Pat Blake, "South East: Strategy or Hypothesis?" *Town and Country Planning*, 36:179–182 (March 1968).

12. Gerald Smart, "Strategy or Hypothesis?", *Proceedings of Conference*, p. C 1.

13. U.S. National Capital Planning Commission and U.S. National Capital Regional Planning Council, *The Nation's Capital: Policies Plan for the Year 2000* (Washington, D.C.: 1961).

14. Peter Hall, "Alternative Urban Forms for the Region," in *Proceedings of Conference*, p. D 1.

15. South East Economic Planning Council Press Notice, April 16, 1968: "Planning Council's Evidence to Hunt Committee."

16. *The Guardian* (May 6, 1968).

17. Standing Conference, "A Venture in Partnership," p. 2.

18. For a review of the progress report, see Maurice Ash, "Back to Earth," *Town and Country Planning*, 38:105–113 (February 1970).

19. *Strategic Plan for the South East: Report by the South East Joint Planning Team* (London: HMSO, June 1970). The five volumes of studies are: *Population and Employment*, Vol. I of the Studies (London: HMSO, March 1971); *Social and Environmental Aspects*, Vol. II (London: HMSO, April 1971); *Transportation*, Vol. III (London: HMSO, publication pending); *Strategies and Evaluation*, Vol. IV (London: HMSO, publication pending); *Report of the Team's Economic Consultants*, Vol. V (London: HMSO, April 1971).

20. *Strategic Plan for the South East: Report* . . . , p. 66.

21. *Ibid.*, p. 71

22. *Ibid.*, p. 76.

23. *Ibid.*, pp. 93–94.

24. *Ibid.*, p. 95.

NOTES TO CHAPTER FIVE, pp. 94–112

1. See Foley, *Controlling London's Growth: Planning the Great Wen* (Berkeley and Los Angeles: University of California Press, 1963), especially Chapters Two and Three.

2. *A Strategy for the South East: A First Report by the South East Economic Planning Council* (London: HMSO, 1967), p. vii.

3. *Ibid.*, p. 1.

4. *Greater London Development Plan: Statement* (London: GLC, July 1969), pp. 10–11.

5. *Tomorrow's London: A Background to the Greater London Development Plan* (London: GLC, October 1969), p. 38.

6. *Greater London Development Plan: Report of Studies* (London: GLC, July 1969), pp. 59–60.

7. Great Britain, *Offices: A Statement by Her Majesty's Government. 4th November, 1964* (London: HMSO, 1964), p. 2.

8. *Financial Times* (February 18, 1969).

9. A. E. Holmans, "Industrial Development Certificates and Control of the Growth of Employment in South-East England," *Urban Studies*, 1:138–152 (November 1964).

10. *Financial Times* (February 18, 1969).

11. *Greater London Development Plan: Statement*, p. 18.

12. *Town and Country Planning*, 38:44–48 (January 1970).

13. *Ibid.*, p. 50.

14. *Review of the South East Study* (London: HMSO, January 1966), MHLG Circular May 1966. Also Brandon Howell, "Review of the South East Study," *Town and Country Planning*, 44:215–216 (April 1966).

15. *A Strategy for the South East*, Table 11, p. 96.

16. For a summary of development mechanisms and policies, see Central Office of Information, *Regional Development in Britain* (London: HMSO, 1968).

17. Department of Economic Affairs, *The National Plan*, Cmnd. 2764 (London: HMSO, September 1965), Table 8.2, p. 88.

18. *Ibid.*

19. This policy was enunciated primarily through a white paper issued on behalf of the government by the Secretary of State for Industry, Trade and Regional Development, *The North East: A Program for Regional Development and Growth*, Cmnd. 2206 (London: HMSO, November 1963). This has also been reinforced by statements in *The National Plan*.

20. British Information Services, *Regional Development in Britain* (New York: August 1965), p. 23.

21. Sources here include: *The National Plan*; Edward Allen, "The North East since Hailsham," *New Society*, 5:16–17 (January 28, 1965); John Parrott, "Northeast England Woos Industry," *The Christian Science Monitor* (January 7, 1966); Northern Economic Planning Council, *Challenge of the Changing North* (London: HMSO, 1966); *Regional Development in Britain* (1968), especially pp. 28–29.

NOTES TO CHAPTER SIX, pp. 113–141

1. Per the *Workplace Tables,* 1961 Census, as reported in "Tracking Down Commuters," *New Society*, 7:21 (June 23, 1966).

2. Unpublished tables. London Transport Planning Notes, 16 (addendum) and 23. Count is for Inner Cordon (London Transport Board, 1968).

3. *The Times* (January 2, May 20, and May 28, 1970).

4. *Sample Census 1966, England and Wales: Greater London* (London: HMSO, 1967), Table 13.

5. Greater London Council, *London's Roads: a Program for Action* (London: GLC, November 1967), p. 3; GLC, *Getting About in London* (London: GLC, September 1966), unpaged.

6. "Homes Before Roads," *New Society*, 15:548 (April 2, 1970).

7. Standing Conference on London Regional Planning, "Road Construction and Improvement Prospects in the Conference Area," LRP 602, March 9, 1966. Also *The Times* (January 22, 1970).

8. *The Times* (May 12, 1970).

9. *Report of the Commission on the Third London Airport* (London: HMSO, 1971). Also *The Times* (December 19, 1970 and January 22, 1971). Peter Hall, "The Roskill Argument: An Analysis," *New Society*, 17:145–148 (January 28, 1971).

10. *Report of the Committee on Housing in Greater London*, Cmnd. 2605 (London: HMSO, 1965). Also J. B. Cullingworth, "London's Housing: Towards an Agreed Policy?" and other summaries of the report, *New Society*, 6:16–21 (March 18, 1965); "The Milner Holland Report," *Housing Review*, 14:79–82 (May–June 1965).

11. *Sample Census 1966 . . . Greater London*, Table 12.

12. *Ibid.*, Tables 11 and 12.

13. Jane Morton, "Housing: Twilight Measured," *New Society*, 13:715 (May 8, 1969).

14. Ruth Glass, "Housing in Camden," *Town Planning Review*, 41:40 (January 1970), Table 5.

15. *Ibid.*, p. 22.

16. *Ibid.*, Tables 3, 5, 6, pp. 34, 40, 48.

17. *Ibid.*, Table 3, p. 34.

18. Jane Morton, *op. cit.*, p. 715.

19. This paragraph and the ensuing discussion have drawn upon John Barr, "What Kind of Homes Do People Want?" and "How Can We Get the Right Homes?" *New Society*, 6:6–10 (November 11, 1965) and 6:15–19 (November 18, 1965).

20. *Sample Census 1966 . . . Greater London*, Table 10.

21. This paragraph has drawn upon *1966 Annual Abstract of Greater London Statistics* (London: GLC, 1968), Tables 151, 155, 158.

22. *The Times* (January 22 and April 13, 1970).

23. Robin Pedley, *The Comprehensive School* (Harmondsworth: Penguin, 1967), pp. 12–14.

24. "Education: Sixth Forms," *New Society*, 13:17 (June 30, 1969).

25. "London's Schools," *New Society*, 8:797 (November 24, 1966).

26. *The Times* (October 5, 1968).

27. *The Times* (April 13 and 28, 1970).

28. Adapted from Ann Corbett, "Comprehensives: The Tally," *New Society*, 15:265 (February 12, 1970).

29. *1966 Annual Abstract of Greater London Statistics*, Table 125, p. 110.

30. *Census 1961. England and Wales: Birthplace and Nationality Tables* (London: HMSO, 1964), Table 2. *Sample Census 1966. Great Britain: Summary Tables* (London: HMSO, 1967), Table 6.

31. "Britain's Colored Population Over 1,200,000," *The Times* (June 18, 1969). The South East Joint Planning Team also assumed a "colored" population of about 500,000 in Greater London. See *Strategic Plan for the South East* (London: HMSO, 1970), pp. 29–30.

32. For reports on the distribution of minority groups within Greater London see Ruth Glass and John Westergaard, *London's Housing Needs* (London: Center for Urban Studies, University College, 1965), Appendix Table E, p. 67; also R. B. Davison, "The Distribution of Immigrant Groups in London," *Race*, 5:56–69 (October 1963).

33. This subject is carefully explored by Philip Mason, Director, Institute of Race Relations, London, in "What Do We Mean by Integration?" *New Society*, 7:8–11 (June 16, 1966).

34. *Sample Census 1966 . . . Greater London*, Table 4.

35. E. J. B. Rose, "Deteriorating Position of West Indians in Britain," *The Times* (May 15, 1970); Brian Lapping's review of Rose, *Color and Citizenship*, in *New Society*, 14:65–66 (July 10, 1969).

36. See "British Housing Criticized," *Christian Science Monitor* (October 25, 1965), p. 2, and Janet Stewart, "Race and Local Government," *New Society*, 5:18–19 (March 19, 1964).

37. Eric J. Thompson, "A Note on Changes in the Boundaries of the Metropolitan Police District and the Greater London Conurbation Since 1946,"

Quarterly Bulletin of the Research and Intelligence Unit, GLC, No. 4 (October 1968), pp. 15–16.

38. *Report of the Commissioner of Police of the Metropolis for the Year 1962,* Cmnd. 2088 (London: HMSO, July 1963); same, 1967, Cmnd. 3659 (July 1968); same, 1968, Cmnd. 4060 (June 1969). Also *1966 Annual Abstract of Greater London Statistics,* Tables 202, 203.

39. *Ibid.*

40. "Police Problems," *New Society,* 7:18–20 (March 25, 1965). Peter Watson, "Becoming a Policeman," *New Society,* 13:921–922 (May 28, 1970).

41. *Report of the Commissioner of Police . . . 1968,* pp. 15–17.

42. *Royal Commission on Local Government in Greater London, 1957–1960: Report,* Cmnd. 1164 (London: HMSO, October 1960), p. 239.

43. This assumes that the distribution of local authority income to the London boroughs followed the national pattern. In fact, the proportion from government grants was probably somewhat lower, reflecting higher average ratable resources within Greater London. *Britain: An Official Handbook, 1969* (London: HMSO, 1969), p. 72.

44. *Annual Budget Programs, 1969–1970* (London: GLC, February 1969).

45. This discussion of rates and government grants was drawn from W. Eric Jackson, *The Structure of Local Government* (London: Longmans, 5th ed., 1966), pp. 96–113; British Information Services, *Local Government in Britain* (London: HMSO, 1965); and *Britain: An Official Handbook, 1969,* pp. 72–73.

46. *1966 Annual Abstract of Greater London Statistics* (London: GLC, 1968), Table 241, pp. 238–239.

47. For a description of the Ilersic proposal, see David Peschek, "London Rate Equilization: The Story Behind the Headlines," *Local Government Chronicle* (February 17, 1968), pp. 258–259, and "Richer Boroughs to Help Poorer in Rates Change," *The Guardian* (February 7, 1968).

48. *1967 Annual Abstract of Greater London Statistics* (London: GLC, 1969), Table 11.03, p. 264.

49. *The Municipal Yearbook 1969* (London: Municipal Journal Ltd., 1969), p. 858. Also Jane Morton, "Rates that Councils Don't Collect," *New Society,* 13:407 (March 13, 1969).

NOTES TO CHAPTER SEVEN, pp. 142–168

1. *Royal Commission on Local Government in England, 1966–1969: Vol. I, Report,* Cmnd. 4040 (London: HMSO, 1969). *Vol. II, Memorandum of Dissent by Mr. D. Senior,* Cmnd. 4040-I (London: HMSO, 1969). *Vol. III, Research Appendices,* Cmnd. 4040-II (London: HMSO, 1969). *Local Government Reform: Short Version of the Report of the Royal Commission on Local Government in England,* Cmnd. 4039 (London: HMSO, 1969).

2. *Local Government Reform,* p. 3.

3. *Ibid.,* p. 4.

4. *Ibid.;* Seebohm Committee report: *Report of the Committee on Local Authority and Allied Personal Social Services,* Cmnd. 3703 (London: HMSO, 1968).

5. *Local Government Reform,* p. 5.

6. *Ibid.,* p. 9.

7. *Ibid.,* p. 20.

8. *Ibid.,* p. 21.

9. *Royal Commission on Local Government in England. Vol. I, Report,* pp. 285–295.

10. *Royal Commission on Local Government in England. Vol. II, Memorandum of Dissent by Mr. D. Senior,* p. 59.

11. *Ibid.,* pp. 256–266.

12. *Royal Commission on Local Government in Scotland, 1966–1969: Report,* Cmnd. 4150 (Edinburgh: HMSO, 1969). *Appendices,* Cmnd. 4150 (Edinburgh: HMSO, 1969). *Scotland: Local Government Reform: Short Version of the Report of the Royal Commission on Local Government in Scotland,* Cmnd. 4150-I (Edinburgh: HMSO, 1969).

13. See John Mackintosh, "The Royal Commission on Local Government in Scotland, 1966–69," *Public Administration,* 48:49–56 (Spring 1970).

14. *Scotland: Local Government Reform,* p. 9.

15. On this point, see Jane Morton, "Commissions in Conflict," *New Society,* 14:516–517 (October 2, 1969).

16. Data here and in the next three paragraphs are taken from *Royal Commission on Local Government in Scotland: Appendices,* Appendix 14, pp. 65–66.

17. *Royal Commission on Local Government in Scotland: Report,* p. 284.

18. "Scotland," *Special Report: British Record* (December 30, 1969), p. 4.

19. *Local Government in Wales,* Cmnd. 3340 (Cardiff: HMSO, 1967).

20. *Local Government Reorganization in Glamorgan and Monmouthshire,* Cmnd. 4310 (Cardiff: HMSO, 1970).

21. *Local Government Commission for Wales: Draft Proposals* (Cardiff: The Commission, 1961); *Local Government Commission for Wales: Report and Proposal for Wales* (Cardiff: HMSO, 1963).

22. *Local Government in Wales,* p. 24.

23. For an excellent discussion of various political implications of the royal commission report, see "Editorial: The Future of English Local Government," *Public Administration,* 47:411–419 (Winter 1969). (Presumably written by the Hon. Editor of the journal, Nevil Johnson, although no authorship was indicated.)

24. *Reform of Local Government in England,* Cmnd. 4276 (London: HMSO, 1970). Also "Local Government Reform," *British Record* (February 26, 1970); "Local Governmental Reform Proposals," *The Municipal and Public Services Journal,* 78:300–301 (February 6, 1970); "Local Government: Carbon-Copy Maud," *New Society,* 15:222 (February 5, 1970); "Local Government Reforms/ White Paper," *The Times* (February 5, 1970).

25. See National Health Service, Department of Health and Social Security (The green paper), *The Future Structure of the National Health Service* (London: HMSO, 1970). Also "Social Services," *British Record* (February 26, 1970).

26. Peter Walker, "More Power at Local Level," *The Municipal and Public Services Journal,* 77:1769 (July 11, 1969). Also reports of debate in House of Commons, *The Times* (February 19, 1970).

27. *Local Government in England: Government Proposals for Reorganization,* Cmnd. 4584 (London: HMSO, 1971). *Reform of Local Government in Scotland,* Cmnd. 4583 (Edinburgh: HMSO, 1971). *Welsh Office: The Reform of Local Government in Wales: Consultative Document* (Cardiff: HMSO, 1971). We have drawn upon the following summaries and analyses: Peter Hall, "The Country Fights Back—and Wins," *New Society,* 16:491–494 (September 17, 1970). David Wood, "Mr. Walker Remaps Local Government," *The Times* (February 1, 1971). Various summarizing articles, *The Times* (February 17, 1971). Terrence Bendix-

son, "Walker Deposes the Rural Gentry," *The Observer* (February 21, 1971). "Walker's Lame Duck Reform for Local Government," *The Economist* (February 20, 1971), pp. 18–19. "The Carve Up," *New Society*, 17:259 (February 18, 1971).

28. Author's calculations based on the Herbert Commission report, the Redcliffe-Maud Commission report, and *1966 Annual Abstract of Greater London Statistics* (London: GLC, 1968), Table 15, p. 10.

NOTES TO CHAPTER EIGHT, pp. 169–189

1. These have been footnoted earlier, but for the reader who may focus on this concluding chapter, we repeat the most relevant references on the Herbert Commission report and its adoption: *Report of the Royal Commission on Local Government in Greater London, 1957–1960*, Cmnd. 1164 (London: HMSO, October 1960). Frank Smallwood, *Greater London: The Politics of Metropolitan Reform* (Indianapolis: Bobbs-Merrill Co., 1965). Gerald Rhodes, *The Government of London: The Struggle for Reform* (London: London School of Economics and Political Science, and Weidenfeld and Nicholson, 1970). And for the reader who wishes to put this further in historic perspective—although a good deal of history is provided in the *Report*—the classic reference is: William A. Robson, *The Government and Misgovernment of London* (London: George Allen and Unwin Ltd., 2nd ed., 1948).

2. These other reviews were reported in Chapter Seven, but for the reader particularly concerned with the conclusions in Chapter Eight we summarize the main commissions and their reports. Redcliffe-Maud Commission for England (excluding Greater London): *Local Government Reform: Short Version of the Report of the Royal Commission on Local Government in England*, Cmnd. 4039 (London: HMSO, 1969); *Royal Commission on Local Government in England, 1966–1969: Vol. I, Report*, Cmnd. 4040 (London: HSMO, 1969) ; *Vol. II, Memorandum of Dissent by Mr. D. Senior*, Cmnd. 4040-I (London: HMSO, 1969); also note 1 to Chapter Seven, above.

Wheatley Commission for Scotland: *Royal Commission on Local Government in Scotland, 1966–1969: Report*, Cmnd. 4150 (Edinburgh: HMSO, 1969); also note 12 to Chapter Seven, above.

Reports for Wales: *Local Government in Wales*, Cmnd. 3340 (Cardiff: HMSO, 1967); *Local Government Reorganization in Glamorgan and Monmouthshire*, Cmnd. 4310 (Cardiff: HMSO, 1970); also note 21 to Chapter Seven, above.

3. Derek Senior, "The Royal Commission Report—a Dissenter's Reply," *Journal of the Town Planning Institute*, 55:344 (September–October 1969).

4. Roscoe C. Martin, *The Cities and the Federal System* (New York: Atherton Press, 1965), especially Chapter Two.

5. Committee for Economic Development, *Reshaping Government in Metropolitan Areas* (New York: February 1970), pp. 19, 42.

6. Communication from Professor W. A. Robson (October 15, 1970).

7. Stanley Scott and Harriet Nathan, "Public Referenda: A Critical Reappraisal," *Urban Affairs Quarterly*, 5:313–328 (March 1970).

Table I

Employment in Greater London, the London Metropolitan Region, the South East Region, and England and Wales, 1951–1966

	Employment (in thousands)			Per Cent Increase (annual averages)		Percentage Distribution of Increase	
	1951	1961	1966	1951–61	1961–66	1951–61	1961–66
Greater London	4,228	4,383	4,430	+0.4	+0.2	16.0	3.3
Outer Metropolitan Area	1,402	1,740	2,063	+2.4	+3.7	35.1	22.8
London Metropolitan Region	5,630	6,123	6,493	+0.9	+1.2	51.1	26.1
Outer South East	1,397	1,500	1,712	+0.7	+2.8	10.7	14.9
South East Region	7,027	7,623	8,205	+0.8	+1.5	61.8	41.0
Rest of England and Wales	12,913	13,290	14,120	+0.3	+1.2	38.2	59.0
ENGLAND AND WALES	19,940	20,913	22,325	+0.5	+1.4	100.0	100.0

SOURCE: *Greater London Development Plan: Report of Studies* (London: GLC, July 1969), Tables 3.4 and 3.5, pp. 40–41.

Table II

Industrial Composition of Increased Employment in Greater London, the South East Region, and England and Wales, 1961–1966

	Employment Increases, 1961–66 (in thousands)					Per Cent Increases, 1961–66 (annual averages)				
	All industries	Primary	Manu-facturing	Construc-tion	Services	All industries	Primary	Manu-facturing	Construc-tion	Services
Greater London	47	0	−125	30	142	0.2	0	−1.7	2.2	1.1
Outer South East	535	−15	151	64	335	3.3	−1.9	3.0	4.7	3.7
South East Region	582	−15	26	94	477	1.5	−1.7	0.2	3.0	2.1
Rest of England and Wales	830	−154	190	197	597	1.2	−2.6	0.7	4.5	2.0
ENGLAND AND WALES	1,412	−169	216	291	1,074	1.4	−2.5	0.6	4.1	2.1

SOURCE: Adapted from *Greater London Development Plan: Report of Studies* (London: GLC, July 1969), Table 3.6, p. 41.

Table III

Population of London, the London Region, the South East Region, and England and Wales, 1931–1981

	Population (in thousands)					Percentage Distribution				
	1931	1951	1961	1968^b	E. 1981	1931	1951	1961	1968	E. 1981
Inner London^a	4,397	3,345	3,173	3,020	2,583^c	11.0	7.6	6.9	6.2	4.9
Rest of Greater London	3,819	4,863	4,812	4,744	4,646^c	9.6	11.1	10.4	9.8	8.8
Greater London	8,216	8,208	7,985	7,764^c	7,229^c	20.6	18.7	17.3	16.0	13.7
Outer Metropolitan Area	2,457	3,505	4,518	5,179	6,086^d	6.1	8.0	9.8	10.7	11.6
London Metropolitan Region	10,673	11,714	12,503	12,943	13,315	26.7	26.7	27.1	26.6	25.3
Outer South East	n.a.	3,501	3,848	4,287	5,220^d	n.a.	8.0	8.3	8.8	9.9
South East Region	n.a.	15,215	16,351	17,230	18,535^b	n.a.	34.7	35.4	35.5	35.3
Rest of England and Wales	n.a.	28,600	29,854	31,363	34,015^b	n.a.	65.3	64.6	64.5	64.7
ENGLAND AND WALES	39,952	43,815	46,205	48,593	52,550^b	100.0	100.0	100.0	100.0	100.0

[a] The former Administrative County of London.

[b] *Registrar General's Statistical Review of England and Wales for the Year 1968* (London: HMSO, 1970), Part II, Table A6; *Britain 1970: An Official Handbook* (London: HMSO, 1970), pp. 13–15.

[c] *Greater London Development Plan: Report of Studies* (London: GLC, 1969), Tables 2.7 and 2.33. The 1981 estimates represent the averages of high and low estimates.

[d] Estimation obtained by allocating the proportionate estimates developed in *A Strategy for the South East* (London: HMSO, 1967), Table A7, p. 75.

Note: n.a. means not available. Figures may not add to subtotals or totals due to rounding.

Table IV

Household Spaces by Tenure and Management, Inner and Outer London, 1966

Type of Housing	Greater London Council, Total		Inner London		Outer London	
	Number	Per Cent	Number	Per Cent	Number	Per Cent
Owner-occupied	1,149,400	43.2	259,500	23.8	889,900	56.6
Renter-occupied, Local Authority	573,900	21.6	293,700	26.9	280,200	17.8
Renter-occupied, Private	852,000	32.0	491,000	45.0	361,000	23.0
Other tenure or not stated	88,300	3.3	47,200	4.3	41,100	2.6
TOTAL HOUSE-HOLD SPACES	2,663,600	100.0	1,091,500	100.0	1,572,100	100.0

SOURCE: General Register Office, *Sample Census 1966, England and Wales: Greater London* (London: HMSO, 1967), adapted from Table 10.
Note: Figures may not add to totals due to rounding.